HUMAN RIGHTS
IN THE AMERICAS:
The Struggle for Consensus

HUMAN RIGHTS IN THE AMERICAS:

The Struggle for Consensus

Edited by Alfred Hennelly, S.J.
and John Langan, S.J.

Woodstock Theological Center
Georgetown University

GEORGETOWN UNIVERSITY PRESS
Washington, D.C.

Copyright © 1982 by Georgetown University Press.
All Rights Reserved
Printed in the United States of America

International Book Number: 0-87840-400-7

Library of Congress Cataloging in Publication Data
Main entry under title:

Human rights in the Americas.

    1. Catholic Church and civil rights—America—
Addresses, essays, lectures.   2. Church and civil rights
—America—Addresses, essays, lectures.   3. Civil rights
—America—Addresses, essays, lectures.   I. Hennelly,
Alfred T.   II. Langan, John, 1940-
BX1401.H85   261.7'097   82-2990
ISBN 0-87840-401-5   AACR2
ISBN 0-87840-400-7 (pbk.)

TABLE OF CONTENTS

PART II
*Human Rights in Other Traditions: Convergence
and Comparison*

PREFACE

This work and a companion volume, *Human Rights and Basic Needs in the Americas,* edited by Margaret E. Crahan, are the products of a research project initiated in 1977 by the Woodstock Theological Center, located in Washington, D.C. Established in 1974 by the Maryland and New York Provinces of the Society of Jesus to stimulate interdisciplinary reflection on contemporary human problems, the Center has undertaken a wide variety of projects and published a series of studies dealing with personal values and public policy, ethics and nuclear strategy, religious freedom, social change, and ethical issues in foreign policy.

A key concern of the Woodstock Center has been issues of justice that have international ramifications. No human problem transcends national boundaries to the degree that violations of human rights do, not only in terms of the causes, but also in the search for solutions. The emergence of human rights as a prime criterion of U.S. foreign policy in the 1970s raised complex questions of definition, emphasis, strategy and objectives. The tendency, for example, in the United States to emphasize violations of civil and political rights to a greater extent than social, economic, and cultural rights raised questions about the intentions and scope of U.S. human rights policies. Domestic challenges concerning the value of strong human rights stances in achieving national objectives, together with international questioning of the U.S. understanding of the relationship between violations of the two sets of rights, prompted the initiation of the Woodstock project. This effort was undertaken to establish major political and economic factors affecting observance and to help clarify the normative, theological, and philosophical bases of human rights in the Americas. It was intended to provide both interested professionals and concerned citizens with a better understanding of the reasons for human rights violations and some insights into how they could be reduced.

In early 1977 consultations were held by the Woodstock Center with policymakers, human rights activists, and scholars in order to obtain suggestions for the conceptualization and organization of the project. Specialists from Latin America and elsewhere were asked to recommend research priorities, modes of analysis, and the most useful formats for the dissemination of the results. This began a dialogue aimed at refining and broadening the project that was to continue throughout the course of the work.

Of particular value were meetings held in Santo Domingo in June 1978 and Bogotá in December of the same year, as well as in Washington in April 1979. They provided input not only for the Woodstock project, but also the simulus for a number of other human rights activities. In the fall of 1977 a core of ten scholars representing the fields of economics, ethics, history, law, philosophy, political science, sociology, and theology began research on the theoretical bases of definitions of human rights and their implications for human rights observance in various cultural traditions in the Americas, focusing on the Anglo-American, Marxist, and Judaeo-Christian traditions. Analysis of historical, political, and economic factors contributing to violations was also begun.

Subsequently, additional scholars were incorporated into the project to cover specific aspects of the overall topic. These individuals examined the economic models underlying basic needs strategies in specific Latin American countries, as well as in some international financial institutions. In addition, the impact of private international capital flows on the fulfillment of needs was analyzed. Issues relating the roles of U.S. bilateral assistance to the promotion of the satisfaction of basic needs and the impact of the Carter administration's policies on general human rights observance in the Americas were also examined. Reflections on legal and philosophic issues raised in countries in which there were substantial violations were contributed by individuals who experienced them first-hand (see Chapters 5 and 11 of this volume). Seminars and meetings from 1978 to 1980 resulted in the incorporation of additional contributors that presented perspectives not covered by the core group.

An integral part of the research and writing was the critique of work-in-progress in seminars, conferences, and consultations. From January to June 1979 a series of six seminars focusing on moral and political implications of policy alternatives relating to basic needs was held. These engaged government officials, human rights advocates, scholars, and other specialists in lively debates that one participant described as raising critical issues that had not been previously raised in discussions among some of the same individuals.

In January 1980, 25 scholars gathered at Woodstock to critique papers dealing with political, intellectual, and cultural barriers to the recognition of social and economic rights, the relationship of the exercise of civil and political rights to the securing of social, economic, and cultural rights and the broadening of normative traditions to give equal weight to social and economic, as well as to civil and political rights. The conference also explored the concept of community necessary to secure the full spectrum of rights and the problem of how to protect the rights of the individual without endorsing excessive individualism. Conclusions from these discussions flowed into analyses of the resources of the liberal,

Marxist, and Judaeo-Christian traditions for dealing with conflict in a creative way. They also informed exchanges on how history and contemporary circumstances shape the impact of these traditions on human rights observance. The various threads of these exchanges were brought together in an exploration of whether or not there was sufficient convergence in the three traditions to provide a foundation for a coordinated defense of human rights. These discussions were used as the basis for revisions of the Woodstock papers prior to their being circulated to an even broader group of specialists throughout the Americas.

In March 1980 seven non-Woodstock specialists gathered to critique papers analyzing political, military, and economic factors affecting human rights and basic needs in the Americas. The focus was on national and international structures of power and their impact on rights. Emphasis was placed on examining the basic character of states that violate civil and political rights and impede the satisfaction of basic needs. The role of the United States in rights observance throughout the Americas was also evaluated. After this meeting some fourteen essays were circulated to government officials, lawyers, labor leaders, members of Congress, church representatives, human rights advocates, journalists, educators, and scholars in the United States and abroad. This was done in preparation for a three-day conference of some 60 specialists at Woodstock in May 1980.

This meeting served not only to assess the conclusions of the project up to that point, but also to disseminate human rights information and stimulate network building. Discussions covered the full scope of the project ranging from communalities in normative values across cultures that can be used to reinforce pressures for the observance of human rights to exchanges on what specific strategies have proven effective in the defense of rights. Emphasis was on exploring the policy implications of the research presented. The discussions revealed that lack of information about current developments and resources in the protection of human rights was substantial, particularly in countries with serious rights problems. While no panaceas were offered, some progress was made in refining existing strategies for the promotion of civil and political, as well as social and economic rights.

These meetings, as well as extensive networking with Latin American colleagues, were funded largely by a grant from the Inter-American Foundation to the Corporación Integral para el Desarrollo Cultural y Social (CODECAL), a nonprofit organization based in Bogotá, Colombia that promotes education for human rights. A substantial portion of the research and writing was funded by a grant from the United States Agency for International Development under Section 116(e) of the International Development and Food Assistance Act of 1977. This legislation was introduced by former Congressman Donald M. Fraser to promote studies and programs to encourage increased adherence to civil and political rights as set forth in the Universal Declaration of Human Rights. Assistance from the Beirne Foundation was especially valuable in facilitating the dissemination of studies produced during the course of the project both in this country and abroad. Throughout, the Maryland and New York Provinces of the Society of Jesus provided very substantial financial backing, as well as unflagging moral support.

An incalculable contribution was made by those individuals, too numerous to name, who participated in the Woodstock seminars, consultations, and conferences. To the Latin Americans who attended the various meetings and critiqued early drafts of the essays that constitute the present volume, and its companion, *Human Rights and Basic Needs in the Americas,* we owe a deep debt of gratitude. Their contributions resulted in improvements in both books, and also generated valuable suggestions for new directions in human rights work at Woodstock and elsewhere.

Several Latin Americans spent extended periods of time at Woodstock during the course of the project, generously sharing with us their knowledge and expertise. These include Marcello Azevedo from Brazil and Patricio Cariola and Santiago Larraín from Chile. In addition, Frank Ivern of Spain provided a breadth of perspective that was very welcome.

Jaime Díaz, Director of CODECAL, not only shared with us his own insights, but put us in touch with a good number of other human rights specialists laboring throughout Latin America. Beyond this, he greatly assisted the project by shouldering a variety of administrative burdens.

Special thanks are due to Roma Knee, Constantine Michalopoulos, Jonathan Silverstone, and Marilyn Zak of the Agency for International Development not only for their ongoing support, but also for their thoughtful suggestions for increasing the utility of the project in various ways. The members of the project particularly appreciated their assistance in translating goals into reality.

A unique contribution was made to the project by José Zalaquett. As a fellow of the Woodstock Theological Center, Pepe brought to bear a keen analytical sense, honed by his work with the legal services department of the ecumenical Committee for Peace which functioned in Santiago de Chile in 1974 and 1975. He not only was able to bridge a multitude of disciplines, but also provided a valuable cross-national perspective. Overall, he helped mold the project intellectually and bring it to fruition.

The administrative burdens on the project Co-Directors, Margaret E. Crahan and Brian H. Smith, were lightened by the substantial assistance of Robert Mitchell, who served as Director of the Woodstock Center from

1976 to 1979 and Gerard Campbell, who succeeded him in September 1979. The realization of the project was also facilitated by the capable assistance of Suzanne Bash, Alice Halsema, Jude Howard, Tam Mehuron, Carol Merrit, Betty Mullen, and Arlene Sullivan.

Henry Bertels and the staff of the Woodstock Theological Center Library provided informed and courteous assistance at all stages of the project. Paz Cohen and Marcelo Montecino, in their patient and skillful work as translators for the conferences held in Washington, helped us and our colleagues to achieve understanding across languages and disciplines. Thanks are also due to Georgetown University for providing facilities for several of the conferences, and to Louis Sharp for special assistance in technical matters during the conferences.

The authors who contributed essays to this and the companion volume all displayed a commitment that went far beyond professional responsibility. Serious scholarship was infused with concern for developing effective strategies to improve human rights observance worldwide. In addition, many of the contributors gave generously of their time to critique the volumes as a whole. Sam Fitch and Jo Marie Griesgraber shared with us their valuable insights and made useful suggestions for the revision of a number of the chapters. Our friends and colleagues at the Center of Concern, especially Philip Land, gave wise counsel and support at many points in the process.

Three individuals made a special contribution to the Woodstock human rights project and to the production of the two books—Bernida Mickens, George Rogers, and Anna Sam. Not only did they work without stinting at a multitude of tasks, they did so with a *joie de vivre* that revived others when they were flagging.

A warm debt of gratitude is owed to all who participated in the Woodstock Theological Center's human rights project. From them we learned a great deal. They were also the source of many of the strengths of the two volumes. For not always realizing their highest expectations, the editors take full responsibility.

Washington, D.C.   MARGARET E. CRAHAN

INTRODUCTION

In the 1970s, human rights became a prominent theme for political argument and for passionate protest, as well as for philosophical and theological reflection. Agitation for human rights has figured in different ways in conflicts between East and West and between North and South. At different times in the decade, Brazil, Chile, Iran, Korea, Uruguay, Argentina, Cambodia, Vietnam, the Soviet Union, Czechoslovakia, Nicaragua, and the Philippines have all been discussed as critical areas for the observance of human rights. Human rights came to be a prominent element both in the shaping of foreign policy, particularly in the United States, and also in the presentation of demands for social and political change within many different countries. Not since the 1940s, when the United Nations Universal Declaration of Human Rights (1948) was drawn up and when the world was still largely united in its reaction to the horrendous violations of human rights involved in World War II, particularly in Nazi Germany, has so much attention been given to human rights issues.

This attention has been partly the result of improved international communications and of increased political awareness, but all too often it has been the result of a serious decline in respect for and observance of human rights in many countries. This decline has led to investigations of violations of human rights and to efforts in defense of human rights by international organizations, by nongovernmental organizations, by concerned governments, and by religious and humanitarian groups. These efforts in defense of human rights have varied in the intensity of their devotion to moral principles, in their sensitivity to political pressures, and in the comprehensiveness of their concern for the victims of human rights violations. Taken together, they constitute an important consensus on the urgency of the defense of human dignity in an age marked by violence and threats of violence, by ideological divisions and economic conflicts, by racial hatred and national ambition.

This consensus on human rights and the elements of human dignity, incomplete and ineffective though it often is, forms one of the important and encouraging signs of our times. It is also a contemporary expression of some central concerns in Western intellectual, political, and religious traditions. It has deep roots in the prophets of Israel and the philosophers of Greece, in the lawyers of Rome and England, in the revolutionaries of Britain, France, the United States, and Latin America.

The concern for human rights is, of course, not a purely Western phenomenon, for two main reasons. First, other cultures and societies have had similar concerns for protecting the welfare and dignity of their members, though they did not use the universalistic and legalistic language of human rights. Second, the language of human rights has in the last two centuries come to be recognized and valued, used and misused around the world.

While the language of human rights has achieved a certain universality and while the protection of human rights is a concern throughout the world, the reader of this volume will notice that it focuses on three particular approaches to human rights. These three approaches or traditions of reflection on human rights are the Catholic, the liberal, and the Marxist. The principal reason for this limitation is that these traditions are of central importance for the discussion of human rights in the Americas, both in the internal political process in the various countries of Latin America and the Caribbean and in the interaction between them and the United States. The liberal tradition on human rights decisively shapes the understanding of most North Americans; it has been both imitated and criticized at different times in Latin America. It emphasizes the importance of subjecting the power of government to moral and legal restraints and of protecting the freedom of individuals. The Marxist tradition, while it is regarded as both alien and dangerous by most North Americans, demands consideration because of its presence in Latin America both as intellectual force and as political alternative. Reference to a Marxist conception of human rights is paradoxical, for Marx himself dismissed talk of natural and human rights as "ideological nonsense." But the subsequent development of the Marxist tradition and the explicit affirmations of Marxist governments and movements make it possible to speak of a Marxist tradition on human rights, a tradition which has roots in Marx's own work and which accords primacy of place to social and economic rights. In Latin America, moreover, this tradition serves a double role as the carrier of hope and as the instrument for interpreting and transforming society for many of those most interested in fundamental social change.

The Catholic tradition plays a similar double role for the hemisphere's largest religious community, a community which has played a central part in the national history of most Latin American countries and which now often serves as a rallying point for opposition to repressive regimes. It is a tradition which attempts to understand human rights in relation to the common good, while avoiding the dangers of individualism and class conflict. This effort gives the Catholic tradition something of a balancing role between the other two traditions. These observations are not meant to bypass the considerable contributions of Protestant, Jewish, and nonreligious thinkers and communities to the advancement and defense of human rights both here and in Latin America, but to indicate the criteria for our selection of a limited number of ways of thinking about human rights which could then be explored and compared in some depth. In presenting and criticizing these traditions, we have taken the United Nations Universal Declaration of Human Rights (1948) as a fixed reference point. This does not mean that every contributor to this volume necessarily endorses every claim advanced in the Declaration, but that we have taken it as a reliable guide to the range and content of human rights and as an indicator of a consensus that is more widely held than any of the particular traditions.

The Universal Declaration of Human Rights, precisely because of its scope and comprehensiveness, poses the problem of achieving an integrated understanding of the conceptual and practical connections between civil and political rights on the one hand, and social and economic rights on the other. This problem runs through most of the essays included in this volume. It has pointed the work of Woodstock's research project on human rights beyond a comparison of different philosophical and theological traditions on human rights, toward an interdisciplinary presentation of the basic economic and political factors affecting the observance of human rights in Latin America. This presentation can be found in the essays of the parallel volume *Human Rights and Basic Needs in the Americas,* edited by Margaret Crahan.

The present volume of essays, which deals with philosophical and legal approaches to human rights, is the fruit of a process of collaborative research, dialogue, and reflection that has been going on at Woodstock since 1977. It began with three presentations of the contemporary Catholic understanding of human rights. David Hollenbach, who focuses mainly on papal and conciliar documents, acknowledges that human rights has become a central theme in Roman Catholic social teaching only in the last 20 years. He stresses the connection between Catholicism's acceptance of pluralism at the Second Vatican Council and its readiness to use the language of human rights. Alfred Hennelly reports on the reluctance of the Latin American theologians to use this language, which they associate largely with the First World. Against this reluctance he sets both the readiness of bishops and episcopal conferences to appeal to human rights and the willingness of those Christians influenced by liberation theology to collaborate with non-Christians (many of them Marxists) in a praxis which aims at protecting human rights. Ignacio Ellacuría, a philosopher and university rector who has worked in El Salvador and Nicaragua, sets human rights in the context of the primacy of the common good as this was affirmed in the social philosophy of St. Thomas. This primacy is to be understood in such a way that what belongs to the common good is not captured by private interests, while at the same time the integrity of the personal is respected. Ellacuría's insistence on the "historicization" of the common good, that is, its being made real in human history, points the way to the problems and possibilities raised in the companion Woodstock volume on human rights and basic needs.

A common theme running through these essays is a desire both on the part of the writers and on the part of the theologians and church leaders whose views they report, to distance themselves from what they perceive as the excessive individualism of the liberal tradition and to preserve a Catholic sense of community and solidarity. This sense of community, they insist, has to be developed to accommodate the challenges of contemporary pluralism and the struggles of the poor and the dispossessed.

John Langan's essay aims at presenting the main features of the liberal conception of human rights, which has been predominant in the political theory and practice of Britain and the United States and has had substantial influence in Latin America. He then argues that social and economic rights can and should be affirmed from within the liberal understanding of human rights. John Haughey sets out from Marx's distrust of the language of human rights as a rationalization for bourgeois individualism and explores the bases and limitations of Marx's understanding of human dignity. These two essays can be regarded as exemplifying in more general and secular terms the contrast between explicit and implicit affirmations of human rights that is found in the different approaches of teaching authorities in the Catholic tradition and of liberation theologians.

The three following essays all involve assessments and comparisons of the three central traditions taken up in the Woodstock project. In the first of them, Max Stackhouse, a professor of Christian ethics and a minister of the United Church of Christ, argues for the necessity of basing our understanding of human rights on God's convenant with his people rather than on secular philosophies. As an illustration of the approach that Stackhouse is commending, he has added to his paper a statement of the United Church of Christ on human rights. Monika Hellwig, a Catholic theologian, directs our attention behind the separate traditions on human rights to the situations of suffering in which cries of pain and cries of rage occur before being transformed into demands for rights. She also points forward to the values to be found in the dialogue among the traditions. Philip Rossi, a moral philosopher, explores the differences among the liberal, Catholic, and Marxist traditions in terms of the varying conceptions that they have of human commonality (what makes you like me) and of human community. This leads him to suggest important differences in the roles of memory, imagination, and hope in the three focal traditions and also in the conceptions of human dignity that are characteristic of the traditions.

The final group of essays examines issues that bear more directly on legal and economic systems. Hernán Montealegre, a Chilean lawyer, traces the inclusion of human rights in international law. He offers an account of state security which, by distinguishing government, territory, and people as elements of the state, enables us to understand how governmental violations of human rights are themselves a threat to state security. Thomas Clarke, a systematic theologian and writer on spirituality, offers a sustained meditation on our need to break bread together, a meditation which opens up new ways of connecting cultural and religious symbols with the shaping of policy. Along with the following essay by Drew Christiansen, this paper stresses the importance of understanding economic and social rights in relation to human dignity rather than in terms of mere survival. Christiansen, a social ethicist, proposes the meeting of basic human needs as a moral test for development strategies in the Third World. His work stresses the importance of need in our understanding of justice and illuminates the obstacles that the North American experience puts in the way of our accepting such a conception of justice. His work also provides a suggestive example of how the claims advanced by the theologians and philosophers writing in this volume can be used to evaluate and to transform the economic and political conditions that are described and explained in the parallel volume of the Woodstock project, *Human Rights and Basic Needs in the Americas.*

JOHN LANGAN, S.J.

David Hollenbach, S.J.

1. Global Human Rights: An Interpretation of the Contemporary Catholic Understanding

The emergence of human rights as a central concern for contemporary Roman Catholicism is a remarkable historical development. From some points of view it is even an astonishing development. The Catholic church was a vigorous opponent of both the democratic and socialist revolutions which were the chief proponents of the civil and social rights enshrined in twentieth-century human rights declarations. [1] In recent years, however, various groups within the Catholic church have become highly visible on the global horizon as advocates for the full range of human rights. [2] Also, the ceneral institutional organ of the Catholic church, the Holy See, has adopted the cause of human rights as the prime focus of its ethical teaching and pastoral strategy in the domain of international justice and peace. This rapid change in the Catholic church's stance toward global human rights is a crucial fact which must be taken into account in any effort to understand current church theory and practice in the rights field.

The interpretation presented here is just that: an interpretation. The Catholic church is a highly differentiated community composed of subcommunities, divided from each other along regional, cultural, economic, and educational lines. This interpretation attempts to grasp the predominant understanding of human rights in the Catholic church, i.e., the one which is setting the course on which the church as a whole seems presently embarked. Therefore, in addition to providing a descriptive account of the prevailing understanding of human rights in the church, what is said here contains an element of prediction. The uncertainty of such an approach may be counterbalanced by the interest it sparks.

The first part of this chapter argues that the impetus for the rapid development of the Catholic understanding of the church's role in the human rights field came from a major event in the modern history of Catholicism: the Second Vatican Council and the pontificate of Pope

John XXIII. Part I tries to show that it was not only the developments in theology which occurred at the Council which brought about this change. Rather, under the leadership of John XXIII, Vatican II was the occasion of a fundamental shift in the church's understanding of its social and institutional place in a pluralistic world. The effort to respond to this newly understood social location caused a rapid development in the church's normative stance on human rights. Part II outlines the content of this development and shows its relationship to the central elements of previous Catholic social thought. It shows how a major and unexpected development was legitimated by appeals to tradition. Finally, Part III makes some suggestions about the contribution which the newly developed Catholic understanding of human rights can make to current discussions. Also, some of the questions about human rights that remain unanswered in Catholic thinking will be highlighted.

I. THE CONTEXT FOR DEVELOPMENT:
A TRANSNATIONAL CHURCH IN A
PLURALISTIC WORLD

Perhaps the single most significant statement contained in the collection of decrees, constitutions, and declarations of the Second Vatican Council is the following apparently innocuous sentence from the first article of the Declaration on Religious Freedom: "This sacred Synod intends to develop the doctrine of recent Popes on the inviolable rights of the human person and on the constitutional order of society." [3] In fact, the statement is far from innocuous, for it represents an an acknowledgment on the highest level of church teaching that Catholic doctrine can develop, can change. The importance of this assertion has been noted by the theologian who was chiefly responsible for the drafting of the Declaration: "In no other conciliar document is it so explicitly stated that the intention of the Council is to 'develop' Catholic doctrine." [4]

In its immediate context the statement was a prelude to the unambiguous affirmation of the fundamental right of every person to religious freedom. In earlier Catholic teaching this right had been variously qualified and even denied. It is remarkable enough to find a reversal of the explicit content of church teaching coming from as traditional a body as the worldwide episcopacy of the Catholic church assembled in council. In the context of the overall influence of the Council on the church's life, however, the statement is even more noteworthy. It suggests that the development in question touches the basic structure of the church's understanding of human rights and constitutional order. The fact that the need for such development is acknowledged most directly in the Religious Freedom Declaration provides a clue for interpreting the fundamental shift in the Catholic understanding of rights which occurred at the Council. The reorganization of the normative foundations of the Catholic understanding of human rights was produced by the same social force which precipitated the Declaration on Religious Freedom, namely, the reality of pluralism. At the Council the modern Catholic church for the first time was compelled to come to grips in an official way with the realities of the religious, cultural, social, economic, political, and ideological pluralism of the contemporary world. The most obvious effect of this acknowledgment of pluralism was the Council's movement from the kind of unitary model of church/state relationships which prevailed through almost all of previous church history to a pluralistic model based on the right of all persons to religious liberty.

The new experience of the reality of pluralism, however, was not limited to the religious sphere. The diversity of political and economic systems and the conflicting social ideologies present in contemporary global society were also a central concern. This concern is evident in the Council's Pastoral Constitution on the Church in the Modern World, which says:

> Today, the human race is passing through a new stage in its history. Profound and rapid changes are spreading by degrees around the whole world. . . . although the world of today has a very vivid sense of its unity and of how one man depends on another in needful solidarity, it is most grievously torn into opposing camps by conflicting forces. For political, social, economic, racial and ideological disputes still continue bitterly. . . . True, there is a growing exchange of ideas, but the very words by which key concepts are expressed take on quite different meaning in diverse ideological systems. [5]

In the Council's view, this diversity of political, social, economic, and ideological systems is a threat to peace and an obstacle to justice. The depth of disagreement between the fundamental social and ideological visions prevailing around the globe leads to disagreement about the meaning of peace itself and justice itself. This basic conflict in interpretations of the central normative foundation of social order was one of the "signs of the times" which inspired the Council's examination of the place of the church in the world today.

Had the Council followed the lead of past Catholic tradition in formulating its response to the reality of contemporary pluralism and conflict, it would have proposed a normative model of social structure and political order chosen on the basis of compatibility with Catholic tradition and faith. Such an approach would have repeated past Catholic solutions to the problem of religious pluralism—the proposal of a single ideal religious order in which Catholicism would hold a privileged place. But just as the option of a single normative social-religious system was rejected as the Catholic ideal in the Declaration on Religious Freedom, so also conciliar and post-conciliar Catholic teaching has rejected the ideal of a single, normative model of political and economic order. This parallelism is also evident in the kind of solution actually proposed for dealing with pluralism and conflict. In the religious sector the Council did not abandon Catholic commitment to the truth of the Christian religion. Far from it. Rather, it asserted that a Christian understanding of the human person, rooted both in the Christian tradition and the tradition of reason, demands that human dignity be respected through the civil guarantee of religious freedom. Similarly, the conciliar response to social and ideological pluralism did not take the form of a retreat by the church from the effort to establish justice and peace in global society. Rather, it affirmed that there are basic rights in the social, economic, political, and cultural fields which all systems and all ideologies are bound to respect. These are the basic rights of the human person, derived from the fundamental dignity of the person.

In the midst of Vatican II, Pope John XXIII issued his encyclical letter *Pacem in Terris* in which he sought to move the Council toward this new perspective. In his words:

Any human society, if it is to be well ordered and productive, must lay down as a foundation this principle, namely, that every human being is a person; that is, his nature is endowed with intelligence and free will. Indeed, precisely because he is a person he has rights and obligations flowing directly and simultaneously from his very nature. And as these rights are universal and inviolable so they cannot in any way be surrendered. [6]

Following John XXIII's lead, the Council affirmed the full array of human rights spelled out in *Pacem in Terris* as the norms to which every society is accountable no matter what its political, economic, or ideological system, and to which the international order itself can be held accountable. These rights include both the civil and political rights generally associated with Western democracies and the social and economic rights emphasized in socialist societies. In following John XXIII, the Council did not propose a single model of society or nostalgically seek the elimination of pluralism. It adopted a normative framework for a pluralistic world.

This move amounts to a definitive shift in Catholicism from a social ethic which proposed a concrete model of society as demanded by the natural law to a social ethic in which all social models are held accountable to the standards of human rights. The difference between the two perspectives is the acceptance of social, political, and ideological pluralism as an inescapable fact in the contemporary world. Human rights norms do not lead to the prescription of any single economic, political, or ideological system as the natural law ethic which dominated past Catholic thought has often claimed to do. Rather, basic human rights set limits and establish obligations for all systems and ideologies, leaving the precise form in which these systems will be organized undefined. In making this somewhat more modest claim, conciliar and postconciliar Catholicism has actually increased its capacity to make a critical and creative contribution to the social life of a pluralistic global society.

How did this substantial shift in the foundation of Catholic social thought come about? There were a variety of intellectual and theological currents operating in the church in the two decades immediately preceding the Council which prepared the way for the change. From the viewpoint of social rather than intellectual history, however, an equally important cause can be discerned. As an event in the social history of the church, the Council had an impact on Catholic thought similar to the influence which the founding of the United Nations exerted on the content of secular political thought in general. Both events gathered representatives from all regions of the globe, persons with vastly different cultural backgrounds, from countries with enormously different levels of economic development and wealth, from societies with opposed political and ideological systems. Though the events leading to the creation of the United Nations and those which transpired at the Vatican Council had evidently different purposes, they had a common concern with the problem of the unity of the human community and the task of finding norms and structures for world peace in the face of ideological pluralism and conflict. It is true that Westerners had the largest voice both in the founding of the United Nations and at the Second Vatican Council. But in both assemblies the conflicts between East and West, between Western and non-Western culture, and between rich nations and poor nations were conflicts *internal* to the two assemblies themselves. The need to find consensus on a normative basis for international justice and peace without suppressing the legitimate differences between regions and social systems led both bodies to a human rights focus. The early years of the United Nations saw the first really significant efforts at the elaboration of a fundamental set of internationally accepted standards for a pluralist globe. The Second Vatican Council attempted the same task for a church newly aware of itself as a transnational, transcultural community.

Theologian Karl Rahner has suggested that the most fundamental significance of the Second Vatican Council lies in the qualitative difference between the broad representation of non-European regional sub-units of the church which occurred at the Council and the Europocentrism of the history of Catholicism since the days of the Apostle Paul. In Rahner's view the Second Vatican Council marked the beginning of Catholicism as a genuinely worldwide community. At Vatican II, "a world church as such begins to act through the reciprocal influence exerted by all its components." [7] In other words, at the Council the Catholic church became, at least incipiently, a genuinely transnational body rather than a European one with missionary outposts. [8] Though the Council was obviously a Christian assembly, the forms of Christianity represented were culturally diverse and had been shaped by very different economic, political, and ideological contexts. At Vatican II these diverse forms of Christianity were brought into direct contact with each other. It should, therefore, have been almost predictable that a new emphasis on the full range of human rights, both civil/political and social/economic, would develop once the decision had been reached to convoke a Council of the transnational Catholic church.

Since the Second World War nongovernmental organizations, like the International Commission of Jurists and Amnesty International, which are both transnational and also advocates for international justice and peace, have increasingly employed the perspective of human rights as the normative basis for their activities. [9] In a world which is simultaneously pluralistic and interdependent, human rights norms have gained a central place because they attempt to articulate the immunities and entitlements which are due every person "simply by virtue of being a human person, irrespective of his or her social status, cultural accomplishments, moral merits, religious beliefs, class memberships, or contractual relationships." [10] This quality of universality and the status of human rights as "moral claims that human persons can make independently of and prior to their acknowledgment by particular societies" [11] are especially important for groups that aim to contribute to a normative foundation for a pluralist world order and for the elaboration of a transnational ethic.

The impetus for the rapid development of a human rights ethic in the Catholic church came in large part from the non-European regions of the transnational church (from the poor countries of the Third World in the area of social/economic rights and from the United States in the area of civil/political rights, especially the right to religious freedom). The recent systematic elaboration of the normative human rights framework of contemporary Catholicism, however, was initiated principally at the center, namely at the transnational assembly of all the Catholic bishops in Council under the leadership of the chief transnational agent of the

church, the Pope. Thus the exigencies of regional and ideological pluralism combined with need for unity at the center to produce a fundamental
reorientation in the church's understanding of the appropriate normative
foundation for global politics and economy.

All this was only incipient at the Council. But as Rahner insists, the
process of developing a transnational perspective and pastoral strategy
was definitively begun at the Second Vatican Council. Since the Council
the normative framework has been developed in greater detail. The
postconciliar period has also seen the development of local, national,
regional, and transnational institutional structures within the church for
the implementation of the new human rights perspective. This process
of implementation has been hesitant, conflictive, and at times self-
contradictory. Nevertheless, the understanding of rights which has been
developing since the Council in Catholic social thought in response to
its newly discovered transnational context is the chief explanation of the
new visibility of the church in the human rights struggle. [12]

II. THE NORMATIVE UNDERSTANDING: AN INTEGRAL THEORY OF RIGHTS

The fact that the Catholic church pursues both its religious mission
and its pastoral role in nearly all the regions of the globe has brought
it into contact with all the major forms of human rights violations and
with the chief ideological interpretations of human rights. In its attempt
to formulate an understanding of human rights appropriate to its transnational existence, the church has inevitably had to face the arguments
about the central focus of human rights theory which divide the Western
democracies from the Eastern socialist bloc. In the liberal tradition of the
West the civil and political freedoms of speech, worship, assembly, press,
and the juridical guarantees of *habeas corpus* and due process are at the
center of human rights thinking. Human rights are rooted in the liberty
of the individual person In Marxist socialism, on the other hand, the
rights to work, to minimum levels of nutrition, and to active participation
in the process of creating a socialist society are central. These rights
are grounded by the conviction that personal freedom is an abstraction
unless it is viewed in the economic and social context which conditions
it. [13] A similar though not identical polarity characterizes the debate
between the industrial powers of the North and the less developed countries of the South. In general, the Northern societies argue for an effort
to meet human needs within the context of a social system based on a
prior commitment to political and economic liberty. In the countries of
the South the emphasis is inverted. Political and economic freedom are

regarded as obtainable for the vast majority of the population of these countries only in the context of policies aimed at meeting basic needs for food, clothing, shelter, and minimum education. [14]

These divergent emphases in thinking about human rights have all had an impact on the content of the contemporary Roman Catholic understanding of rights. It is one of the deep biases of the Catholic tradition to respond to basic intellectual and social choices by saying both/and rather than either/or. John XXIII's *Pacem in Terris* includes all the rights emphasized on each side of these East/West and North/ South debates. It includes all the rights enumerated in the UN Universal Declaration and its two accompanying Covenants. It affirms the rights to life, bodily integrity, food, clothing, shelter, rest, medical care, and the social services necessary to protect these rights. It includes the rights to freedom of communication (speech, press), to information, and to education. In the area of religious activity it affirms the right to honor God in accord with one's conscience and to practice religion in private and in public. In the area of family life the rights to marry, to procreate, and to the economic and social conditions necessary for the support of family life are all included. Economic rights include the rights to work, to humane working conditions, to a just wage, to appropriate participation in the management of economic enterprises, and to the ownership of private property within limits established by social duties. The rights of assembly and association and the right to organize are also affirmed, as are the rights to freedom of movement and to internal and external migration. Finally, the encyclical asserts the political right to participate in public affairs and the juridical right to consitutional protection of all other rights, including *habeas corpus* and due process. [15]

The appeal of this comprehensive list of human rights is certainly a powerful one, as the enthusiastic reception which *Pacem in Terris* received in many parts of the world testifies. Several questions must be raised about such an all inclusive understanding of rights. The strength of such a universal and integral approach to rights may also be a weakness. In seeking to incorporate the emphases of both East and West, of North and South, the church's understanding of human rights may be in danger of rising above the actual conflicts of global society which generate human rights violations. It can be asked whether some more recent statements from the Holy See do not show unmistakable signs of using abstract comprehensiveness as a substitute for concrete choice and action in the midst of conflict. For example, Pope Paul VI, after an analysis of capitalism, socialism, liberalism, and Marxism, affirmed that the foundation of Christian engagement in political action "is above and sometimes opposed to the ideologies," and is "beyond every system." [16] At their Third General Conference held in Puebla, Mexico, in 1979, the

Latin American episcopate expressed ambivalence about how the commitment of the church to human rights should be related to the major ideologies which currently motivate political action in Latin America. [17]

A response to this problem involves three points. The first concerns the ultimate foundation of the Catholic rights theory. The second deals with the historical background of the theory in modern Catholic thought. And the third addresses once again its relationship to the current context for the protection and violation of human rights in global society.

First, then, the foundational principle of the theory must be distinguished from an abstractly inclusive harmonization of the rights emphasized by the various competing ideologies. The fundamental value which undergirds it is neither simply the liberty of the individual person stressed in the liberal democracies nor simply the social participation and economic well-being stressed in various ways by Marxism and socialism. Rather the theory maintains that respect for freedom, the meeting of basic needs, and participation in community and social relationships are all essential aspects of the human dignity which is the foundation of all rights. The institutional protection of personal freedom is emphasized by liberal democracy. The fulfillment of human needs is stressed by the emerging "basic needs" strategies at the center of the North-South debate. And the restructuring of the social and economic order in a way that allows genuine communal participation in the corporate life of society is the program of socialist thought. Each of these ideologies links its fundamental understanding of human rights with a particular structural obstacle to the realization of human dignity. The contemporary Catholic understanding, however, refuses to tie its notion of human dignity to only one of these three spheres of life in which persons can be either violated or protected by the structure of the social order. As John XXIII put it, "The cardinal point of this tendency is that individual men are necessarily the foundation, cause, and end of all social institutions. We are referring to human beings, insofar as they are social by nature, and raised to an order of existence which transcends and subdues nature." [18] Any political, economic, or social system which is to be morally legitimate must provide respect for these spheres of freedom, need, and relationship. Thus the foundational norm of human dignity does not claim to be an ideological principle of social organization but rather a principle of moral and political legitimacy.

The Catholic tradition offers two warrants for the validity of the foundational principle. The imperative arising from human dignity is based on the indicative of the person's transcendence over the world of things. The ability of persons to think and to choose, their hopes which always outrun the historical moment, and the experienced call to discriminate between good and evil actions—all these indicate that persons are more than things. This warrant for the foundational principle of Catholic rights theory is held to be accessible and plausible apart from the particular doctrines of the Christian faith. The Christian faith does provide, however, a second explicitly Christian warrant for the principle of human dignity. The beliefs that all persons are created in the image of God, that they are redeemed by Jesus Christ, and that they are summoned by God to a destiny beyond history serve both to support and to interpret the fundamental significance of human existence. The theological doctrines both illuminate general human experience and are themselves illuminated by such experience. With this as the basic relationship between theological and philosophical approaches to the norm of human dignity, the Catholic tradition does not hesitate to claim a universal validity for the way it seeks to ground human rights in the dignity of the person rather than in convictions about institutional and structural means for the protection of this dignity.[19]

A full response to the charge that this notion of human dignity is the result of a false abstraction from the realities of social conflict and the need for choice leads to the consideration of a second point. As a norm of political legitimacy the standard of respect for human dignity affirms that political and economic institutions are to serve human persons as free, needy, and relational beings. The primary referent of the term is not abstract and conceptual but concrete and existential: actually existing human beings. At the same time, however, the notion of human dignity is nearly empty of meaning. Unless it is further specified, the notion of human dignity lacks all reference to particular freedom, needs, and relationships. It is for this reason that most ideological systems can appeal to human dignity for moral legitimacy. Therefore, unless the relationship between the transcendental worth of persons and particular human freedoms, needs, and relationships can be specified, the notion of dignity will become an empty notion.[20] The task of determining the concrete political and economic conditions which are in fact required to protect human freedom, meet human needs, and support human relationships is an historical task. The move from the affirmation of the worth of persons to the proposal of *specific* rights which can legitimately be claimed from society is mediated by historical experience and historically accumulated understanding.[21] Historical memory and continuing historical experience are thus the only means by which the notion of dignity gains enough concrete content to support particular rights claims. Therefore every theory of rights which claims human dignity as its foundation necessarily presupposes a tradition of historical memory about the human effects of different kinds of social and political systems in the past. It also presupposes an understanding of the human effects of present patterns of social organization.

Over the past hundred years the Catholic ethical tradition has been self-consciously engaged in a protracted effort to determine more precisely just what conditions *are* necessary if human persons are to be protected in their dignity. During the years of Leo XIII's pontificate, two of these conditions were brought to the fore. The first was the indispensability of minimum economic levels for all, in the form of adequate wages and broad distribution of property. Second, in the political realm it was recognized that the freedom of the majority in a democracy or of the ruling powers in other forms of polity must be limited by their obligation to serve the common good of the whole society. This is the principle of the limited state, a principle which places a check on all forms of totalitarianism by making government accountable for the basic rights and liberties of all citizens. These two principles are respectively the bases of social/economic rights and civil/political rights.

The history of the church's understanding of these principles has followed a circuitous path through the past century. Opposition to anticlerical interpretations of religious liberty led to a limited understanding of the way persons would be protected in their dignity by a constitutional guarantee for civil liberties and political rights. Also resistance to the totalitarianism and irreligion of the Soviet Union led to a narrowed understanding of the potential human benefits of other kinds of socialist models. [22]

Despite the hesitant movement of Catholic understanding of the concrete exigencies of dignity, however, one basic insight was ingrained in the historical memory of the church by its efforts in this area: the conviction that dignity would be violated by any system which denied political freedom in the name of economic rights or which appealed to the primacy of individual liberty as justification for its failure to meet basic human needs. This insight was often expressed in the form of proposals for a "third way" between capitalism and socialism. This middle path was variously elaborated in the social models known as corporatism, solidarism, and Christian democracy. All of these models were based on the assumption that respect for civil and political rights could be combined with protection of social and economic rights in a harmonious, nonconflictual social order. The supposition that this inclusive vision of human dignity could be protected concretely without the continuing presence of social conflict was the chief reason why Catholic concern has often been one step removed from the actual sources of conflict and rights violations. The reluctance to address the reality of conflict often cut the nerve of action which leads to social change. Thus the predominant Catholic disposition to seek resolution of the problem of the pluralism of ideologies and diversity of social systems by direct appeal to social harmony was linked with a reluctance to deal with the realities of power and conflict. This negative side of Catholic human rights thought was, however, directly linked with its experience and memory of the indispensability of both civil/political and social/economic rights.

The shift in appreciation of the reality of ideological and social pluralism which was begun by Vatican II is the focus of the third point to be considered in discussing the charge of abstractness leveled against the current Catholic approach to rights. The transnational and transcultural institutional self-consciousness of the church has reinforced its historic bias against opting for one of the competing ideologies or social models which shape the context in which the church exists. However, the beginning of the legitimation of pluralism which occurred at the Council has freed the church to approach the issue of conflict in a new way. Though this development is still incipient, the post-conciliar church has begun to look for the realization of the fullness of human dignity in the midst of political and economic conflict. Rather than proposing a model of social organization that claims to protect human dignity in every nation or culture, recent statements from Rome have emphasized the ways that the interconnected package of civil/political and social/economic rights is today threatened by a variety of oppressive power configurations. The post-conciliar church's normative statements have increasingly argued that civil/political and social/economic rights are interconnected and that respect for one set of rights is dependent on respect for the other. The historical memory of the church is combining with its present historical experience as a community to produce what amounts to a transnational human rights ideology. The elements of this new ideology are a respect for social pluralism, a conviction that all human rights are interconnected, and a willingness to stand for the rights of those who are simultaneously denied their political and economic rights against those whose disproportionate political and economic power is the cause of this denial.

The basis of this new "human rights ideology" was particularly evident at the 1971 Synod of Bishops, an assembly which, significantly, was a transnational one. The interconnection of all rights was highlighted in the Synod's assertion of the "right to development." This right was defined as "the dynamic interpenetration of all those fundamental human rights upon which the aspirations of individuals and nations are based." [23] It is also evident in the assertion of the right to participation —"a right which is to be applied in the economic and in the social field. [24] Both the "right to development" and the "right to participation" are shorthand ways of affirming the interconnected rights of those deprived of development and excluded from economic and political participation.

These two "synthetic" rights are in the best tradition of the Catholic bias to say: *both* political liberty *and* basic human needs. In the light of the other studies of this project, the *both/and* which is lodged in the Catholic historical memory may have new relevance in the context of an interdependent and pluralistic world.

III. IMPLICATIONS: THE RIGHTS OF THE OPPRESSED

Several conclusions about the implications of the contemporary Catholic church's understanding of human rights can be drawn from the generalizations proposed in this essay. [25] If the historical memory and present transnational experience of the Catholic community is in any way accurate, it would seem that the argument between those who say "bread first" and those who say "freedom first" has reached a dead end. And increasingly those without political freedom and access to political power seem to end up without bread. The interconnection of rights has become evident not only in theory but in practice. As J. P. Pronk, Minister for Development Cooperation from the Netherlands put it:

> In Latin America and elsewhere we see in a dramatic way how people set about achieving social justice, how they need to exercise political freedom to do this, and how they are oppressed and become the victims of inhuman tortures. The link between the different categories [of rights] is shown clearly not only in the preambles to treaties but also in the practical exercise of human rights. [26]

The empirical evidence for this interconnection of rights is presented in other papers of this study. But if such an interpretation of the situation is correct, then the charge of "abstractness" and indecisiveness against the inclusive Catholic approach to rights is unfounded. The same can be said about similar charges against the UN Universal Declaration.

Those who would learn from the mistakes of the past, however, should realize that this inclusiveness of Catholic rights theory has hindered the church's capacity for action and frequently fostered a reactionary stance. The condition for translating an inclusive theory of rights into a strategy for action and policy is the recognition that pluralism is inevitably accompanied by conflict. Defense and support of the full range of rights for every person under current patterns of economic and political conflict, therefore, calls for a choice. This choice is one which will orient policy toward preferential concern for the rights of those who have neither bread nor freedom. It means that the rights of the oppressed, those deprived of both political and economic power, should take priority in policy over privileged forms of influence and wealth.

The contemporary Catholic understanding of human rights has just begun to move in this direction. But the leaders of both liberal and authoritarian governments and of capitalist and socialist economies have something to learn from transnational organizations like the Catholic church. It may even be that a community with as long a memory and as pragmatic a style as the Catholic church has something unique to contribute to a global understanding of a new human rights ideology. The potential for such a contribution will become an actuality if and only if the church continues on the course charted at Vatican II.

NOTES TO CHAPTER 1

1. See Bernard Plongeron, "Anathema or Dialogue? Christian Reactions to Declarations of the Rights of Man in the United States and Europe in the Eighteenth Century," in Alois Muller and Norbert Greinacher, eds., *The Church and the Rights of Man, Concilium,* no. 124 (New York: Seabury, 1979) pp. 39–47; and Arturo Gaete, "Socialism and Communism: History of a Problem-Ridden Condemnation" *LADOC* IV, 1 (September, 1973), pp. 1–16.

2. See, for example: Brian H. Smith, "Church Strategies and Human Rights in Latin America," unpublished Working Paper, Woodstock Theological Center, 1979; Alfred T. Hennelly, Chap. 2 of this volume; Muller and Greinacher, eds., *The Church and the Rights of Man,* pp. 77–121.

3. *Dignitatis Humanae,* no. 1, The translation is that found in Walter Abbott and Joseph Gallagher, eds., *The Documents of Vatican II* (New York: Guild Press/America Press, 1966), p. 677.

4. John Courtney Murray, "Commentary and Notes on the Declaration on Religious Liberty," in Abbott and Gallagher, p. 677, n. 4. See also Murray, "Vers une intelligence du développement de la doctrine de l'Église sur la liberté religieuse," in *Vatican II: La Liberté Religieuse* (Paris: Cerf, 1967), pp. 111–147.

5. *Gaudium et Spes,* no. 4, in Abbott and Gallagher, p. 202–203.

6. *Pacem in Terris,* no. 9. In Joseph Gremillion, ed., *The Gospel of Peace and Justice: Catholic Social Teaching since Pope John* (Maryknoll, N.Y.: Orbis Books, 1976), p. 203.

7. Karl Rahner, "Towards a Fundamental Interpretation of Vatican II," *Theological Studies* 40 (1979), p. 717.

8. For a fuller discussion of this shift and its implications for the structure, function, and self-understanding of the Catholic church, see Joseph Gremillion, *The Gospel of Peace and Justice* (Maryknoll, N.Y.: Orbis Books, 1976), pp. 57–68; *idem, Harvard Seminar on Muslim Jewish Christian Faith Communities as Transnational Actors for Peace and Justice:*

Report and Interpretation (Washington, D.C.: Interreligious Peace Colloquium, 1979, privately circulated), pp. 20–29 and *passim;* and J. Bryan Hehir, "The Roman Catholic Church as Transnational Actor: Amending Vallier," unpublished paper, International Studies Association, Washington, D.C., February 23, 1978.

9. See José Zalaquett, "The Scope of Human Rights: Consensus and Priorities among Practitioners," and John A. Coleman, "The Role of International Non-Governmental Organizations in Promoting Human Rights," unpublished Working Papers, Woodstock Theological Center, October, 1979.

10. John Langan, Chap. 4 of this volume.

11. *Ibid.*

12. See Gremillion, *The Gospel of Peace and Justice,* Section II, "The Church as a Social Actor," pp. 125–132.

13. See John Haughey, "Individualism and Rights in Karl Marx," Chap. 5 of this volume.

14. See Drew Christiansen, "Basic Needs: Criterion for the Legitimacy of Development, Chap. 11 of this volume, and John Weeks and Elizabeth Dore, "Basic Needs in Development Strategies: The Journey of a Concept." Chapter 4, *Human Rights and Basic Needs in the Americas.*

15. *Pacem in Terris,* nos. 9–27. See also Pontifical Commission on Justice and Peace, *The Church and Human Rights* (Vatican City: Vatican Polyglot Press, 1975); and David Hollenbach, *Claims in Conflict: Retrieving and Renewing the Catholic Human Rights Tradition* (New York: Paulist Press, 1979), pp. 62–69, 89–100.

16. Pope Paul VI, *Octogesima Adveniens,* nos. 27, 36, in Gremillion, *The Gospel of Peace and Justice,* pp. 498, 501.

17. For an analysis of this ambivalence, see Gregory Baum, "The Meaning of Ideology," in the Catholic Theological Society of America, *Proceedings of the 34th Annual Convention,* 1979, pp. 174–175.

18. *Mater et Magistra,* no. 219. In Gremillion, *The Gospel of Peace and Justice,* p. 190.

19. For a more detailed discussion of these warrants, see Hollenbach, Chapter 3 of this volume and *Claims in Conflict,* pp. 107–137

20. For a somewhat similar though not identical argument, see Bruno Schuller, "Die Personwürde des menschen als Beweisgrund in der normativen Ethik," *Theologie und Glaube* 53 (1978), pp. 538–555.

21. See John Courtney Murray, "The Problem of State Religion," *Theological Studies* 12 (1951), p. 170.

22. For an account of this history of modern Catholic reflections on the specific rights essential to the protection of human dignity, see Hollenbach, *Claims in Conflict,* Chapter 2, pp. 41–106.

23. "Justice in the World," no. 15, Gremillion, *The Gospel of Peace and Justice,* p. 516.

24. "Justice in the World," no. 18, in Gremillion, *The Gospel of Peace and Justice,* p. 517.

25. What is said here is argued in somewhat greater detail in Hollenbach, *Claims in Conflict,* Chapter 5, pp. 187–207.

26. J. P. Pronk, "Human Rights and Development Aid," *International Commission of Jurists Review* 18 (June, 1977) pp. 35–36. See also Patricia Weiss Fagen, "The Links Between Human Rights and Basic Needs," *Background* (Center for International Policy) (Spring 1978).

ALFRED HENNELLY, S.J.

2. Human Rights and Latin American Theology

The objective of this chapter will be to synthesize and reflect upon a perspective on human rights that is derived from Latin American theology in the past 20 years. This new theological development is of great importance, not only for Latin America but also for the developing nations of Asia and Africa, where it has been carefully studied and creatively adapted in recent years. [1] Its importance lies in the fact that, for the first time in centuries, a Christian vision and practice is being produced within the context of the poor majority of the human race. In examining this development, therefore, my hope is to offer a contribution to the enormously difficult task of achieving whatever consensus is possible concerning human rights in a global context.

The historical background of recent Latin American theology will be sketched here in cursory fashion, since I have treated it at greater length in other publications. [2] A pivotal year was 1960, when the Uruguayan Jesuit Juan Luis Segundo initiated a theological approach that transcended the customary European and North American models and began instead from his own continent's situation of massive human suffering and injustice. [3] A dramatic impetus along this line was then provided by the Second Vatican Council (1962–1965), especially in its epoch-making Constitution on the Church in the Modern World (*Gaudium et Spes*). Finally, the Latin American bishops' conference (CELAM) contributed both official endorsement and further development of the new approach in continent-wide assemblies at Medellín, Colombia (1968) and Puebla, Mexico (1979).

In the recent efflorescence of theology in Latin America, the topic of human rights does not constitute a central *explicit* theme. This is not to deny the existence of some works that treat specifically of human rights, but their number is not large. [4] However, the thesis of this study is that the *reality* of human rights (including socioeconomic rights as well as individual political rights) does have central importance, although this centrality is usually articulated with different concepts and terminology than the ones that we are accustomed to in North America.

The next section of my study, then, discusses some basic themes that are common among Latin American theologians, but which also concern the issue of human rights. It should be strongly stressed that the authors themselves do not usually make the explicit connections that I suggest.

The relative lack of explicit attention to human rights derives from the exercise of what Latin Americans call "ideological suspicion." In this case, it is the suspicion that North American emphasis on human rights (understood as individual freedoms) serves as an ideological mask to conceal the massive human suffering on the socioeconomic level that envelops great masses of human beings in the southern continent, but more importantly to conceal North American complicity in contributing to this situation of suffering. The role of the United States government and business interests in creating and sustaining the Somoza dynasty in Nicaragua for almost 50 years—years of incredible plunder of the poor—provides only one dramatic illustration of the bases for such suspicion.

Indeed, Segundo has complained recently that "if my country could apply to the rich nations the economic and political mechanisms which they now apply to us, then we would be the ones who would go to investigate—hypocritically, to be sure—the violations of human rights in those countries." And he concludes that "the tragedy of the situation is that the ones who determine and control the defense of human rights . . . are the very ones who make human rights impossible in three quarters of the planet." [5] I shall return to this argument in the course of my analysis.

Turning to a consideration of what I believe to be the major themes both of Latin American theologians and of the Latin American episcopal conference during the past 15 years, I shall then present my own views concerning the linkages between these ideas and the question of human rights. Because of limitations of space, my treatment is necessarily brief, but references are provided to sources where the issues are analyzed more fully.

I: THE REALITY OF SOCIAL SIN

The concept of social sin is a rather new topic in theology, but it is not one that is confined to Latin America. In an important article, Peter Henriot has traced the development of the idea in the official teaching of the Roman Catholic Church and of the World Council of Churches, as well as in the Latin American episcopal meeting in Medellín in 1968. [6]

Henriot points out the elements that together comprise social sin: "In general, social sin refers to: 1) Structures that oppress human beings, violate human dignity, stifle freedom, impose gross inequality; 2) Situations that promote and facilitate individual acts of selfishness; 3) The complicity of persons who do not take responsibility for the evil being done." [7] He cites a key passage from the Second Vatican Council which clearly shows the awareness of this concept by the Roman Catholic church:

> To be sure, the disturbances which so frequently occur in the social order result in part from the natural tensions of economic, political and social forms. But at a deeper level they flow from man's pride and selfishness, which contaminate even the social sphere. When the structure of affairs is flawed by the consequences of sin, man, already born with a bent toward evil, finds there new inducements to sin, which cannot be overcome without strenuous efforts and the assistance of grace. [8]

Granted that the concept of social sin has come into general use, what is peculiar to the Latin American situation is the *emphasis* given to this reality as well as to the acute *urgency* of the Christian response needed to transform the unjust structures that perpetuate social sin. This emphasis and urgency result from a primal fact of the Latin American reality: the vast majority of human beings in the continent live in situations of deprivation and suffering that are everywhere evident and that simply cannot be evaded. Ignacio Ellacuría has expressed this succinctly: "Who the poor are in the real situation of the Third World is not a problem whose solution requires scriptural exegesis or sociological analysis or historical theories. . . . As a primary fact, as the real situation of the majority of humanity, there is no room for partisan equivocations." [9]

Perhaps the rationale for such emphasis and urgency can best be understood, not in theological syllogisms, but in the more journalistic description offered by George H. Dunne. In describing a *mocambo* or slum of Recife in Northeast Brazil, Dunne observes

> . . . it is inhabited by some 50,000 wretches made, so the catechism says, in the image and likeness of God, who live, eat, sleep, copulate, bear babies, bury babies, raise families, suffer, laugh, cry and die on a garbage dump. I do not know where they are buried. Perhaps in the garbage. It seems unreasonable to expect a society which could not find them a better place to live to provide them with a more decent place in which to lie dead. [10]

Dunne also takes pains to point out that this is not an isolated phenomenon, for

> one-half million of Recife's population of 1,250,000 live in its *mocambos*. A quarter of Rio's population of more than 3,000,000 are crowded into its hillside *favelas*. The same ghastly statistics, with little proportional variation, would describe the demographic situation in Caracas, Lima, Fortaleza, Salvador, and other Latin American cities. [11]

The situation of social sin, then, is the theological concept which lies at the root of Latin American reflections. Whatever positive steps might be elaborated to change the structures that cause this sin, it is clear that, negatively, it demands opposition. That is to say, it constitutes the very antithesis of the kingdom of God and requires of the Christian an unconditional "no." [12]

In the context of human rights, it is also glaringly obvious that the reality of social sin consists in an almost total deprivation of socioeconomic rights: food, clothing, housing, medical care, literacy, work, security, and the barest minimum of human culture. Faced with such comprehensive deprivation, the only possible reaction of the masses is either resignation or rebellion. To ensure that the response continues to be resignation and to preclude a successful rebellion, political and other organizational rights have been largely suspended, while such flagrant crimes as arbitrary arrest, torture, and murder have been inflicted on numerous persons in a generalized campaign of intimidation. The ideology of "national security," [13] also known as "permanent war," has been elaborated to justify these glaring violations of rights as well as to preserve the status quo of the powerful. Here, as in much of the third world, the point to be emphasized is that the deprivation of socioeconomic rights lies at the core of the problem and thus must be given primary consideration in any elaboration of a human rights policy.

II. THE CHURCH OF THE POOR

Faced with the situation of social sin, the Latin American church in the past two decades has been confronted with a truly formidable choice: either it would take the side of those who were suffering from social injustice or it would support the ones causing or maintaining the situation of injustice. With increasing firmness, the church has committed itself to the poor, and I will now briefly survey this decision in its official documents and in the writings of theologians.

In the Second Conference of Latin American Bishops (CELAM II) held at Medellín, Colombia, in 1968, the participants manifested a keen awareness of the prevalence of injustice in their countries. The very first document, on justice, begins as follows: "There are in existence many studies of the Latin American people. The misery that besets large masses of human beings in all of our countries is described in all of these studies. That misery, as a collective fact, expresses itself as injustice which cries to the heavens." [14] Faced with this collective fact, the bishops emphasize that "the Church, the People of God, will lend its support to the downtrodden of every social class so that they may come to know their rights and how to make use of them. To this end the Church will utilize its moral strength and will seek to collaborate with competent professionals and institutions." [15] Later, in the context of a poor church, the bishops state that the church "experiences the urgency of translating that spirit of poverty into actions, attitudes, and norms that make it a more lucid and authentic sign of its Lord. The poverty of so many brothers cries out for justice, solidarity, open witness, commitment, strength, and exertion directed to the fulfillment of the redeeming mission to which it is committed by Christ." [16]

The realization of the need for solidarity with the poor and with their cause was taken up with even greater clarity and decisiveness in CELAM III more than ten years later at Puebla, Mexico. In an entire chapter entitled "A Preferential Option for the Poor," the bishops commit themselves "to take up once again the position of the Second General Conference of the Latin American Episcopate in Medellín, which adopted a clear and prophetic option expressing preference for, and solidarity with, the poor . . . We affirm the need for conversion on the part of the whole Church to a preferential option for the poor, an option aimed at their integral liberation." [17]

Moving to the area of concrete options, the bishops adopt the following, among others: "Committed to the poor, we condemn as anti-evangelical the extreme poverty that affects an extremely large segment of the population. . . . We will make every effort to understand and denounce the mechanisms that generate their poverty. . . . Acknowledging the solidarity of other Churches, we will combine our efforts with those of people of good will in order to uproot poverty and create a more just and fraternal world." [18]

Here and in other places in the documents the bishops caution that the commitment to the poor is "preferential but not exclusive." Lest this seem to absolve the rich of any responsibility, however, the text clearly states the implications for them: ". . . the witness of a poor Church can evangelize the rich whose hearts are attached to wealth, thus converting them and freeing them from this bondage and their own egotism." [19]

Besides the official documents, there is a large and continually growing theological literature on the church of the poor, which can be referred to only cursorily here. Foremost in this field has been the Peruvian priest Gustavo Gutiérrez, who has emphasized the creation of a theology "from the reverse side of history," that is, from the standpoint of the poor, [20] and the need for rereading history "with the eyes of the poor." [21] The book that brought him to world attention, *A Theology of Liberation* (first published in 1971), concluded with an eloquent chapter on "Poverty: Solidarity and Protest," where he insists that "Christian poverty, an expression of love, is solidarity *with the poor* and is a protest against poverty." [22] Recently, other authors have devoted much more detailed attention to the church of the poor as a basic source—in their view *the* basic source—for an authentic Christian theology. [23]

These developments have affected the renewal of the Catholic human rights tradition recently espoused by David Hollenbach. [24] All of Hollenbach's strategic principles concern the rights of the poor, the dominated, and the marginalized in the global society. The option of the Latin American church (which constitutes almost half of Roman Catholicism) appears destined to exert enormous pressure for the incorporation of such principles in the teaching of the universal church. [25] At the same time, the wealth of theological analysis now under way regarding the church of the poor should provide theological depth and solidity for such a renewal. The more practical implications of the Latin American option will be discussed in the following section.

III: THE ECCLESIAL BASE COMMUNITIES

In the book cited, Hollenbach concluded his argument with a prudent warning regarding his three strategic principles: "Whether they are in fact strategically suited to the formation of policy in a pluralistic and conflicted world can finally be determined only by the test of action." [26] One of the major achievements—if not *the* major one—of the Latin American bishops both at Medellín and at Puebla was to translate their commitment to a church of the poor precisely into concrete mechanisms of action. They accomplished this through their endorsement of the pastoral importance of "ecclesial base communities." [27]

These *comunidades eclesiales de base* (henceforth referred to as CEBs) consist of small groups of a few dozen members which emphasize the active participation of all in worship, reflection, and action, and which foster strong interpersonal bonds through this process of cooperation and sharing. In most of them there has occurred a process, popularized by the Brazilian educator Paulo Freire, called conscientization, that is, a technique of raising awareness among the poor of their situation of misery, its causes, and possible remedies for their plight. [28] This type of grassroots church had begun to flourish during the early 1960s, and has since increased its numbers to an estimated 100,000 to 150,000 cells, many of them in Brazil but with others scattered in varying density throughout all the nations of Latin America.

The Medellín conference had endorsed the CEBs, but did not enter into much detail: "The Christian ought to find the living of the community to which he has been called in his 'base community,' that is to say, in a community, local or environmental, which corresponds to the reality of a homogeneous group and whose size allows for personal fraternal contact among its members." [29] Despite a struggle because of the fear that Marxist ideas would infiltrate the CEBs, the Puebla conference not only endorsed them, but elaborated in detail their achievements during the decade since Medellín. [30]

Thus, in an analysis of the ecclesial reality in Part One of the Puebla document, it is asserted that the CEBs have both multiplied and matured since Medellín and that they now constitute a motive of "joy and hope for the Church." In accordance with the desires of Medellín they are also said to have become "centers of evangelization" and "moving forces for liberation and development" (#96). And in the very last paragraph of the lengthy document, this theme is taken up again as the communities are hailed as one of "the signs of joy and hope" in the church (#1309).

In various places throughout the Puebla conclusions, the bishops also point out more specific accomplishments of the CEBs. They contribute to a more personalized (#111) or familial (#239) style of evangelization, contrasted with the increasing coldness of modern society; they lead to a more profound understanding of the Word of God and participation in the Eucharist (#641); they promote self-examination as well as reflection on the social reality (#629); and they foster active commitment to the new commandment of love, to the struggle for justice (#640) and to the construction of a new society (#642). Finally, they have been successful in fostering vocations (#97), have encouraged the emergence of new types of lay ministry (#629), and have developed a very effective style of catechesis for simple people, both the young and adults. Consequently, when mapping out pastoral strategy, the bishops strongly emphasize their own desire "to promote, guide and accompany" the CEBs as well as to discover and train leaders for them, especially in the large cities (#648).

A good deal of pastoral and sociological study has already been done on the CEBs, usually including salutary criticism concerning their strengths and weaknesses. [31] One accomplishment has special importance with regard to human rights. José Marins has pointed out that the CEBs reject the "massification" of the people and strive to make them true *subjects* of their own history (an essential element in the pedagogy of Freire). [32] One result is that the Word of God has become the "collective property of the people" and no longer a clerical monopoly. [33] Consequently, "the members of the Ecclesial Base Communities acquire a greater sense of equality, overcoming the barriers which divide human beings into classes or castes. And they encourage new types of service (charisms) which arise from the midst of the community." [34]

In a continent, then, where for the most part governments exert total control and subsidiary institutions have been largely suppressed, the CEBs clearly function as a grassroots "school of human rights," where the dignity and equality of persons is respected and their freedom to speak and act is encouraged and cultivated. The influence of such training, in my opinion, cannot fail to have a profound impact on the struggle for human rights in Latin America and other parts of the world in the years that lie ahead.

This new model of the church has problems and dangers as well as promise; both aspects are clear in the recent empirical studies of Thomas C. Bruneau, [35] as well as in the more theoretical analysis of Alexander Wilde. [36] The development in Latin America of other types of church organizations besides the CEBs is also very important. For example, the wide proliferation of human rights groups in various countries has been documented and analyzed by Brian Smith, [37] while the growth of even broader organizations, such as the Priests for the Third World, has been studied by Michael Dodson. [38]

A final aspect of the CEBs may serve as a transition to the next section of this chapter. The conscientization process mentioned earlier is clearly laying the groundwork for a prophetic church, that is, one that *denounces* structures or actions of injustice and oppression, while at the same time it *announces* alternatives that better embody the justice and love characteristic of the kingdom of God. [39] What is ultimately at work in this activity is a process of social, economic, and cultural analysis of society; thus I shall now consider this process and its relationship to theology.

IV. THEOLOGY AND THE SOCIAL SCIENCES

The Brazilian Leonardo Boff has recently advanced a schema which may serve to coordinate the next two sections. Boff is speaking of the specific field of Christology, but I believe his remarks pertain to any area of liberation theology: "Any liberation Christology is fashioned through two basic mediations on the theoretical level. One is that of *social analysis* concerned with the reality to be changed; the other is *hermeneutics*, which considers the theological relevance of the social analysis." The latter activity "considers the socioanalytic text in the light of Jesus Christ the Savior and the word of divine revelation, thereby guaranteeing the theological character of liberation theory and praxis." [40] Thus, without negating the mediating role of philosophy, Latin American theology gives special emphasis to the need for dialogue with the social sciences in order to understand the historical situation within which religious faith must be incarnated.

The Medellín conference broke new ground in beginning its deliberations with a social analysis of the Latin American situation, rather than relying on European or more global but abstract points of reference. Thus, after a description of "tensions between classes and internal colonialism," [41] the bishops move on to a discussion of various "international tensions and external colonialism." [42] Their conclusion is the following:

> . . . in many instances Latin America finds itself in a situation that can be called institutionalized violence. . . . This situation demands all-embracing, courageous, urgent, and profoundly renovating transformations. We should not be surprised, therefore that the "temptation to violence" is surfacing in Latin America. One should not abuse the patience of a people that for years has borne a situation that would not be acceptable to anyone with any degree of awareness of human rights. [43]

Although written in 1968, the last sentences appear prophetic with regard to more recent events in Central America.

Puebla, also, after a brief history of evangelization, begins with a "Pastoral Overview of the Sociocultural Context." [44] In one now wellknown passage, the bishops present a poignant description of the various "faces" of poverty in their continent, concluding with the assertion that

> We share other anxieties of our people that stem from a lack of respect for their dignity as human beings, made in the image and likeness of God, and for their inalienable rights as children of God. Countries such as ours, where there is frequently no respect for such fundamental human rights as life, health, education, housing, and work, are in the position of permanently violating the dignity of the person. [45]

However, despite its strong criticism of existing structures, the Puebla document has been criticized by social scientists present at the meeting for adopting a descriptive and static methodology rather than an analytic and causal one. [46] Despite many suggestions made by this group for a more rigorous method, the necessary episcopal majority for changing the document was not achieved.

At this point, in order to achieve greater precision regarding the relationship of theology and the social sciences, I will focus on a treatment of the issue that was recently prepared for the use of religious orders throughout Latin America, entitled *Pueblo de Dios y comunidad liberadora.* [47] The book's main concern is with a renewal of ecclesiology, in response to the needs of religious who are either working or planning to work among the poor, an increasingly common phenomenon throughout the continent. After a brief historical survey similar in many ways to Puebla's, it moves on to a long and detailed survey of "the contribution of the social sciences" to this work. [48] Here I can only touch on some of the more important areas.

In understanding any society, the book asserts the need for sociological theories that are relevant to the facts. Although they recognize the possible danger of an "ideological residue" behind any theory, the authors nevertheless assert their determination to pass judgment on the various models. [49]

The first to be analyzed is the development model, in which the situation of Latin America is understood as analogous to that of pre-industrial Europe. Within this framework, development depends on the *acceleration* of industrialization by capital investment and the acquisition of the most modern technology.

The second model is that of marginalization, wherein the basic problem is viewed as the existence of two strata of society, which are superimposed but not integrated. The first stratum, predominantly white, espouses the values and culture of the West and is integrated with these, both internally and externally; the other, predominantly mestizo or indigenous, is locked into the ancestral culture, without real access to the goods and services which the society produces (passive marginality) or to the making of decisions (active marginality). Development strategy in this model consists in providing *greater access* to goods and services and *greater participation* for the marginalized stratum.

The last model to be considered is that of dependence. Here the problem focuses on the two poles of center and periphery, both on the international level (macro-system) and on the national level (micro-system). The two centers are well integrated, sharing economic interests and cultural values, but their integration takes place to the detriment of the peripheries, which are marginalized as regards economic benefits, political decisions, and possibilities for expressing their cultural identity.

Development from this perspective requires the *overcoming of both external and internal colonialism,* which requires in turn a radical transformation of structures and an alternative form of social organization.

The book then carefully elaborates the reasons why the first two models are rejected, while the third is considered to be both the best explanation and the best solution to the problems of underdevelopment. Space forbids the delineation of the authors' arguments, but it is important to note that a process of *discernment* is essential, in order to adopt a solution which is not only effective but also human and Christian: "The discernment unites both levels in an option which permits us to arrive at the concrete (an effective solution) but from the perspective of a transcendent judgment on human destiny (an ethical solution)." [50]

After making this discernment, the authors move on to a critique of ecclesial practice and theological discourse, both of which are based, explicitly or implicitly, on one of the aforementioned models, and which the book is intent to bring to explicit awareness and analysis. In summary, it emphasizes that the social sciences enable us "to point out the social 'alienations' which, under the appearance of free actions, are nothing but an alienating use of activities created for the legitimation, functioning, and reproduction of the established society and its structures." [51] On the other hand, faith and theology are not merely passive recipients of the data of the social sciences, but offer their own positive contribution by enabling these sciences to transcend the three dangers or risks of all scientific thought: immanentism, determinism, and ideologization. [52] These three dangers will be further analyzed later in this chapter.

Clearly, then, dependency theory provides the linchpin for Latin American social analysis and, ultimately, for understanding the basic causes of human rights violations. But, if it is to avoid the traps of oversimplification and glittering generalities, the theory demands further development and, if possible, empirical verification. Thus Michael Dodson, while acknowledging the essential correctness of the dependency insight, argues that the Latin Americans have "employed a subtle but imprecise and still largely untested tool of analysis as though it were a finished and verified product." [53] In a constructive spirit, he suggests that advocates of the theory should pay greater analytic attention to the unique social and political experiences of each Latin American nation and should exercise greater critical detachment regarding Marxist categories of social analysis within the varied national contexts. In a similar spirit of dialogue, a team of social scientists at Yale University is currently engaged in the elaboration of a much more rigorously scientific model of dependency theory that would facilitate empirical testing. [54]

V. A SOCIAL HERMENEUTIC

At this point, further attention should be given to the second mediation mentioned by Leonardo Boff, that of hermeneutics (interpretation) and the theological relevance of social analysis. Again, it should be kept in mind that the act of theologizing occurs in the Latin American situation of massive human suffering and the preferential commitment of the church to the poor discussed previously.

In general terms, theology is envisioned within a constant *dialectical* process. [55] Fidelity to the gospel and recent church teaching leads to solidarity with the poor; this in turn leads to an experience of their suffering, but it goes still further. Through struggle with the poor to better their situation, the profound causes of inequity gradually begin to become apparent. These causes are perceived not as the result of blind fate or inevitable destiny, not as the will of God, and not as the inevitable result of certain laws of human nature. Rather they are seen to be rooted in structural mechanisms that regulate the distribution of possessions, of power, and of knowledge in ways that lead to the virtual exclusion of the poor.

In the next stage of the dialectic, one returns to Scripture and the documents of the church and attempts a rereading of them from the new perspective that has been experienced. Fundamental to this process is the axiom of the sociology of knowledge that one's perception and articulation of the world is always greatly conditioned by one's "social location," whether of profession, status, wealth, or race. Entering into a new social location, that of the poor, results in a new interpretation of the basic texts of Christianity, which I have referred to as "theology through the optic of the poor." This rereading opens up new demands arising from the commitment to the poor, as the dialectic of theory (faith) and praxis continues in a permanent spiral. The process has been analyzed in great detail in the work just mentioned and in many others; thus here I will restrict myself to one concrete example.

In a recent book on liberation theology, [56] Robert McAfee Brown illustrates the rereading process very succinctly. He takes the well-known text of Luke 4:16-18 which Jesus uses to begin his ministry: "The Spirit of the Lord is upon me, because he has anointed me to preach good news to the poor. He has sent me to proclaim release to the captives, and recovering of sight to the blind, to set at liberty those who are oppressed, to proclaim the acceptable year of the Lord." [57] Brown then turns to several standard commentaries for an accepted interpretation of this rather straightforward passage. One example from the Moffit Bible Commentary will suffice to show the general tenor: "The term *the poor* is to be taken in its inward spiritual sense . . . and similarly the expressions *captive, blind, oppressed* indicate not primarily the down-trodden victims of material force, such as Rome's, but the victims of inward repressions, neuroses, and other spiritual ills due to the failure of life's energies and purposes." [58] In response to this and similar bourgeois interpretations, Brown comments: "The consistency with which Jesus' message is confined to the 'inward' and the 'spiritual' is astounding. The harsh, angular, strident, and threatening implications of the passages have been successfully muted: one need not be upset by them nor view them as a threat to the way things are." [59] In the rest of the chapter the author presents many other texts from both Old and New Testaments as illustrations of the obscuring of the original sense of the text by bourgeois preconceptions and of the need to reinterpret the texts from the viewpoint of the poor.

A corollary of such rereading is that "ideological suspicion" has become a necessary instrument for Latin American theology. This has been analyzed in great detail in Juan Luis Segundo's recent book and indeed has been utilized by him in all his published works. [60] Its basic premise is that the dominant ideas of any epoch are usually those of the ruling classes, and are used to disguise and legitimate the preservation of their interests. The "suspicion" contends that these ideas have also infiltrated theology, especially since the theologian as a professional occupies a position among the dominant classes. Thus the question is constantly raised as to whose interests are being served by the choice, emphasis, omission, and development of themes for theological reflection. However one reacts to this hermeneutical tool, it should be kept in mind that it is very widespread, and consequently will influence any attempts to reach a broad international understanding on the question of human rights.

At this point, I would like to expand somewhat on the question of theology's use and critique of the social sciences that was mentioned earlier. For theology, as systematic and critical reflection on the faith, is not a mere passive recipient, but rather asserts that the dialogue initiated by God offers a perspective for criticism of the ideologies behind the models of the social sciences and indeed for criticism of the dangers that are involved in all scientific thought. [61]

Immanentism constitutes the first of these dangers. Certainly it has its rationale in a sound principle of scientific methodology: relationships of causality must be sought within the immanent order of the world. But from this sound principle there often arises a tendency to move to the denial of every explanation or structure of meaning which considers human life in relation to the transcendent. From this flows the attempt to restrict all attribution of meaning to human life within the framework of a world that is experienced empirically. an attempt which theology opposes consciously and vigorously.

The second major danger is determinism, that is, the necessary search for relationships of cause and effect. However, the necessity of elaborating "laws of human behavior" often leads to overlooking the possibility of the transcendence of human liberty over determinisms and to ignoring the fact that these "laws" do not have the same rigor as the laws of the natural sciences. Again, theology takes its stand decidedly against both these exaggerations.

Finally, there exists the danger of ideologization. This occurs because the social location of those who do scientific work tends to make their work selective and biased, with results that are in harmony with their interests. Thus science tends to be instrumentalized in favor of that social location, a tendency which is again countered by theology.

All of the foregoing could be expressed synthetically by saying that theology strives to keep social science open to a triple modality of transcendence. First there is the transcendence of God in his dialogue with man, a dialogue which decides the ultimate meaning of human life. Next is the transcendence of human liberty faced with social mechanisms that are considered rigid and absolute. And finally there is the transcendence of the poor, when confronted with a form of science that has become an ideological justification for the interests of the powerful.

In the context of a theological discussion of human rights, therefore, it is of the utmost importance to achieve clarity and honesty regarding one's own perspective or social location. That the latter will have enormous influence on the choice or omission of certain themes, as well as on the emphasis and mode of development accorded them, is by now a commonplace in the sociology of knowledge. [62] Moreover, I believe that an alleged neutrality on this issue collapses inevitably into accommodation with the status quo, so that the option for the perspective of the poor and oppressed is absolutely decisive. Without this, any discussion concerning a more universal framework for human rights will be blocked by the interests that lurk behind the framework of the discussion. Clearly, this applies to those who do social science as well as to those who do theology.

VI. THEOLOGY AND PRAXIS

At the conclusion of his long and erudite argument for a theology of liberation, Gustavo Gutiérrez concludes with an assertion that appears to undermine all his theological labors: ". . . we can say that all the political theologies, the theologies of hope, of revolution, and of liberation, are not worth one act of genuine solidarity with exploited social classes. They are not worth one act of faith, hope, and love, committed—in one way or another—in active participation to liberate man from everything that dehumanizes him and prevents him from living according to the will of the Father." [63] Thus, for Gutiérrez and indeed for all the better-known theologians in Latin America, theology is interpreted as a "critical reflection on praxis." [64] The praxis involved is a very definite one, that is, "real charity, action, and commitment to the service of men." [65] Even further, given the continent's situation of massive human suffering, the privileged form of praxis is to be found in the struggle to eliminate suffering and to transform the structures that perpetuate it.

I have analyzed this method in much greater detail elsewhere, and will not repeat that discussion at this point. [66] Rather, I would like to show how Gutiérrez's rather general ideas have been applied to the classical treatises of theology in the past decade. One of the more important accomplishments of Latin American theology has been an overcoming of the division between theology and spirituality. An excellent example of this may be found in Segundo Galilea's spirituality of liberation. [67] In relating spirituality to praxis, Galilea emphasizes five central intuitions that should be prominent in a liberating spirituality. [68] The first intuition centers on the fact that true conversion is not just an inner process but implies a change of commitment in favor of the oppressed. Next, he insists on the intimate link between salvation history and the liberation of the poor. Third, he holds that the commitment must be seen both as an anticipation and as a concrete advancement of the kingdom of God, a kingdom characterized by the attributes of justice, equality, fraternity, and solidarity. The fourth intuition stresses that Christian love has to be made incarnate in history and that one of the most important exercises of love is the praxis which transforms society on behalf of the oppressed. Lastly, he emphasizes the value of voluntary poverty, which entails an identification with the poor and also with their struggle for justice. In working out the implications of the five intuitions throughout his book, Galilea has produced a spirituality that is dominated by a praxis that seeks the human rights of the poor.

Another significant advance has been made in the critical area of Christology with the publication of the recent book of Jon Sobrino. [69] This author first voices dissatisfaction with past and current Christologies within the Latin American context for three basic reasons. [70] The first is their tendency to reduce the historical figure of Christ to a sublime abstraction, which allows for any number of alienating interpretations of him and his message. This has permitted the creation of images of Christ that serve to legitimate those in power: "These are the symbols that they have used, wittingly or unwittingly, to maintain the Latin American continent in its present state." [71]

Sobrino has a second difficulty with the presentation of Christ as the embodiment of universal reconciliation, in a historical and not eschatological sense. Relying on this undialectical understanding, some "present a pacifist Jesus who does not engage in prophetic denunciations, a Jesus who pronounces blessings but does not pronounce maledictions, and a Jesus who loves all human beings but who is not clearly partial to the poor and the oppressed." [72] In this way Christians have become blinded to the sinfulness (including the sinful structures) of the world and to the conflictual nature of history.

Lastly, Sobrino is dissatisfied with the tendency to absolutize Christ, which he believes would lead to an individualistic reduction of the Christian faith, since one who already possesses the absolute would tend to lose interest in the nonabsolutes of history. Sobrino, on the other hand, is convinced on evangelical grounds "that our history has absolute importance and that it is only through history that we can envision and arrive at the absolute." [73] What also vexes him is the way in which the absoluteness of Christ is used as a justification of the present unjust system in Latin America. Thus, his own objective is "to attain an understanding of Jesus based on a praxis that follows Jesus in proclaiming the coming of the Kingdom, in denouncing injustice, and in realizing that kingdom in real life—even if only partially." [74] The entire book, then, contains the elaboration of a Christology that stresses the absolute need of a commitment to the human rights of the poor in order to be related to and thus know the authentic Jesus of the gospels.

To move to another field, Leonardo Boff has produced a book on the subject of grace, which reviews the much controverted history of that concept and presents a creative modern interpretation. [75] Because of his synthesis of what has been a very fragmented treatise in the history of theology, the entire book is in itself a valuable contribution; my focus, however, will be limited to his understanding of the relation of his subject to praxis.

In a chapter on experiencing the reality of grace in Latin America, Boff accepts and elaborates the theory of dependence mentioned earlier, therefore stressing the existence of "dis-grace" as well as grace in the continent. [76] In a subsequent chapter, he discusses the Christian response to this situation by summarizing his own understanding of liberation theology. This approach, which is also his own, "begins with an analytical, sociological, and structural reading of reality that is as scientific as possible," and then "proceeds to its own theological reading based on the word of God." [77] The last step is most germane to my purposes in this section, for he asserts that liberation theology "culminates in a new praxis of the faith that aids human beings in their liberation process." [78]

In developing this within the context of grace, Boff insists that "when Christians take cognizance of the link between the personal and the structural levels, they can no longer rest content with a conversion of the heart and personal holiness on the individual level. They realize that if they are to be graced personally, they must also fight to change the societal structure and open it up to God's grace." [79] As regards the church itself, he asserts that "the grace of God can be seen in the new-found awareness of the Latin American church, which now seeks to do penance for its past complicity with the status quo and to ally itself with the liberation process" and also "in the emergence of so many prophetic figures who fight passionately for justice and are persecuted even unto death for their defense of those who have no voice." [80] Boff is a young and extraordinarily productive theologian, as well as being editor of Brazil's leading theological periodical, and it is clear that his influence will continue to expand throughout the continent.

A number of other works along the same line could be cited in the areas of sacramental theology, eschatology, biblical studies, and social ethics, [81] as well as in ecclesiology. However, the foregoing survey is sufficient to demonstrate the close relationship between recent developments in theology and praxis in favor of human rights in Latin America. These developments affect the issue of human rights on two levels. The first concerns the Latin American insistence that all theological work should lead to and constantly be informed by Christian praxis, with priority given to the struggle for the human rights of the poor and oppressed, including both socioeconomic rights and individual political rights. This should at least serve as a reminder to those working for human rights in other parts of the world that their efforts should not be limited to speculative theory (although this is necessary), but that their work must issue in the choice and implementation of strategies for social change in favor of human rights, both nationally and internationally. It should also be noted that the Latin Americans have displayed a greater openness to collaboration with secular approaches (Marxist and other) on both the theoretical and practical level than is common in the churches of the West. This collaboration, despite its dangers and difficulties, appears to me essential if the rights of all human beings are to be defended, and not merely the rights of those in the Christian churches.

On a second level, the competent and scholarly works I have surveyed seem destined increasingly to function as basic texts for the formation (or updating) of priests, religious and pastoral agents throughout Latin America. Thus, the leadership of almost half of the Catholic Church in the future will be influenced by a vision of Christian existence that places unswerving emphasis on the struggle for human rights. And it is worth repeating that the same vision is spreading rapidly to Asia and Africa, thus contacting the majority of the world's inhabitants, although the process has not yet attained the level of sophistication that exists in Latin America. [82]

My conclusion is that a long-range strategy for human rights demands the same type of theological grounding in other parts of the world, and specifically in North America. The rationale for this integration has been presented by Robert McAfee Brown in his study of the official teachings of both Catholic and Protestant churches over the past two decades. [83] This work has started in North America, but the task for this generation of theologians is surely an enormous one. [84] As in Latin America, the integration should affect every theological treatise or theme, for without this basic theological vision the struggle for human rights in the churches will continue to be seen as a praiseworthy work for the few who are interested instead of as an imperative that is at the core of all authentic Christian praxis.

CONCLUSION

From a very general perspective, it appears that Latin American theology and episcopal teaching regarding human rights have adopted a basically eclectic stance with regard to the Roman Catholic, Marxist, and liberal traditions. [85] The fundamental criteria that govern their choices from the traditions include the analysis of the actual condition of their continent, a preferential commitment to the cause of the poor, and an emphasis on the centrality of justice in the Bible and tradition.

In regard to Roman Catholic social doctrine, Latin American thought has adopted a dialectical relationship. Thus, there are constant references to the astonishing production of official teaching on social issues, beginning with Pope John XXIII's *Christianity and Social Progress* (*Mater et Magistra*) in 1961, continuing through the Second Vatican Council, and including such documents of Pope Paul VI as *On the Development of Peoples* (*Populorum Progressio*) in 1967, *The Eightieth Anniversary of Rerum Novarum* (*Octogesima Adveniens*) in 1971, and *On Evangelization in the Modern World* (*Evangelii Nuntiandi*) in 1975, as well as the document of the Synod of Bishops on *Justice in the World* in 1971. More recently, careful attention has been paid to the many speeches of Pope John Paul II, delivered both in Latin America and in other countries as well.

Along with this use of tradition, however, there exists also a constant effort to move the tradition forward, to examine how it must be expanded and concretized within the reality of the Third World. Among other things, this effort highlights the need for historical strategies for social change, not merely general pronouncements; the existence of real conflict among classes, not premature reconciliation; and the struggle for justice as essential to Christian knowledge of God, not merely an ethical consequence for some concerned Christians. I believe that these and other emphases are destined to affect universal church teaching in the future. A striking contemporary instance is provided by Pope Paul VI's apostolic exhortation on evangelization. In an important chapter regarding the very content of evangelization, the Pope devoted no less than 11 of 15 sections to a dialogue regarding issues emphasized in recent Latin American theology. [86] A promising example of such development has been provided by Ignacio Ellacuría in his essay in this volume. Latin America also offers an example of fruitful borrowing from the Marxist tradition. The fundamental reason for this, it appears to me, is Marxism's emphasis on the social dimensions and conditions of human existence, as opposed to the West's exaltation of individualism. Among Marxism's contributions are the focusing on the alienation of the popular classes, the use of social sciences to understand and overcome repressive structures, and the insistence on the dialectic between theory (e.g., theology) and praxis in the struggle for justice.

On the whole, I would say that Latin American theology has kept its Christian vision intact and central throughout this symbiosis. In fact, it has been helped to recover fundamental biblical themes that have been obscured by Western rationalism and materialism. At the same time, it remains to be seen whether Christianity can help to transcend doctrinaire and petrified versions of Marxism, and thus contribute to the project of realizing socialism with a human face that has been embraced by many nations in the Third World.

Latin American theologians have been wary of the tradition of liberalism, both for historical reasons in their own national experience and because at present it appears to bolster the status quo and to mask the enormous disparity in the distribution of the world's goods. Individual bishops and bishops' conferences, however, have had frequent recourse to this tradition in defense of human dignity against disappearance, arbitrary arrest, torture, murder, and the suppression of freedom of speech and a free press. In practice, too, the many human rights organizations referred to earlier are solidly grounded in the liberal tradition. Perhaps, then, the Latin American theologians have dismissed the liberal tradition prematurely, for in any present or future socioeconomic system they must surely support the need for moral, constitutional, and legal guarantees of the freedom and rights of the human person.

Here I will conclude by offering some suggestions which may facilitate the process of dialogue necessary to achieve consensus on a normative theory of human rights for the Americas. I will do this by commenting on each of the six main directions of Latin American theology outlined earlier, presupposing the links already mentioned between this theology and human rights.

I) In speaking of social sin, I stressed that "what is peculiar to the Latin American situation is the *emphasis* given to this reality as well as to the acute *urgency* of the Christian response needed to transform the unjust structures that perpetuate social sin." I think it is important that we share and communicate this sense of urgency. The Latin Americans I have met do not appear willing to waste precious time in merely abstract or academic theorizing. A major focus of discussion on human rights in the Americas, if it is to be fruitful, must be the widespread deprivation of socioeconomic rights or, more simply, the right of the poor to a decent human existence in which their basic needs are met. Unless this is done, there will be no real confrontation with the *root causes* for the increasing suppression of individual rights that has occurred in recent years. This implies also, as the Medellín and Puebla documents noted explicitly, that major economic and political transformations are necessary if these socioeconomic rights are to be provided and a path opened for the restoration or inauguration of structures that protect individual rights.

Some of the difficulties that North Americans may encounter in discussing both these key issues are the following: a) The campaign for human rights in this country is heavily influenced by the liberal tradition, with its concentration on the protection of individual freedoms. b) The social location of North American interlocutors, both social scientists and theologians, tends to insulate them from exposure to the human suffering that accompanies deprivation of basic socioeconomic rights. c) The changes mentioned pose a threat to powerful economic interests in the United States, which are supported by an enormous ideological apparatus, including most of the media and the academy. d) Traditional Catholic social thought, articulated largely from a first world perspective, places great emphasis on order and the avoidance of conflict, and thus does not provide a strong encouragement for economic and political transformation.

II) The Latin Americans will be deeply interested in discussing what precisely is the preferential option of United States Christians. Since I do not think there is theological justification for a preferential opinion for the rich, it seems to me that the North American position should be the same, but with the necessary adaptation to our different historical and cultural milieu. Paths to this goal are provided by David Hollenbach's priority principles [87] and the various "basic needs" documents, including the excellent normative analysis of basic needs by Drew Christiansen. [88]

III) The CEBs have by now accumulated years of experience in educating people to seek both their socioeconomic rights (through conscientization about causes and possible solutions for violations in this area) and their individual rights (through active participation and re-lationships of equality in the communities). This experience could be of value in building an awareness of and commitment to human rights among Christians in the United States, which would be essential for the implementation of any common human rights strategy. So far, the major practical use of the CEB concept has occurred among U.S. Hispanic Catholics; [89] this is quite important, however, because of the increasing influence that the Hispanics are destined to have on the evolution of the U.S. Catholic church.

IV and V) The most important issues that will be raised in any North-South dialogue involve the relationship of theology and the social sciences. In my opinion the major problem concerns the correct analysis of the political and economic relationships that exist between the United States and Latin America. North Americans will have to decide whether they conceive these relationships according to the development model discussed earlier (which appears to be the position of the United States government and corporations) or according to the dependence model (which has been accepted by the liberation theologians and the continent-wide Conference of Religious). The recent empirical research on de-pendency theory in the United States and elsewhere suggests that a creative synthesis of various aspects of the two models may be possible. At any rate, a basic position on this point will be necessary if we are to move beyond the question of human rights violations to the question of the basic *causes* of these violations and to possible remedies. The same may be said for an analysis of the role of the transnational corporations and the various international development and lending agencies.

VI) Finally, Latin Americans, as we have seen, place great em-phasis on the praxis on which theological reflection should be based and which will continually revitalize it in a dialectical process. Thus it is likely that they will attach greater importance to the implementation phase of any human rights project than to foundational theory. At the same time, because of the theory/praxis relationship, it appears that future development and refinement of normative theory must depend heavily on the analysis of efforts at implementation. Only through this dialectic, then, will there be real progress in actually achieving both socioeconomic and political human rights in the Americas.

NOTES TO CHAPTER 2

1. With full recognition of many historical and cultural differences, the influence is clear in the reports of two recent conferences: *African Theology en Route,* Kopi Appiah-Kubi and Sergio Torres, eds. (Maryknoll,

N.Y.: Orbis Books, 1979) and *Asia's Struggle for a Full Humanity,* Virginia Fabella, ed. (Maryknoll, N.Y.: Orbis Books, 1980).

2. Alfred T. Hennelly, "Courage with Primitive Weapons," *Cross Currents* 27 (Spring 1978), pp. 8–19; and "Theology through the Optic of the Poor," Chapter 2 of *Theologies in Conflict* (Maryknoll, N.Y.: Orbis Books, 1979), pp. 23–49.

3. Juan Luis Segundo, *Etapas precristianas de la fe* (Montevideo: Cursos de Complementación Cristiana, 1962). These lectures were originally delivered in 1960.

4. See, for example, the series of articles entitled "Direitos Humanos y Evangelização," in *Revista Eclesiástica Brasileira* 37 (March 1977); the entire issue of *Christus* 43 (November 1978); and Ignacio Ellacuría, "Derechos humanos en una sociedad divida," *Christus* 44 (October 1979), pp. 42–48 (included in this volume). I stress that human rights is not a prominent theme in *theology;* for an illustration of its *pastoral* importance, cf. Brian Smith, "Churches and Human Rights in Latin America: Recent Trends in the Subcontinent," *Journal of Interamerican Studies and World Affairs* 21 (February 1979), pp. 89–128.

5. Juan Luis Segundo, "Derechos humanos, evangelización e ideología," *Christus* 43 (November 1978), pp. 33–34. He also charges that the churches in the rich nations "continue to preach a strange universal good news, without conversion" (*ibid.,* p. 34).

6. Peter Henriot, "The Concept of Social Sin," *Catholic Mind* (October 1973), pp. 38–53. Cf. also the more lengthy treatment of Patrick Kerans, *Sinful Social Structures* (New York: Paulist Press, 1974).

7. Henriot, "Social Sin," p. 40. The concept is also in use in Africa, as can be seen in this excellent text of Laurenti Magesa: "The worst type of sin, in fact the only 'mortal' sin which has enslaved man for the greater part of his history, is the institutionalized sin. Under the institution vice appears to be, or is actually turned into, virtue. Apathy towards evil is thus engendered; recognition of sin becomes totally effaced; sinful institutions become absolutised, almost idolised, and sin becomes absolutely mortal. The prerequisite of repentance in the Holy Scriptures . . . is recognition and admission of sinfulness. But recognition of evil, and therefore repentance for sin, is made practically impossible when sin is idolised as an institution." Quoted in *Concilium 124: The Church and the Rights of Man* (New York: Seabury Press, 1979), p. 118.

8. *Gaudium et Spes,* no. 25; Walter Abbott and Joseph Gallagher, eds., *The Documents of Vatican II* (New York: Guild Press/America Press, 1966), pp. 224–225.

9. Ignacio Ellacuría, "La Iglesia de los pobres, sacramento histórico de liberación," *Estudios Centroamericanos* (October/November 1977), p. 717.

10. George H. Dunne, *The Right to Development* (New York: Paulist Press, 1974), p. 15. Dunne, commenting on the army of rats who contest every foot of the terrain, continues with bitter irony: "Were the rats dis-

ciplined in scholasticism they could argue, not unjustly, that this invasion is a violation of the natural law, since it seems patent that nature fashioned rats rather than humans to inhabit garbage dumps" (*ibid.,* p. 16).

11. *Ibid.,* pp. 17–18. Dunne notes that these statistics are based on a visit in 1967 and undoubtedly have increased considerably since then.

12. Cf. the comments of Jon Sobrino in a discussion of Christian prayer: "Analyzing further the 'action for justice' as the place of Christian contemplation, it must be noted first that it is in the contact with and orientation toward the oppressed masses that one encounters the unconditional and radical 'no' which God pronounces on the world of sin," "La oración de Jesús y del cristiano," *Christus* 42 (July 1977), p. 41.

13. Cf. José Comblin, *The Church and the National Security State* (Maryknoll, N.Y.: Orbis Books, 1979).

14. *The Church in the Present-Day Transformation of Latin America in the Light of the Council* (Washington, D.C.: USCC, n.d.), p. 40.

15. *Ibid.,* p. 49.

16. *Ibid.,* p. 191.

17. *Puebla and Beyond: Documentation and Commentary,* John Eagleson and Philip Scharper, eds. (Maryknoll, N.Y.: Orbis Books, 1979), p. 264. For the Spanish version, see *Puebla: La evangelización en el presente y en el futuro de América Latina* (Bogotá: CELAM, 1979).

18. *Puebla and Beyond,* p. 267.

19. *Ibid.* Cf. the remarks of Leonardo Boff: "This option for the poor . . . was sanctified by the third Latin American Episcopal Conference, and it will certainly constitute an ineradicable framework for the further history of the church in the continent." In "Puebla: Ganhos, Avanços, Questões Emergentes," *Revista Eclesiástica Brasileira* 39 (March 1979), p. 51.

20. Gustavo Gutiérrez, *Teología del reverso de la historia* (Lima: CEP, 1977).

21. *Theology in the Americas,* Sergio Torres and John Eagleson, eds. (Maryknoll, N.Y.: Orbis Books, 1976), p. 310.

22. Gustavo Gutiérrez, *A Theology of Liberation: History, Politics and Salvation* (Maryknoll, N.Y.: Orbis Books, 1973), pp. 300–301. Italics are the author's.

23. Ignacio Ellacuría, "La Iglesia de los pobres," pp. 707–721. See also the section entitled "Iglesia de los pobres: Presencia y anuncio de una Iglesia nueva," in *Cruz y Resurrección* (Mexico City: CRT, 1978), pp. 47–273.

24. David Hollenbach, *Claims in Conflict,* pp. 203–207. The author's three strategic principles are: "1) The needs of the poor take priority over the wants of the rich. 2) The freedom of the dominated takes priority over the liberty of the powerful. 3) The participation of marginalized groups takes priority over an order which excludes them."

25. For an example of such influence already, see Pope Paul VI, *On Evangelization in the Modern World* (Washington: USCC, 1976). A

perceptive analysis of the extent of such influence . . . this document may be found in Jon Sobrino, "Evangelización e Iglesia en América Latina," *Christus* 43 (February 1978), pp. 25–44.

26. Hollenbach, *Claims in Conflict*, p. 207.

27. The term used throughout the Puebla document is *comunidades eclesiales de base*. The usual term during the past two decades was *comunidades de base;* the bishops thus appeared to want to stress the ecclesial nature of the communities, i.e., their incorporation into the larger structure of the church and its episcopal authority. For an excellent historical and analytic study of the CEBs, cf. Thomas C. Bruneau, "Basic Christian Communities in Latin America," in *Churches and Politics in Latin America,* Daniel H. Levine, ed. (Beverly Hills, Calif.: Sage Publications, 1979), pp. 225–237.

28. The technique of *conscientização* is described and justified by Freire in *Pedagogy of the Oppressed* (New York: Seabury Press, 1970). For an annotated bibliography of 184 publications by and about Freire, cf. Stanley M. Grabowski, *Paulo Freire: A Revolutionary Dilemma for the Adult Educator* (Syracuse: Syracuse University Publications in Continuing Education, 1972), pp. 96–136. For a brief life of Freire, cf. Denis Collins, *Paulo Freire: His Life, Works and Thought* (New York: Paulist Press, 1977).

29. *The Church in the Present-Day Transformation II*, p. 201.

30. I have discussed this struggle in greater detail in "The Grassroots Church," The Catholic Theological Society of America, *Proceedings of the 34th Annual Convention* (New York: Manhattan College, 1979), pp. 183–188. All references in this section are to *Puebla and Beyond* (n. 17).

31. Cf. *Iglesia de los pobres y organizaciones populares* (San Salvador: UCA Editores, 1979); "Comunidades eclesiales de base: Una Iglesia que nace del pueblo," *SEDOC* (May 1975); *Basic Christian Communities: LADOC Keyhole Series #14* (Washington: USCC, 1976); Jacques Van Nieuwenhove, "Puebla and the Grass-Roots Communities," *Lumen Vitae* 34 (4, 1979), pp. 311–330. Especially important are the works of José Marins: *Comunidades Eclesiales de Base y conflictividad social en América Latina* (Bogotá: Ediciones Paulinas, 1976) and *Realidad y praxis en la Pastoral Latinoamericana* (Bogotá: Ediciones Paulinas, 1976).

32. Marins, *Realidad y praxis,* p. 32.

33. For an excellent example of this popular exegesis in the CEB's of Nicaragua, see the series of works by Ernesto Cardenal, *The Gospel in Solentiname* (Maryknoll, N.Y.: Orbis Books, 1977–1980).

34. Marins, *Realidad y praxis,* p. 33.

35. Bruneau, "Basic Christian Communities" (n. 27). Cf. also the author's book *The Political Transformation of the Brazilian Church* (Cambridge: Cambridge University Press, 1974).

36. Alexander Wilde, "Ten Years of Change in the Church: Puebla and the Future," *Journal of Interamerican Studies and World Affairs* 21 (August 1979), pp. 299–312.

37. Smith, "Churches and Human Rights in Latin America" (cf. n. 4).

38. Michael Dodson, "Liberation Theology and Christian Radicalism in Contemporary Latin America," *Journal of Latin American Studies* 11 (1, 1979), pp. 203–222.

39. For an analysis of Paulo Freire's concepts of denunciation and annunciation, see Gustavo Gutiérrez, *A Theology of Liberation*, pp. 233–235.

40. Leonardo Boff, *Jesus Christ: A Critical Christology for Our Time* (Maryknoll, N.Y.: Orbis Books, 1978), p. 272.

41. *Medellín II: Conclusions*, pp. 54–56.

42. *Ibid.*, pp. 56–58.

43. *Ibid.*, p. 61.

44. *Puebla and Beyond*, pp. 126–132.

45. *Ibid.*, p. 129.

46. Xavier Gorostiaga, ed., *Para entender América Latina: Aporte colectivo de los científicos sociales en Puebla* (Panama: CEASPA, 1979), p. 11.

47. *Pueblo de Dios y comunidad liberadora* (Bogotá: Editorial Stella, 1977). This book was produced by a group of theologians and social scientists from a very active organization called CLAR (Confederación Latinoamericana de Religiosos).

48. *Ibid.*, "Contribución de las ciencias sociales," pp. 25–59.

49. Discussion of the models occurs in *ibid.*, pp. 35–41.

50. *Ibid.*, p. 39.

51. *Ibid.*, p. 56.

52. *Ibid.*, p. 57.

53. Dodson, "Liberation Theology and Christian Radicalism," p. 208.

54. Steven Jackson, Bruce Russett, Duncan Snidal, and David Sylvan, "An Assessment of Empirical Research on *Dependencia*," *Latin American Research Review* 14 (no. 3, 1979), pp. 7–28. Cf. also Fernando Cardoso and Enzo Faletto, *Dependency and Development in Latin America* (Berkeley: University of California Press, 1979).

55. Here I am reflecting on ideas developed at greater length in *Pueble de Dios y comunidad liberadora*, pp. 19 ff.

56. Robert McAfee Brown, *Theology in a New Key: Responding to Liberation Themes* (Philadelphia: Westminster Press, 1978).

57. *Ibid.*, p. 82.

58. *Ibid.* The reference given for this quotation is William Manson, *The Gospel of Luke* (New York: Harper, n.d.), pp. 41–42.

59. *Theology in a New Key*, pp. 83–84.

60. Juan Luis Segundo, *The Liberation of Theology* (Maryknoll, N.Y.: Orbis Books, 1976).

61. Here I am following and reflecting on the ideas expressed in *Pueblo de Dios y comunidad liberadora*, pp. 57–59.

62. For a very perceptive recent analysis of this process, see Alvin W. Gouldner, *The Dialectic of Ideology and Technology: The Origins, Grammar, and Future of Ideology* (New York: Seabury Press, 1976). For the relationship of theology, see Gregory Baum, "The Impact of

Sociology on Catholic Theology," Catholic Theological Society of America, *Proceedings of the 30th Annual Convention* (New York: Manhattan College, 1975), pp. 81–100.

63. Gutiérrez, *A Theology of Liberation,* p. 308. For a very nuanced analysis of the relationship between theology and praxis, cf. Clodovis Boff, "Theologia e Prática," *Revista Eclesiástica Brasileira* 36 (December, 1976), pp. 789–810.

64. *Ibid.,* p. 6.

65. *Ibid.,* p. 11.

66. Alfred T. Hennelly, "Theological Method: The Southern Exposure," *Theological Studies* 38 (December, 1977), pp. 709–735.

67. Segundo Galilea, *Espiritualidad de la liberación* (Santiago: Ediciones, ISPAJ, 1973).

68. *Ibid.,* pp. 7–10.

69. Jon Sobrino, *Christology at the Crossroads: A Latin American Approach* (Maryknoll, N.Y.: Orbis Books, 1978).

70. *Ibid.,* pp. xv–xix.

71. *Ibid.,* p. xvi.

72. *Ibid.*

73. *Ibid.,* p. xviii.

74. *Ibid.,* p. xxv.

75. Leonardo Boff, *Liberating Grace* (Maryknoll, N.Y.: Orbis Books, 1979).

76. *Ibid.,* pp. 65–75.

77. *Ibid.,* pp. 79–80; italics omitted.

78. *Ibid.,* p. 81.

79. *Ibid.,* p. 85. Boff continues: "Insofar as the latter does not happen, their personal goodness will remain terribly ambiguous. It will generate grace and dis-grace whether they will it or not."

80. *Ibid.,* p. 86. World attention was directed to such prophetic witness by the murder of Archbishop Oscar Romero of San Salvador on March 24, 1980.

81. E.g., Juan Luis Segundo, *The Sacraments Today* (Maryknoll, N.Y.: Orbis Books, 1974); Leonardo Boff, *El destino del hombre y del mundo* (Santander: Sal Terrae, n.d.) and *Hablemos de la otra vida* (Santander: Sal Terrae, n.d.); José Miranda, *Marx and the Bible: A Critique of the Philosophy of Oppression* (Maryknoll, N.Y.: Orbis Books, 1974); and Francisco López Rivera, *Biblia y sociedad: Cuatro estudios exegéticos* (Mexico City: CRT, 1977); Enrique Dussel, *Para una ética de la liberación latinoamericana* (3 vols.; Buenos Aires: Siglo XXI, 1973).

82. As examples in Asia, see, in sacramental theology, Tissa Balasuriya (Sri Lanka), *The Eucharist and Human Liberation* (Maryknoll, N.Y.: Orbis Books, 1979); in Trinitarian theology, see Samuel Rayan (India), *The Holy Spirit: Heart of the Gospel and Human Hope* (Maryknoll, N.Y.: Orbis Books, 1978); and for the whole field of theology, see the continuing series of *Loyola Papers* (Manila: Cardinal Bea Institute, 1971 forward).

83. Brown, *Theology in a New Key,* pp. 11–49.

84. See *Theology in the Americas* (Maryknoll, N.Y.: Orbis Books, 1976).

85. For an analysis and critique of the Marxist position on human rights, see Chap. 5 in this volume; for expansion of liberal thought to include socioeconomic rights, see Chap. 4; future directions for Catholic thought on human rights are suggested in Chap 1; finally, an excellent comparison of the three traditions may be found in Chap. 8. Another probing critique of the Catholic tradition has recently been published by Christine E. Gudorf, *Catholic Social Teaching on Liberation Themes* (Lanham, Md.: University Press of America, 1980).

86. Pope Paul VI, *On Evangelization in the Modern World* (Washington, D.C.: USCC, 1976), pp. 20–26.

87. Hollenbach, *Claims in Conflict,* pp. 204–207.

88. See, in the companion volume, *Human Rights and Basic Needs in the Americas,* Ed. Margaret Crahan (Washington, D.C.: Georgetown University Press, 1982), Chaps. 4 and 5; and Chap. 11 of this volume.

89. See the emphasis on base communities in the report of the Second National Pastoral Conference of Hispanic Catholics in *Origins* 7 (November 1977), pp. 353–368.

IGNACIO ELLACURÍA, S.J.

3. *Human Rights in a Divided Society*[1]

The issue of the common good has a long philosophical and theological history. Aristotle and St. Thomas, with their many followers, are a proof of this and, from another point of view, so is Rousseau with his idea of the general will as a reality that transcends the will of all. At the same time, the topic of human rights has a long philosophical and theological history, and in a certain sense it can be understood as the continuation and historical realization of the common good. The issue is not a question, then, of new themes nor of problems that are accidental to the evolution of society and of history. But why have these themes, which are so important for the correct ordering of personal and political ethics, had so little effect on the ethical development of the person and of society? On the contrary, why have they functioned and why are they functioning as a permanent denial of the common good and of human rights? How should this problem be focused to make a real contribution to an effective common good and the actual exercise of human rights? These are the questions I will try to answer in the two parts of this brief essay.

The first part is a formal analysis of the topic with its strong and weak points. The second part will discuss the historicization of the common good and human rights as the test of its truth or falsehood.

I. FORMAL CONSIDERATION OF THE COMMON GOOD AND HUMAN RIGHTS

There is no need to consult contemporary authors to emphasize the importance of the common good and, deriving from that, of human rights. For example, St. Thomas produced a powerful theological analysis of this topic, based on the philosophical thought of Aristotle. The treatment of his principal ideas will help us understand the importance of the problem, both in its positive and negative aspects.

1. The idea of the common good is based on two fundamental

assertions: society in the sense of the *polis, civitas,* or political society is a necessary reality for the individual; and society cannot be what it is nor do what it should do if it does not have sufficient material resources at the disposition of all and of each one of its members.

St. Thomas, in effect, follows Aristotle in considering it to be an undeniable fact that the human person cannot provide for himself or herself everything that is necessary to lead a human life. Therefore, the existence of political society is both a necessity and a good. This political society must be distinguished not only from individuals but also from those social groups which do not represent the whole society, since they cannot guarantee the sufficiency of goods necessary to lead a human life. This society has its own proper reality, its own proper goal, and its own proper good, which is expressed as the common good.

But there is something further: the relation of the individual to society is the relation of the part to the whole, and the relation of the particular good to the general or common good is also the relation of the part to the whole. Thus, the whole is prior to its parts and has primacy over them; this is a fundamental idea of all structuralist thought. More generally it is an idea that is self-evident wherever there exists a whole which is really such. However "totalitarian" this concept may appear, it is held very explicitly by Aristotle and St. Thomas and also by Rousseau and Hegel. The relationship, then, between the common good and the individual good is that of the whole with the part, which leads to the evident conclusion that the common good is above the particular good.

St. Thomas is very explicit in his affirmations. The goodness of a part is seen in relation to the whole to which its belongs. "Since the human person is part of civil society, it is impossible for the person to be good except in relation to the common good" ("cum igitur homo sit pars civitatis, impossibile est quod aliquis homo sit bonus nisi proportionatus bono communi," *Sum. Theol.,* 1-2, q. 92, a.l, ad 3). No one is good except in relation to the common good; furthermore, one who prefers his or her private good to the common good is not an ethical person. The goods of the person are not excluded from this, because the common good prevails over the particular good of each person ("in quantum bonum commune praeminet bono singulari unius personae," ibid., 2-2, q. 58, a. 12). And thus St. Thomas holds that "it is not correct for someone to seek a particular good without reference to the common good as its end" ("non est recta voluntas alicujus hominis volentis aliquod bonum particulare, nisi referat illud in bonum commune sicut finem," 1-2, q. 19, a. 10). The part receives its meaning from the whole, and thus any good of a part is related to the good of the whole.

This provides the foundation for the assertion that the acts of every virtue are linked to the virtue of justice and that justice has priority over any other moral virtue. The justice that holds priority in the life of the individual and of society is not the justice of judges nor the justice of individuals, but rather the so-called legal justice, that is, the justice of civil society which seeks the promotion and defense of the common good. In a parallel manner, the best way of providing for the good of persons is by promoting this civil justice, this correct organization of civil society. The best way of achieving the good of persons and achieving it justly so that all can develop their personal lives is by working for the promotion of the common good. Furthermore, the just form of seeking one's own good is by seeking the common good.

Certainly the followers of St. Thomas have discussed how the priority of the common good over the particular or private good should be understood and in what areas it applies. It is unnecessary for us to enter into this discussion between personalists and communitarians; let us simply emphasize two fundamental points of view. First of all, both the common good and the particular good are seen as personal goods. Only someone who has identified the person with his or her individuality can consider the personal element diminished by stress on the common good. Secondly, the discussion considers goods of a more internal character, but what interests us here is not those goods but rather the ones that belong to the person as a citizen who is part of a political society. In the case of the latter goods, especially economic ones, which are fundamental in the structuring of society, the disputants are in agreement and leave no doubt about priority of the common good over particular goods.

St. Thomas bases the theological character of this whole consideration on the notion of God as the good by definition. Although the idea is not fully developed, and is even less sufficiently developed from the point of view of Christology, it is still proposed as the key for interpreting the common good. In the community of the common good, God becomes present as the common good that communicates itself and leads to further communication. The primacy of the common good over the particular good is thus proposed as the starting point in the argument against the privatizing of goods.

2. Human rights can be understood as the unfolding of the common good for humanity as a whole. This does not mean that in the classical treatment the good of the whole of humanity or even of the whole of the universe was forgotten. However, given the historical circumstances, it was difficult to speak historically of a single humanity which could be viewed as involved in the realization of a single common good. But once the condition of a single history of the human race was fulfilled, the worldwide consideration of human rights became an urgent issue.

It should not be overlooked that the concept of the common good cleared the way for a strict understanding of justice, which is prior to the will of individuals and the foundation of rights as such. The latter must be recognized and promoted by the laws of society.

These human rights are the rights of the human being as such, pertaining to a single humanity. In itself humanity has a single universal common good, however much this is divided into distinct national common goods, which are always subordinate as parts of the whole which is humanity. This understanding of international society as a whole was certainly impossible in the Middle Ages. Today, however, it is a reality, since the entire world historically constitutes one single humanity, a fact made clear by the necessity of worldwide economic and political exchange. Humanity today is a single humanity and its common good is obligatory, because it is necessary both for the existence of humanity itself and for the sake of justice.

Thus, we can treat human rights and the common good as a single problem. This is not only because it is impossible to speak of a common good where there is denial of human rights but also because the fundamental community of the good is nothing else but humanity, which is one and cannot cease to be so. Locating human rights in relation to the common good provides them with their foundation and frame of reference, while it provides a principle of concreteness and obligation for the common good. If human rights are derived from the common good, then they will appear as obligatory for all who make up humanity, since all would have a fundamental right to share in the common good as well as to contribute to its realization.

3. This formal consideration of the common good and human rights has much to recommend it. Before entering into a discussion of its limitations, it will be useful to examine its positive aspects to which we shall return when considering the process of historicization. The following are the three principal aspects.

a) There is no particular good without the common good, and without the real existence of the common good one cannot speak of a particular good except as a selfish and unjust gain. Clearly, it is impossible for any individual to achieve his or her good without availing himself or herself of what is offered by the common good as it exists in a political society. In effect, something is required which the particular good does not produce in order for it to be able to be what it should be and to do what it should do. But this something goes beyond the individual, and by its nature denies that private appropriation which makes the common good cease to be common. The fundamental sin here would consist in the private appropriation of what is common, in effect, the negation of what is common in favor of what is particular, and the denial

of the structural whole in favor of separate parts. The private appropriation of that which is by nature social and thus common is a fundamental injustice, which renders all its effects unjust. Consequently, there
is no ethical possibility of private appropriation of the common good
to the detriment of the community. It may happen that the private
sphere and private interests determine the distribution of the common
good. This exploitative use of the common good means that a few appropriate from it what cannot be theirs without the diminishment of others
and thus prevent the others from making use of what they have a right to.
When that occurs, we are in the presence of an absolute negation of the
common good and the destruction of a just social order.

b) The common good is not achieved by the accumulation of individual goods, that is, by pursuing an individual interest, but by the
primary search for the common good. Each one cannot be allowed to
pursue his or her particular interest in the belief that this would be the
best way of achieving automatically the good of all. This is so for two
basic reasons: first, the whole is not the result of its parts and, secondly,
the common good or the good of the whole is qualitatively distinct from
the good of the parts. This involves the denial of individualistic liberalism and the affirmation of social communitarianism, whatever the historical political forms which individualism or communitarianism may
take.

c) The common good is basically a union of structural conditions
and finds its expression through justice in society. Both the conditions
and justice must be provided by the society as a whole and concretely
by organs that are truly representative of the society. No structuring of
society and no government is legitimate, if they do not foster an effective
promotion of the common good. The real proof of such promotion occurs
when no one feels deprived of the basic conditions for personal development and when no one profits from the common good at the expense of
the right of others to avail themselves of this common good. As a result,
justice, which fosters the common good, is the fundamental virtue of the
state and the guiding star of the citizen and the politician. The government, as the custodian of the common good, must not only have the
power to punish violations against the common good, but also must
possess the basic means to prevent such violations. Thus it would be
absurd if the one who held political power were the representative of
one group of individuals, especially if the group consisted of those who
had unlawfully appropriated what is fundamental to the common good.

Nevertheless, the realization of the common good does not presume
the denial of the personal good and thus of the rights of the person.
This is so because the common good exists as a means or instrument for
the realization of personal life, and an authentic common good cannot be

achieved if it entails the violation of human rights. It is true also because the common good itself implies the empowerment of persons and also the fullest development that is possible for them What is proposed, then, is a common good which transcends each one of the individuals, but without being extrinsic to them. It is a common good, moreover, which surpasses each one considered individually, but in the same way that each one surpasses himself or herself in his or her communitarian and social dimension. A common good which would nullify the realm of the personal, or even one which would not encourage the development of the person to the maximum, would cease to be an authentic common good. What often happens, however, is that the development of the person is confused with what is merely an individualistic understanding of the common good.

4. What is lacking, then, in this whole discussion, so reasonable and progressive on a formal level, that makes it in fact unsatisfactory even as a way of posing the problem? What is the element of mystification in the idea of a common good which is supposed to be superior to a particular good? The answer is clear: it is its formal character itself and its interpretation along the lines of idealist abstraction. The result is that it becomes unclear what the content of the common good should be in each historical situation and what the means are for attaining it. In parallel fashion, it is unclear what the ranking of human rights is or what the true cause is of permanent structural violations, which are often beyond what could be considered as personal decisions. Let us look at this briefly, first as regards the case of the common good and then as regards the case of human rights.

a) The example of the situation in Athens at the time of Aristotle (similar events can be seen in the political society of St. Thomas) shows where the fault lies in an idealist consideration of the common good. Hegel has shown in a somewhat romantic fashion how the Greek city is the prototype of the unification of the particular will and the universal will, of the will of the individual and that of the citizen. The Greek citizen saw the good of the city as his own good and participated in it as his own. Thus he could easily adapt his particular will to the universal will of the city. It is clear that Hegel himself saw that among the Greeks and Romans only some persons were free and not the human being as such, and that only Greek citizens, not all who lived in the city, were free. Aristotle did not raise nor draw the consequences of the following question: Who were the ones whose material labor made the existence of free citizens possible? Who constituted the real material base of the city itself and of its common good? In this Aristotelian—and Thomistic —perspective, the common good ceases to be a totality and becomes a partiality, in which not only do all the individuals not share, but a few share because they have prevented others from enjoying what they have produced. The democratic structure and social stratification of Athens and Rome, with their enormous base of slaves, provide a convincing proof of the real denial of the common good.

If we move from the example to the ideological mechanism that makes this radical conception of the common good possible, we find that the search for a common good is affirmed in an idealistic way, but that this formal and idealist affirmation is not realized in history. And this happens in two ways. First, there is no examination of how common this good proposed as the common good really is, that is, for how many and in what way it is effective. Secondly, a common good is defended in the abstract order, without establishing the material conditions for its realization, while at the same time material conditions are established which make the realization of an authentic common good impossible.

There is yet another fundamental mechanism used to mystify the common good. It consists in a selfish acceptance of the established order as a fundamentally just one or at least as the indispensable condition for working toward a just order. Thus law, order, peace, etc., are considered to be fundamental elements of the common good, while anything that opposes these is regarded as a negation of the common good. There is no inquiry into the real situation of injustice that can exist under the appearance of order, peace, and legality. And there is a denial of the proposition that order and peace are not authentic if they do not lead to the existence of the common good and that their only value lies in their relationship to the common good.

In contemporary terms, a doctrine of the common good which does not take into account the real possibility of internal conflicts in society and which does not consider the existence of opposed classes with contrary interests can neither pose nor adequately resolve the problem of the common good. A doctrine of the common good which does not take into account the suspicion that the State, instead of guaranteeing the common good, is actually the policeman of an order favoring a minority in the society, can only offer mystifying solutions when faced with the real needs of the common good. How does one avoid the simple question of who benefits most from what by definition should be common? Who really profits from the common good? Are we going to understand the common good as the crumbs which fall from the table of the opulent?

b) The issue of human rights has to be judged in similar terms. The affirmation of some human rights can become a mask to conceal the fundamental violation of the most basic human rights. If it is taken as a fundamental human right that a definite economic order should exist and that a political order should exist to reinforce its permanence and development, then every possible ethical defense of human rights crumbles at its base. This does not imply a disregard for protection against individual abuses nor for the promotion of formally democratic models, especially in cases of openly dictatorial regimes. But such protection and promotion cannot make us forget the fundamental rights of human existence and the indispensable minimal conditions that are necessary if speaking about human rights is to have real meaning. To defend some human rights which are not fundamental and radical or to defend fundamental ones without concern for the real conditions that make them possible is to mystify the whole problem of human rights and the common good. Only the consistent affirmation of the right to life, including the right of freedom, can be the crucial test of what the real understanding of human rights is, as opposed to its self-interested mystification.

II. HISTORICIZATION OF THE COMMON GOOD AND HUMAN RIGHTS AS A PRINCIPLE OF VERIFICATION

1. Without historicizing the common good and human rights, it is impossible either to overcome their abstract, mystifying formality or to define their truth or falsity. The presupposition that there is a common good for all peoples and all epochs reduces its reality to a minimal content, and also ignores the conditions for its realization. Historicization consists in seeing how what is abstractly affirmed as an "ought to be" of the common good or of human rights is actually being realized in a given circumstance. Secondly, it consists in the establishment of those real conditions without which there can be no effective realization of the common good and of human rights.

As an example, let us suppose that the right to work is considered a fundamental right and an indispensable part of the common good. If it is found that half the active population does not hold a permanent job and that a certain kind of economic system is not going to be able to solve that problem, we would have to say that that economic order and the society which maintains it are really denying the preeminence of the common good and are thwarting a fundamental human right. In such a case, the common good demands in principle the restructuring of that society by a basic change of its economic order. Examples can be multiplied, since in most of the countries of the Third World the national reality constitutes the most blatant denial of constitutional rights. Those who permanently violate the constitution are the ones who defend an economic and social system which renders impossible the fulfillment of the rights considered fundamental by the constitution itself.

It is only through such a historical mediation that it is possible to verify whether a supposedly general good is genuinely common, whether it is in fact communicated to all the members of the society. The common good is really common only if it fosters a common life. It is impossible to speak of a common good as unifying in a situation where opposed and exclusive goods are claimed, where in effect there is nothing in common or very little in common. It may be said, then, that a primary demand of the common good is the establishment of a real community in the society in question.

This formulation, however, can be interpreted in two very different ways. It can be understood in the sense of not being conscious of the real disunion that exists in the community because of unequal or discriminatory participation in the common good. Or it can be understood in the sense of becoming aware of the disunion and opposition in order to overcome them by overcoming the real causes of the division. Only the second interpretation is correct. Thus it is a mystification of the problem to attempt to eliminate the class struggle without seeking to make the struggling classes disappear. Disunion and the denial of the common good are located in the real existence of opposed classes, an existence which flows necessarily from socioeconomic causes. The affirmation of the common good and of union will lie in overcoming the socioeconomic causes which produce the disunion and the negation. A society in conflict, then, which is the one that really exists, demands that we pose the problem of the common good and thus of human rights in very specific terms, which cannot be hidden by an ingenuous and abstract understanding of the common good.

Historicization, therefore, consists in examining how the common good and human rights exist in a definite historical situation, and in establishing the mechanisms which either impede or favor the effective realization of the common good. Hegel has said that Spirit can achieve consciousness of itself and full realization only through concrete historical determinations. Thus, it should be stressed that the truth of the common good is the truth of its determinations in practice. Naturally, this is not a question of a static common good, since the important thing in the process of historicization is not the achievement at any specific moment but the orientation of the process. And this means its real orientation and not an idealized one.

2. From this historical perspective, it is easy to show that we cannot speak today of a common good or a common participation in human rights, whether in the totality of international relations or in the countries that constitute the periphery in a structure of dependency. The empirical proof of these affirmations can be found in the specialized literature of dependency theory. Here it is sufficient to show briefly that we must speak of a fundamental negation of the common good in the present moment of history, and thus of a structural situation of injustice which uses violence to prevent the achievement of human rights.

It is evident that the historical structures which would allow us to speak of the common good do not exist on a global level. In effect, there exist many things in common, that is, things that are transmitted from the centers of power to the oppressed periphery and things that are taken from the periphery to the great advantage of the centers. However, this community of things cannot be called a good, since it is a source of oppression and not of liberty. It is not merely a case of a scandalous and radical disproportion in the possession and use of the goods of the earth, (which as such have humanity as a whole as their principle owner), since this disproportion is achieved at the expense of those least favored by denying them access to resources which in principle should be common. This means that it is not merely a question of an inequality between members of a single history who are fundamentally equal, but of an inequality that is increasing and that is based upon exploitation. In effect, the existence of very specific economic and political mechanisms (such as unequal exchange, multinational companies) seeks the good of those who possess the most productive capital rather than the good of those who either do not possess it or possess it under unfavorable conditions. In these circumstances, one group's particular good denies the more general good of another; in short, the negation of the common good occurs.

In the framework of this structure of international commerce, each nation manifests its own internal conflict which denies the common good. The enormous inequality in the enjoyment of goods in a single nation, which should constitute a whole in which the totality has primacy over the parts, shows that the common good has been appropriated by a few individuals (this includes not only formally economic goods but also cultural, political, and health benefits). The result is that we cannot speak of a common good. The phenomenon of pauperization, that is, of a structure which makes the poor poorer while at the same time it makes the rich richer, provides the true picture of the supposed common good on a national level. The existence of social classes in conflict in the present economic structure reveals the existence of contrary interests, which prevent speaking of a common good. In this context, the supposed common good is only a formal framework that legally permits the denial of the common good. Thus, in a bourgeois capitalist structure it is clear that the smaller part prevails over the larger part. When this happens, the common good is denied for the sake of a particular good, which can no longer be called a good but simply utilitarian egotism.

Perhaps this mystification of the common good can be best appreciated in the structure of the State. The State presents itself as the representative of the entire sociey and as the executor of the common good, and because of this it provides legal structures within which the realization of the common good and of human rights is pursued on a formal level. In practice, however, it becomes one of the principal mechanisms for identifying the common good with the good of those who have most influence on the sources of the common good. Instead of favoring the common good, the State privatizes it and places it at the service of a privileged part and not of the whole. Therefore, the State exists not as the realization of the actual common good, but as the realization of the good of minorities who appropriate for themselves the material resources of the common good. Thus it is the defender of the common good only in the sense that it represents those who have unjustly appropriated the common good.

Furthermore, the production and distribution of the common good should not in principle oppose fundamental human rights or even less fundamental rights, at least methodically and over a long period of time. Thus, the defense of human rights pertains to the concrete totality of the common good. For this reason, the defense of human rights is a task of justice, but those who undertake it cannot avoid asking whether they themselves are the ones ultimately causing the fundamental violations of human rights. This may occur with regard to the citizens of their own country, but also with regard to other persons beyond their borders "whose life and existence depend on their precious liberty," as Hegel has said, and who nevertheless, because of their situation of exploitation, can enjoy neither life nor liberty.

3. How then should we pose the problem of the common good and of human rights in a conflictive society? This is a real question and not a purely theoretical one, because the unity of the world and the unity of many societies is a unity of opposites; and because in the present era of history the common good and human rights appear as the denial of the communality of good and of the humanity of rights. To answer the question, the following points should be taken into consideration.

a) The real truth of a historical process lies in the objective results of that process. Intentions and goals count for little in history; the truth of what is intended or proposed is the results obtained, the historical actions. The intention and goal can legitimate to some extent—and only to some extent—the individual subject, but they cannot legitimate the course of history nor the global conduct of nations. It is useless to claim a more just international order as an expression of the common good or a more just structuring of society, when historical reality demonstrates that that international order is continually becoming more unjust and the social structures continually more dehumanizing.

b) More concretely, the true picture of a historical process is not found in the actual results which should have been the common good, nor still less is it found in the minorities which appropriate those results for themselves. The truth lies rather in the participation in this common good and in the real situation of the majority of persons and citizens. Thus, the Third World is the truth of the First World, and the oppressed classes are the truth of the oppressing classes. It may be argued that without the accumulation of capital and the plundering of resources, and without the deflection of resources away from their primary goal of satisfying basic needs, the scientific, technological, and cultural development which is necessary for the contemporary historical process would not occur. But one has to ask if this development is good in itself, especially since it entails the subdevelopment of the great majority of humanity. Only when we understand that the real condition of this development is the oppression and dehumanization of the majority of humanity will we see that this development in its concrete reality is not development but rather its total opposite. Only when the opulent nations are seen as actually creating oppressed nations, only when the opulent classes are seen as actually creating oppressed classes, will they know who they really are. The truth also is that this will not happen until the historical praxis of the latter nations and classes "makes" the opulent see who they really are.

c) It is undeniable that the present organization of the world has brought many technological advances and an immense production of consumer goods. Thus it could be said that the common good, once its abstract and formal aspects are realized in history, is the sum total of goods produced; one could almost say that the common good in this case is identical with the gross national product. If we look at the problem from this perspective, it is clear that the problems of participation in the common good and the more general problems of justice (let us not forget the classical link between the common good and justice) receive no answer at all. In other words, the common good proposed today is neither good nor common.

d) If this is so, the achievement of the common good in a conflictive society, whether that society be the totality of nations or a single nation, is a process which must extend to the liberation of oppressed people and classes. This is so because it is only through such a process that one can come to speak of a true common good which can be equitably shared in by all those who make up the human race. In the same way, human rights must be primarily the rights of the oppressed, since the oppressors can have no rights insofar as they are oppressors; at most, they will have the right to be freed from their oppression. It is only by doing justice to the oppressed peoples and classes that an authentic common good and truly universal human rights will be fostered. Given the present historical situation, this "doing justice" will have to take the form of "making oneself just." The reason for this "making oneself just" is found precisely in the central importance of the common good as well as in the denial of the common good which is brought about by those who monopolize common goods and their legal representatives.

e) It may be argued that this historicization of the common good and of human rights involves the rejection of the ordinary meaning of the common good. This may be answered in two ways. The first response holds that the common good follows the same contours as society so that, if the society is really divided, so will the common good be divided. The common good, therefore, would involve the process which would lead a divided society toward the creation of a true society, where contradictory social interests would not exist. The common good would thus function as a utopia which would recognize the ideological disguise of the common good as currently propounded, as well as the real though concealed denial of the common good. After this, it would become a process with actual stages, leading to a common good which would become a historical reality.

The second response, which is more formal and juridical, holds that the common good refers to the whole and not to the parts which are making the unity of the whole impossible. Thus, where an unjustly structured society exists, there can be no way of arriving at the common good except by overcoming whatever is causing the injustice. In other words, the common good belongs to the whole of society, but it cannot belong to all members of society in the same way, if there are some sectors in it that deny the common good.

f) The struggle to prevent a specific social sector from unjustly monopolizing the material bases of the common good does not in principle involve a hate-filled struggle against specific persons. By its very nature, the common good must be considered on a formal level in structural terms and not in individual ones; it is pertinent to the latter only insofar as they impede or do not promote the common good. The situation is different with regard to human rights which, although they derive from the human person and the universal community of persons, can be said to refer formally to individuals (although they also refer to peoples, social groups, nations, and the totality of nations). Therefore, the promotion of the common good cannot progress by denying the individual rights of the human person, precisely because the promotion of those rights is an integrating part of the common good. But it can happen in a specific historical situation that it is necessary to establish priorities in the enjoyment of individual human rights. For example, the refined cultural activities of a few cannot have primacy over the fundamental education of the majority of a people, and even less can the enjoyment of some convenience have primacy over the right to have what is necessary for survival. Since almost everything in human life is superfluous in the countries which suffer from extreme poverty, anyone who wishes to enjoy superfluities should join a society where this massive poverty is absent and where the voice crying to heaven of those in need cannot be heard. But although human rights should be regulated by the common good, it is impossible to conceive of a common good which would require the permanent and grave violation of human rights in order to maintain itself.

g) This way of posing the problem of the common good and human rights may give rise to a totalitarian interpretation, but that is not necessarily the case. Although the State today should be the one that secures the common good, it has to do this in subordination to the whole society. The discussion of the common good should be proposed in terms that are predominantly social and thus with the immediate participation of the majority of those who make up the society. When the common good is seen from the viewpoint of society, it consists in the utopian task of the communication of goods. Behind that goal lies the conviction that both the person and the communitarian society are realized by denying private interests of individual egotism. There is only a single step from here to the death that gives life, a life superior to that which was ended in death, as well as to real love, both as personal realization and as historical utopia. It is a theological step which, especially in the theology of liberation, can show the internal unity between the history of salvation and the salvation of history. For St. Thomas already tried to point out the connection between the common good of the world and the common good which is God, with the result that the common good of society would become one of the preeminent ways of making God present in history.

NOTE TO CHAPTER 3

1. This article originally appeared in the October 1979 issue of the Mexican periodical *Christus* and has been translated by Alfred Hennelly.

PART II

Human Rights in Other Traditions: Convergence and Comparison

John Langan, S.J.

4. *Defining Human Rights: A Revision of the Liberal Tradition*

At the same time that the idea of human rights has moved to the forefront of political discussion, it has also come to play a much more prominent role in American political philosophy. John Rawls's magisterial work, *A Theory of Justice* (1971), rejected a purely utilitarian approach to the fundamental issues of political philosophy in favor of a contract theory. Robert Nozick's widely admired book, *Anarchy, State, and Utopia* (1974), took as a postulate the view that human beings have rights which impose moral constraints on what governments and other individuals may do to them. And the most significant recent book in legal philosophy, Ronald Dworkin's *Taking Rights Seriously* (1977), rejected the dominant schools of legal positivism and legal realism, and argued for the view that individuals have rights prior to legislative enactments and judicial decisions. Dworkin has also offered an important interpretation of Rawls's theory as fundamentally a theory of the right of individuals to equal concern and respect.

The present paper then builds on the work of American political philosophers in the analytic tradition. In the first three sections of the paper I propose a certain understanding of what a human right is and deal with some of the objections to including economic and social claims in the scope of human rights. In the fourth, I sketch a line of thought designed to show the compatibility of this acceptance of economic and social rights with traditional liberal concerns. The problems in both sections are dealt with in the hope not of offering a strict demonstration of conclusions, but of providing some philosophical clarification of issues present in current debates.

In calling the paper a revision of the liberal tradition and in speaking of the liberal tradition on human rights, I do not wish to adopt a restrictive view of what is a rich and diversified tradition of political thought and practice. I should say that I regard Locke and not Hobbes as the fundamental liberal philosopher, and that I regard with special sympathy the efforts of both theorists and politicians to incorporate the concerns of social democracy and demands for basic social services into the framework of a constitutional polity that aims to protect individual freedoms. In aligning myself with the liberal tradition, I do not want to endorse the psychological egoism of Hobbes or to accept a system of unrestricted economic liberty. These comments are of more than personal importance, for the sort of liberalism that I will argue for is one that has roots in the experience of the English speaking peoples in constitutional government. It continues to attract both wide support and lively criticism.

The liberal tradition has sometimes been identified with social contract theories of the origin of society and of the state. I should observe that the basic conception of rights advanced in this paper is more in the tradition of natural law than of social contract, for in my view the human rights of persons and their correlative duties derive from our common status as human persons and not from our consent or the consent of others. Consent is, however, an essential factor in the establishment of legitimate political institutions and in the choice of ways to fulfill our common duties and to make our rights effective.

I. WHAT A HUMAN RIGHT IS

Before raising the question of what specific rights should figure on a list of *the* human rights, I propose that we begin by considering what a human right is. First, it is a right that a human person has simply by virtue of being a human person, irrespective of his or her social status, cultural accomplishments, moral merits, religious beliefs, class memberships, or contractual relationships. It is true that some rights movements have arisen precisely because members of certain groups (women, blacks in the United States, Catholics in Northern Ireland, Jews in the Soviet Union, members of leftist political parties in Chile) have been denied certain human rights. Particularly in the United States, there has been extensive discussion of the need for special treatment for members of certain groups in order for them to attain and exercise rights which are owed to them as human beings and also as citizens. But the rights which are affirmed and striven for in these movements are essentially rights which are owed to all persons or citizens on an equal basis. If rights movements aim at preferential treatment as a goal in itself or at rights which would be restricted in principle to certain groups of persons, they would cease to be movements for human rights. In maintaining the view that human rights are those rights that a person has simply by virtue of being a human person, we are in effect distinguishing these rights from rights that human persons have because of particular characteristics or actions. Thus, rights that one possesses by reason of being a citizen of France, or being a child, or being the recipient of a promise, are rights that belong to human persons; but they are not what we mean by human rights.

This understanding of human rights as rights held by all human persons is compatible with efforts to integrate a theory of human rights into a specific religious or philosophical tradition, by affirming its compatibility with or its derivability from the principles of that tradition. This, I take it, is one of the concerns raised by Max Stackhouse, in his chapter in this volume. Though I would agree with his point that "all sorts of universally true matters derive from particular histories and insights," [1] and with his stress on the importance of religious factors in the shaping of the common Western understanding of human rights, it seems to me both possible and desirable for us to develop our understanding of the meaning and implications of human rights claims without explicit reliance on the authority of specific religious traditions.

The distinction between human rights and rights that belong to human persons tends to get blurred because the exercise of certain human rights often creates rights that are not themselves human rights. Thus, a person's exercise of his or her right to enter into agreements or contracts with other persons can create in other parties to the agreement rights to goods or to the performance of certain actions, which the other parties cannot claim as matters of human right, though they may well be consequences of the exercise of human rights. It should also be recognized that affirming the existence of a human right does not commit one to the view that every exercise of that right is right or is immune from moral criticism. Actions that involve the exercise of rights are subject to other moral norms and may be made subject to various forms of social regulation. Thus, the exercise of the right of free speech is subject to moral norms of honesty and truthfulness and charity, and may be regulated in the interest of public order. This last possibility, of course, creates the need to distinguish between regulation that respects the right and regulation that restricts or even extinguishes the right that is to be exercised. Recognition of these points should prepare us to accept the possibility that certain rights of human persons to enter into legal and economic transactions, though they may be remotely derived from the exercise of human rights, may need to be regulated or restricted for the sake of other important values or in order to fulfill the unsatisfied and urgent rights of others. Such regulation and restriction need justifying reasons if they are to be compatible with respect for fundamental human freedoms.

Several consequences of this definition of human rights as rights held by human persons in virtue of their humanity should be pointed out. First, human rights are necessarily universal, that is, they are possessed by all human persons. There may, of course, be disagreement about whether an individual is or is not a human person, as in the case of the human fetus in the abortion controversy. But no one who holds that the fetus is a human person can deny that it has human rights, given the notion of human rights that we are proposing here. There may also be cases of incomplete or damaged personhood (e.g., minors, the mentally retarded, the mentally ill, the senile, the permanently comatose) where one may argue for denying or withholding certain human rights. Cases of these types involve many difficult moral and legal problems; but it is preferable to hold that there are reasons for abridging the human rights of human beings in these conditions than to say that they are not persons and so do not have human rights.

A second important consequence of this way of conceiving human rights is that they are moral claims that human persons have and that they can appeal to independently of and prior to their acknowledgment by particular societies. In saying this, we are not claiming that human beings ever existed in some presocial condition or that the concept of rights is intelligible outside of a social context of institutions and practices. Thus, we can grant the point that the notion of rights originates and has its home in that eminently social institution, the law. Rather, we are pointing to the ideal status of human rights, that is, to their independence of particular constitutional arrangements, legislative enactments, and judicial decisions. Human rights are neither granted nor abolished in such actions, though they may be acknowledged or violated by them. Thus South African statutes cannot abolish the human rights of South African blacks. The Thirteenth Amendment to the United States Constitution did not confer a human right to freedom on American blacks; it should be taken as recognizing such a right and according it constitutional status and legal protection. Human rights are ideal rights, not positive rights, and do not depend on legal recognition and social practice for their validity as moral claims. There may, however, be considerable overlap between human rights and positive rights; in fact, such an overlap is inherent in the constitutional or legislative establishment of a bill of rights and in ratification of the United Nations Covenants on Human Rights. It is also worth noting that cultures and polities without a developed notion of human rights may meet the moral claims that are involved in explicit assertions of human rights, at least for their own members. This point is particularly important in thinking about ways of implementing human rights in non-Western cultures. The way to achieve progress may not be to focus on explicit affirmations cast in the universalist rhetoric of 1776 and 1789, but rather to look to those elements in the local culture that inculcate respect for other persons and concern for their needs and freedom.

The second main aspect of the notion of human rights that should be considered here is the question of the weight to be accorded to human rights in moral and political argument. Our first answer may well be that human rights have or should have overriding weight and that any position that allows human rights to be overridden is morally defective. As Ronald Dworkin has put the matter in his recent book on rights: "Individual rights are political trumps held by individuals." [2] Even if we want to give human rights claims priority over other considerations in our moral and political decisions, we have to remember that there is a plurality of human rights that are in at least potential conflict with each other. Further, there are certain rights, such as the right of free speech, in which one person's exercise of a human right may be in conflict with another person's exercise of the same right, for instance, when hecklers shout down a speaker expressing unpopular opinions. [3]

The problem is to understand respect for rights in such a way that rights are not absolutized, but that at the same time rights are indeed taken seriously. For if respect for rights is taken in such a way that rights cannot be overridden, then we shall have to make do with a very restricted list of rights. [4] For the purpose of our inquiry, we need an understanding of rights that does not require us to hold that it is always right to satisfy a rights claim and always wrong to leave it unsatisfied. [5] Joel Feinberg has indicated one way in which we could be said to respect a right even while not satisfying the claim that is being made. He writes:

> A human right must be held to be absolute in the sense that rights to life, liberty, and the pursuit of happiness are most plausibly interpreted as absolute, namely, as 'ideal directives' to relevant parties to 'do their best' for the values involved. . . . If a human right is absolute only in the sense in which an ideal directive is absolute, then it is satisfied whenever it is given the serious and respectful consideration it deserves, even when that consideration is followed by a reluctant invasion of its corresponding interest. [6]

In adopting this view, we would be assigning to human rights a prima facie status which would put the burden of justification on those who propose to override these claims; and we would be affirming a corresponding prima facie obligation on other persons to satisfy these claims. [7] We would also preserve the general obligation to respect the rights of others. This does not exclude the possibility that some rights, e.g., the right not to be tortured, may be absolute in the stronger sense that they are categorically exceptionless. Feinberg observes that such absolute rights in this stronger sense are likely to be "passive negative rights, that is, rights not to be done to by others in certain ways."[8]

Taking a somewhat weaker view of rights claims in general comes closer to the world of actual political argument in which such claims have no clear overriding status, and reflects the difficulty of legal and political decisions in situations in which conflicting rights have to be weighed and in which time, energy, and resources are often insufficient to meet all the morally justifiable claims that can be advanced. To develop Dworkin's figure, rights may be trumps; but there are many other cards in the deck, and not all trumps are of equal value. The work of balancing claims and interests that is a central task of political leadership is not eliminated by the notion of human rights, but the moral constraints on that process are made more clear and more emphatic. The moral evaluation of restrictions on or infringements of human rights depends on the correctness of the reasons offered in justification of the decision, on the nature and standing of the other values that are being aimed at, and on the readiness of those who decide not to satisfy a right to take other actions to preserve the rights and the well-being of persons adversely affected by their decision. The point to bear in mind is that human rights have both a presumption of priority, which requires that infringements be justified by morally acceptable reasons, and a graduated urgency corresponding to the varying importance and necessity of the values that they protect.

II. CAN THERE BE SOCIAL AND ECONOMIC HUMAN RIGHTS?

Limiting the absoluteness of rights is also relevant to the difficult topic of whether human rights are to be understood to include economic and social rights of the type enumerated in Articles 22-28 of the Universal Declaration of Human Rights of the United Nations. Among these are rights to social security, to work, to education, and to a "standard of living adequate for the well-being of himself and of his family, including food, clothing, housing and medical care, and necessary social services."[9] Feinberg's view is that "rights to be given certain essentials—food, shelter, security, education—clearly depend upon the existence of an adequate supply, something that cannot be guaranteed categorically and universally."[10] We can readily imagine situations of famine or disaster where the supply of essential goods falls short of meeting even normally justified claims. We also know that there are societies in which the level of resources and skills is continually insufficient to meet minimal claims to adequate nutrition and health and to education. As Maurice Cranston

observed in 1962 (and the situation in 1980 is not noticeably different):
"For a government to provide social security, it needs to do more than
make laws; it needs to have access to very great wealth; and most governments in the world today are poor and cannot raise money." [11] Feinberg
draws the conclusion that if human rights are held to be absolutely exceptionless, then social and economic claims of the type being discussed
cannot qualify as human rights. If, however, we adopt the proposed view
that human rights should not be defined to be exceptionless, then the
question of whether social and economic rights should be included in
human rights still remains open.

This question remains open despite two further difficulties. The first
has to do with the obligation of respecting these economic and social
rights, which are also spoken of as positive rights. We should observe
that in this context positive rights are contrasted with negative rights
rather than with ideal or moral rights; in speaking of economic and
social rights as positive rights, we are pointing to the fact that they are
claims to certain kinds of goods, claims which can only be satisfied by
providing the appropriate goods, and that they are not satisfied by the
mere absence of constraint or harm. A right to social security, for instance, can be positive in this sense and be merely an ideal right in a
society which does not give this right the status of law. On the other
hand, the right of free speech is a positive right in American society because of the First Amendment while it is at the same time a negative
right, since it bars interference with my expressing my opinions as I
choose. A right to broadcast time would, however, be a positive right in
the sense we are considering here. Now the obligation to respect most
negative rights falls on governments, private individuals, and voluntary
associations. The right to free speech bars not merely government interference and censorship but also coercive interventions by other individuals
and groups. A negative right of this type is respected as long as individuals, groups, and governments refrain from coercive activity infringing it.
Cranston observes about rights to life and liberty: "Such 'political rights'
can be readily secured by legislation. . . . Moreover, the legislation by
which political rights are secured is generally simple. Since those rights
are for the most part rights against government's interference with a
man's activities, a large part of the legislation needed has to do no more
than restrain the government's own executive arm." [12]

Cranston's account of what is needed to make negative political and
personal rights effective in a society simplifies matters somewhat, since
he disregards the possibility of private interference with these rights
(e.g., the limiting of free speech in a company town) and since he takes
for granted the network of social conditions that are necessary for the
existence of a stable and effective minimal state; but he does have hold

of a very important point. Given the necessary social conditions and the existence of what Richard Claude terms a "human rights system," which he defines as "a set of institutional arrangements for securing legally binding guarantees beneficial to the individual" and which must include "a secure and procedurally regularized legal system," [13] then it is possible for a society to undertake to satisfy the central negative rights or liberties by establishing a system of constitutional guarantees. Such a commitment was undertaken in this country with the adoption of the Bill of Rights, well before serious thought was given to measures involving either state or federal governments in providing goods and services or money to satisfy positive claims for food, shelter, education, etc. As our own history should remind us, there is a considerable gap between undertaking to guarantee negative rights on a legal and constitutional basis and making those guarantees effective for all regardless of race, creed, and sex. There is need of careful activity and of "eternal vigilance" to protect persons, even in a constitutional democracy, from infringements of negative rights by other individuals, pressure groups, police, bureaucrats, and even legislators. But it remains true that negative rights are satisfied by the omission of activities that infringe them, that such omission is normally within the power of both individuals and governments that acknowledge the rule of law, and that such omission is obligatory in the absence of suitable justifying reasons. I would further argue that the moral obligation to respect these rights is universal, that is, that it falls on all persons. For obvious reasons, however, the obligation is likely to be expressed and given legal form only with regard to those persons or institutions that might actually infringe the rights of persons in their vicinity or under their jurisdiction.

Now with regard to positive rights, specifically the social and economic rights of the Universal Declaration, the question arises of who the persons or institutions are on whom the obligation of satisfying these rights falls. Feinberg holds that "these positive (as opposed to negative) human rights are rights in an unusual new 'manifesto sense,' for, unlike all other claim-rights, they are not necessarily correlated with the duties of any assignable persons." [14] Feinberg grants that human persons clearly need food, shelter, education, and social security, but regards talk of their rights to such things as at best "a valid exercise of rhetorical license." He makes the basis of his reluctance to grant full standing to positive economic and social rights more explicit in the following revealing passage: "If we persist in speaking of those needs as constituting rights and not merely claims, we are committed to the conception of a right which is an entitlement to some good, but not a valid claim *against* any particular individual, for in conditions of scarcity there may be no determinate individuals who can plausibly be said to have a duty to provide the mising goods to those in need." Feinberg admits to a certain sympathy with the manifesto writers and approves their principle that basic human needs should be regarded as claims deserving consideration; but he denies that these claims serve as grounds of duties for others. I would agree with Feinberg's view "that a man has a moral right when he has a claim, the recognition of which is called for—not (necessarily) by legal rules—but by moral principles, or the principles of an enlightened conscience." [15]

But, while admitting the real difficulties in assigning the persons or the institutions on whom or on which the duty falls of meeting the basic needs of others, I would argue that indeterminateness about the subject of the duty does not alter the status of the claim; and I would suggest that Feinberg's insistence that there must be an assignable individual to be the subject of the duty overlooks the possibility that this duty may fall on institutions or on the community at large. It is true that meeting the basic needs of other human persons exceeds the resources and the skills of most individuals and that individual efforts to meet these needs, while often noble in intention and heroic in execution, can also lead to conflicts of duties for the individuals who undertake them and to an inequitable distribution of burdens and benefits in society to the disadvantage of the conscientious. Satisfying those positive social and economic rights of human persons that involve the fulfillment of their basic needs requires positive action on the part of organized communities, at least if this satisfaction of rights is to be on a stable and permanent basis. The primary form that fulfilling the duty corresponding to these rights takes is working to bring about the kind of community arrangements that can meet these needs and thus respect these rights. The establishment of these arrangements, the effectiveness and justice of which varies with changing social conditions, is not to be accomplished by a definite constitutional guarantee but normally has to be worked out and revised by political processes.

As we shall see, the level at which basic needs are to be met will be relative to the state of development and the resources available to a given society, and to the plans of life which its members are likely to adopt. Arrangements for meeting basic needs will specify duties that fall on assignable individuals within society (paying taxes, providing goods and services, reporting needs), and so will complete the circle of rights and duties of individuals that Feinberg is looking for. It can, however, be the case that society will transpose the process of meeting basic needs from the sphere of legal right and duty to the sphere of economic exchange by enabling those in need to purchase goods and services that satisfy their needs or by compensating those who provide the necessary goods and services. Or a more intimate society might rely on private associations, such as extended families or clans or guilds, to provide for their members. The duty to provide for the basic needs of human persons would remain fundamentally the same, whatever arrangements a society might choose to adopt to fulfill it; it would serve as a moral standard for assessing the outcome of the arrangements. The secondary form in which this duty could be fulfilled would be by the voluntary actions of individuals responding to the needs of other persons. (In speaking of this as a secondary form of fulfilling the duty of meeting basic human needs, I do not mean to assign it lesser moral worth, only to indicate the greater social importance and effectiveness of the primary form).

Allowing this sort of flexibility in the ways in which societies can satisfy human needs and rights has certain advantages. First, it leaves open the larger questions concerning social organization and constitutional arrangements which are ideologically divisive. Second, it recognizes the possibility that even within the limits of one society some needs may be more effectively met in some ways than others. Thus, health care needs in a given society may be more effectively satisfied by state provision of essential goods and services, whereas satisfying food needs in similar fashion might be economically counterproductive or socially divisive. This is particularly important when we broaden the notion of basic human needs to include certain social and psychological conditions, such as family stability, culturally cohesive communities, loving relationships, that may be indispensable for human flourishing but that can be provided only indirectly, if at all, by state action. Third, it enables us to avoid turning arguments for the universal observance of a wide range of human rights into requirements that diverse cultures and nations adopt the organizational patterns and institutional arrangements of modern welfare states or centrally planned economies. Fourth, it preserves the distinction between arguing for the existence of a specific human right and arguing for a certain kind of social arrangement or institution as a way of meeting the claim present in that right. It thus keeps before our minds the importance of looking at the actual performance of social institutions or policies that ostensibly serve the cause of human rights.

This flexible approach to different ways of satisfying human rights does not foreclose the possibility that in a modernized society there may be one and only one set of institutional arrangements and policies that can satisfy the full range of rights claims, but it does require that such a conclusion be reached by a series of specific arguments confirmed by experience. Even if a series of such arguments can be made, however, the approach recommended here involves us in assessing different social forms and institutions as means to the realization of human rights rather than as ends themselves. This sets the human rights theorist in critical opposition to those whose overriding concern is the achievement of a certain form of social order, whether this be a classless society or an Islamic republic or a free market economy or a legitimate monarchy or a national state. But it need not exclude the possibility that larger communities, and particularly those political communities that consistently show a general respect for the human rights of their citizens and of other persons whom their policies affect, may earn a moral loyalty which goes beyond the regard that we have for reliable means for achieving our objectives. This loyalty is appropriate to what Rawls speaks of as "the social union of social unions," which honors the principles of justice and which is an end transcending the interests and claims of individual agents. [16]

The Catholic tradition following Aquinas has made a special point of insisting on the common good as the end of laws and of public policy. [17] Maritain, in his presentation of a theory of human rights in the 1940s, was anxious to show that a proper understanding of this notion required respect for the rights of individuals and did not involve a totalitarian subordination of the individual to the state or movement. [18] But it remains true that both the Catholic and the Marxist traditions work with a sense of the larger social community (not necessarily or even normally the state) as moving to a certain fulfillment, even though its progress to fulfillment is marked by profound divisions and violent struggles and even though the content of its fulfillment is not agreed on. Both the Catholic and the Marxist traditions offer comprehensive interpretations of the direction of human history, into which particular movements by various groups and individuals for the realization of specific human rights fit as relatively minor episodes. Individuals are summoned to participate in this general history in more informed and generous ways and to fashion more adequate social institutions. But they are not conceived, as they are in most forms of the liberal tradition, as capable of setting up new moral bases for human cooperation or as sitting in independent judgment on the outcomes of particular types of cooperation as these affect their interests or justifiable claims. In the liberal tradition, the fundamental alternative to a society that observes human rights is a condition of anarchy (Hobbes) or rebellion (Locke). In the Marxist and Catholic traditions, the fundamental alternative is a regime or system that is exploitative and oppressive. In the Marxist and Catholic traditions, there is always the presupposition of participation in a continuing social and historical reality, even if only as victim.

The contrast I have just sketched can be regarded as a negative aspect of my earlier characterization of most forms of liberalism (including my own) as abstract. There is also a more positive aspect of this abstractness. The effort to enunciate moral demands that individuals can make on any society whatever, simply by virtue of their standing as human beings, can, if successful, provide a moral basis for assessing the performance of societies and regimes in different ideological and religious traditions, a basis that is applicable whether or not we approve of the society's long-term direction or the regime's political objectives. By treating human rights claims as morally justifiable demands that are independent of the projects, policies, and ideological objectives of particular regimes, and that serve as constraints on how particular regimes and societies are to behave, the general liberal conception of human rights can give us clearer norms for present moral judgments that preserve the urgency and special standing of rights claims. Liberalism, in its classic eighteenth century form, sets fences around individuals to protect them against certain things that governments or social groups or other individuals might want to do to them. Liberalism, in its social-democratic form, provides a floor in terms of welfare benefits of various sorts which enable individuals to meet those needs that must be met if they are to pursue any of the goals they desire. In neither form does a liberal theory of rights erect a proud tower of shared purposes and civic accomplishments. This, in a liberal theory of the type I would argue for, must come from other sources if it is to come at all. I would observe, in support of this view, that, while liberal regimes normally entrust the shaping of policy and the setting of national goals to the executive and the legislative, they assign the protection of rights and the provision of benefits to the judiciary and to administrative units which are supposed to be sheltered from the storms of political debate and the surges of popular feeling.

It seems to me that the Marxist tradition would argue that guarantees of certain minima with regard to protection against invasions of personal freedom and with regard to provision of goods meeting basic needs are either unnecessary or ineffective. In the prerevolutionary situation of feudal or capitalist oppression, such guarantees are unnecessary for the rich and the powerful and ineffective for the poor and the weak. [19] In the situation of full communism, these guarantees are unnecessary since the possibility of any extensive or systematic denial of rights claims will be removed. The moral demands that these guarantees attempt to meet are justified, but the practices and institutional arrangements involved in claiming, exercising, and acknowledging rights are fundamentally irrelevant. But I would argue that, even if one accepts the Marxist account of social development and the Marxist objective of a society that is equalitarian, democratic, and in some sense free, one can still make a case for the relevance and, indeed, the necessity of the concept of human rights and its associated practices and institutions precisely for the inevitably long and complex period of transition that our society is called to live through. In their refusal to deal candidly with the moral issues of this period, and in their readiness to justify policies that violate the rights of many in order to attain a desirable outcome for the majority, many Marxist movements and thinkers have sinned gravely.

The Catholic tradition, on the other hand, affirms a wide variety of rights and makes extensive use of the concept. The content of the rights enumerated in papal teaching, especially in *Pacem in Terris* (1963), is not notably different from the United Nations Declaration or from the demands of most European social democrats. In most Catholic presentations, there is an evident concern to situate rights claims within an already given social context, which is regarded as the natural setting for the fulfillment of human life. Within this social context, rights are to be balanced with duties, and individual claims are to be integrated into the pursuit of the common good. The Catholic tradition shows more sensitivity to the dangers of absolutizing rights claims and less concern for giving them effective legal and constitutional form than does the liberal tradition, particularly in its American form. I suggest that as a consequence, rights claims in the Catholic tradition have less bite and urgency and come closer to being important items on the political agenda rather than constraints on the political process. [20] This tendency is also a consequence of the fact that the church's social function in this area is to endorse and to encourage rather than to enact and to enforce.

III. TWO TESTS FOR HUMAN RIGHTS

The crucial point to be defended is that even before the establishment of specific social and institutional arrangements for meeting basic human needs, and so before the positive recognition of economic and social rights, and before any imposition of duties by positive law or social custom, there can be a human right, a moral right, that is, a valid moral claim on others. As we shall see, this claim is subject to certain limitations and it is not absolute. But we have already seen that a human claim can be a moral right without being unlimited or absolute. I would further maintain that the duty corresponding to this right, namely, the duty of meeting basic human needs, is one that falls on all human persons to the extent of their ability. It can be argued, I believe, that this duty is a consequence of what John Rawls speaks of as our natural duty of mutual aid, which he defines as "the duty to help another when he is in need or jeopardy, provided that one can do so without excessive risk or loss to oneself." [21] Rawls points out that natural duties "hold between persons irrespective of their institutional relationships; they obtain between all as equal moral persons." [22] It should, however, be pointed out that Rawls himself would not draw this conclusion, since his approach emphasizes considerations of mutual advantage arising from social cooperation, and neglects considerations of need. Furthermore, he objects to utilitarianism on the ground that it requires a sacrifice of life prospects, which the view that there is a duty to provide for the basic needs of other persons seems to require even more clearly. Thus he argues against utilitarianism: "When society is conceived as a system of cooperation designed to advance the good of its members, it seems quite incredible that some citizens should be expected, on the basis of political principles, to accept lower prospects of life for the sake of others." [23]

Maurice Cranston takes a more polemical line on the subject of economic and social rights, which, he points out, "were unknown to Locke and the natural rights theorists of the eighteenth century." [24] He attributes the introduction of this extended form of the language of rights into the Universal Declaration to Communist exploitation of Western good intentions. He asserts that the Communists have appropriated "the word 'rights' for the principles which they believe in," among which are "social security, universal education, free health services, guaranteed employment, and other material benefits for the mass of the people." [25] He holds that, while the Universal Declaration does correctly state the natural rights of traditional Western political thought, it does more harm than good by its confusion of rights and ideals, which has the effect of "pushing all human rights out of the clear realm of the morally compelling into the twilight world of utopian aspiration." [26] Here we are not concerned with the historical question of the extent to which Communists did or did not influence the decision to include economic and social rights in the Universal Declaration. But it is worth remembering that concern for such things as social security, free health services, guaranteed employment, and universal education figured prominently in the aspirations of the New Deal in the United States and in the program of the British Labour government after 1945, and that the provision of such goods was regarded by serious non-Communist social reformers as a matter of justice and right, and not simply as a utopian aspiration. But, even while we leave historical considerations to one side, it is worth considering the systematic basis of Cranston's refusal to accept an understanding of the notion of human rights that will allow for economic and social rights. Perhaps, for Cranston himself, the most fundamental reason is his view that human rights must be absolute. Thus he avers: "The natural rights to life, liberty and so forth have always been understood as categorical rights, rights nobody could find any excuse for not respecting." [27] We have already seen reasons for holding that such an understanding of human rights is untenable even with regard to traditional freedoms which need limitation and regulation for the sake of their own preservation and which cannot reasonably be regarded as absolutely exceptionless.

Cranston also proposes two tests for the authenticity of a universal moral right; and these, I think, represent a positive contribution to elucidating the notion of a human right. Such tests are important because of the difference between moral and positive rights, which makes the determination of just what moral rights human beings possess a question to be settled by moral reflection and argument, and not by statutes and legal decisions. Now it is unfortunate that the particular economic and social right that Cranston picks to apply his tests to is the right to holidays with pay, which is affirmed in Article 24 of the Universal Declaration, which reads: "Everyone has the right to rest and leisure, including reasonable limitation of working hours and periodic holidays with pay." Now it is quite easy for Cranston to show that, while the idea of paid holidays is an attractive proposal, it is not "a matter of paramount importance, like freedom of speech or equality before the law." [28] What this shows is that not every right mentioned in the Universal Declaration is necessarily to be acknowledged as a moral right and that the Universal Declaration is a fallible guide in the task of defining human rights. But it does not show that no economic or social right is of paramount importance; for it can readily be held that rights to a nutritionally adequate diet, to work in decent and healthy conditions, to security in the event of disability, are claims of paramount importance. The test of paramount importance, which, as Cranston admits, is necessarily vague, cannot be plausibly and fairly applied in such a way as to show that political and personal rights are of paramount importance and that economic and social rights are not. The test of paramount importance, rough and intuitive as it is, is valuable for the development of a consensus on the things that should be guaranteed to people because they are essential to the welfare of human beings or to their dignity as free and equal persons in society. For it can serve to control a proliferation of "rights" to various things that might well be desirable or beneficial for particular groups or individuals, but that lack of the moral urgency that is a proper characteristic of human rights issues. It would be very unfortunate if all significant political and economic disputes were to be transformed into disputes over human rights. Such a development would be very likely to produce both a moralistic obscuring of the real issues involved (e.g., in Quebec separatism or in energy policy) and a depreciation of the worth of human rights language. This is not to deny that many social and political disputes affect the observance of human rights, but to remind us that in many cases more progress may be made by dealing with aspects of the problem which can be approached in a more pragmatic and less moralistic fashion.

In applying the admittedly loose test of paramount importance, we should remember that the judgment whether something is or is not of paramount importance cannot be applied in isolation. For it is obvious that not everyone has even a prima facie right to everything he or she takes to be of paramount importance. In the first place, the question whether the thing claimed is of paramount importance is asked in an effort to determine whether there is a human right to the sort of thing that is being claimed, that is, whether there is a universal moral right to it. A satisfactory theory of human rights cannot be structured to match the preferences of individuals or even of particular groups, no matter how fervently or tenaciously these preferences may be held. Thus, the intensity of a person's desire to be in a position of predominant power and the overriding importance that this desire might come to have in the person's life would do nothing to establish that the person had a right to such a position. No social system could propose to make a claim expressing this desire a universal moral right. Nor, for that matter, can a desire or claim for a thing or a state of affairs which logically involves the denial of moral rights of others be made the basis of a universal moral right. Thus, devout Catholics or Muslims might consider it a matter of paramount importance that all persons in their society acknowledge the true God and accept his revealed word. They would be correct in this judgment, for truth in such matters is of paramount importance. But it is clear that bringing about such a state of affairs would necessarily involve an infringement of the freedom of thought and of expression and of conscience of members of such a society; and so the good to be realized in this state of affairs could not be the object of a human right. Similar considerations would, I suggest, apply to the good of national security when this is conceived in such a way as to require the silencing of criticism and permanent restriction of personal and political rights. The test of paramount importance should be applied to pick out those goods of which a person cannot be deprived without serious harm to his or her well-being or personal dignity. The difference here is between what is of paramount importance because it is most strongly desired and what is of paramount importance because it is necessary as a recognized minimum for all. This difference reflects the difference between the deontological character of human rights doctrine and the teleological orientation of most political actors and movements and of economic systems. [29] It is a philosophic pointer to the gap between what individuals, groups, and governments desire and what is owed as a right to all human persons. It is this gap that underlies systematic violations of human rights and that makes concerted action to protect rights both necessary and difficult. A fundamental reason why human rights are subject to violation (as contrasted with their limitation and regulation for the sake of order and with their occasional abridgement in cases of conflicts of rights) is that respect for them cuts across the cherished plans and projects of powerful individuals and governments. [30]

A comprehensive system of rights which includes legal, political, and religious rights, as well as social and economic rights, stands as a challenge to every major government in the world. Even if rights are given official acknowledgment in a political system, the defense of human rights and their continued exercise in freedom often requires an adversary relationship to important centers of power within the political and economic system. The claims made in a comprehensive theory of human rights are likely to be so extensive that continuing tension will be felt between those demanding their rights and those who are managing the political system, even when the plans of the rulers do not include goals that directly violate human rights.

A public strategy that takes the promotion of human rights as central and that adopts a comprehensive concept of human rights calls for the limitation of the power of the state and of centralizing institutions so that individuals are free to develop themselves as self-determining persons within a social space, and for the redistribution of goods and opportunities in such a way that the liberty and the self-respect of those in less favored situations is not diminished in value. A fundamental commitment to human rights requires that one be critical of abuses of power and neglect of the needs of the disadvantaged, whether these occur under oligopolistic capitalism or state socialism or the national security state. For any political system, a comprehensive doctrine of human rights is burdensome; for it converts many of the demands of dissidents and the disadvantaged into moral obligations that are restraints on political and economic processes. Insistence on human rights is likely to be perceived as an unrealistic and moralistic interference in the "natural" working of political and economic systems. This can be true for protest groups and liberation movement as well as for the political and economic establishment.

The other test that Cranston proposes for determining whether a claim is an authentic human right or a universal moral right is the test of practicability. Here again, the basic idea of the test is more acceptable than Cranston's use of it to criticize the idea of economic and social rights. Cranston starts from Kant's dictum that "ought implies can" and argues that there can be neither duties nor rights to things that cannot be done. He goes on to conclude: "It is utterly impossible at present, and it will be for a long time yet, to provide holidays with pay for everybody in the world. . . . At best it is a hypothetical right, something they should have if they could have. But because they cannot have it, the so-called universal right to holidays with pay is not a right at all." He also points out that "economic and social rights can rarely, if ever, be secured by legislation alone." [31]

Now we have already seen reason both to doubt whether the right to holidays with pay meets the test of paramount importance and also to think that conclusions that apply to this "right" may not apply to economic and social rights in general. We may grant, at least for present purposes, that Cranston is right in his factual claim that it is impossible to provide holidays with pay for all the workers in the world, as well as in his general principle that rights and duties are about what is possible. But there are several points in his argument that need to be questioned.

First, it is not true that there cannot be a right to what cannot be provided, unless one makes the assumption that rights are absolute in such a way that they must be satisfied. For, as we have argued earlier, there can be prima facie rights, which it is right, when all things are considered, to override. The fact, if it is a fact, that a thing cannot be provided, shows that a claim to it is not an absolute right, and is at the same time a good reason for holding that the claim is merely a prima facie right and not a final right, and that consequently there is no obligation to provide it. In the approach we have been taking, there is no difficulty in holding that there are prima facie rights that can be overridden and that still retain a moral force that is more than merely hypothetical.

The second point in Cranston's argument that should be questioned is his restriction of the notions of possibility and practicability to the present. Cranston overlooks our responsibilty in shaping a social order that will determine future possibilities. A prima facie right to a good that cannot be provided here and now imposes an obligation—not to provide it since this is ex hypothesi impossible—but to bring about the social conditions that will make it possible to provide the good in question. When these conditions obtain, then the obligation of providing the good and satisfying the prima facie right comes into force. If we allow that a prima facie right can function in this way, then it is simply a mistake to hold that such a right is merely hypothetical or is no right at all. It is also a mistake to treat the satisfaction of such a claim as merely realizing an ideal or an optional moral value, which agents are under no moral obligation to realize.

A third point that should be brought into our assessment of Cranston's argument is the variety of contexts within which we make our judgments of possibility and practicability. In discussing the Kantian dictum, Cranston observes that a man cannot have a duty "to do what it is not physically possible for him to do." [32] The further judgment that the millions who live in preindustrial societies in Asia, Africa, and Latin America cannot have holidays with pay seems to require a more specific judgment of what is possible given certain economic conditions. Now there is nothing inherently suspect in such a judgment. But it is worth remembering that most of our judgments of what is possible or practicable are inductive in character (except where we are dealing with logical impossibility), and that they are made against varying background assumptions which we regard as fixed for purposes of deliberation. Our choice of what assumptions to keep constant makes most of our judgments of possibility and practicability, especially in the policy area, dependent, at least to some extent, on our values and choices.

An example will serve to illustrate this point, which, even though I have put it rather abstractly, is a very common feature of our practical life. If we grant that some people in Cambodia died of starvation after the triumph of the Khmer Rouge, the question can be asked whether we could have satisfied their human right to adequate nutrition. There seems to be little doubt that food was available and could have been provided and delivered to these people, at least to those who could be located. So the question about physical possibility can be answered affirmatively. But if we add the requirements that the operation of feeding these people be carried on without violence or without serious risk to the lives of those delivering the food, then there is good reason to think that the operation was not possible or practicable under those conditions If we add the further requirements that such operations be carried on with general international approval or with the consent of the de facto government, then there is even more reason to think that the operation was not possible or practicable. There is no strict logical requirement that we adopt one set of conditions rather than another in making a judgment of possibility or practicability. We should remember that the sets of conditions which we use in making these judgments are often not explicitly stated or chosen; and they may be internalized at a fairly deep level. Bringing them to light, especially when we are dealing with a complex policy matter, may take considerable analysis and may require honest and intensive self-scrutiny. It is one of the functions of moral critics and prophets to raise questions about these background assumptions or implicit conditions.

Once we have some clarity about the conditions which we are assuming in making our judgments of possibility, how do we deal with a situation in which we hold that given these conditions it is not possible to satisfy certain prima-facie rights claims? There are two fundamental alternatives: one is to accept the conditions as given and hold that the claims must yield because they cannot be satisfied; the other is to alter the set of conditions and ask the question of possibility anew. In effect, one asks the question: what would have to be different for me to judge that this prima facie right can be satisfied? Now it seems to me that there is no universally decisive reason for preferring in all cases the situation where fewer restricting conditions are present and where there is accordingly greater likelihood of making an affirmative judgment about satisfying a rights claim. For one thing, some of the conditions normally present in our judgments of possibility involve respect for other rights and values. The variety of conditions that we accept in making our judgments of possibility also depends to some extent on our social location. Thus, a federal civil servant, in making such judgments (which are implicit in many policy recommendations), normally has to take the Constitution and statutes of the United States as invariable conditions for making his or her own judgments as to what is possible or practicable. Such a limitation would not hold for a citizen or a legislator trying to promote new legislation or for a moral philosopher or theologian. The diversity of conditions or assumptions under which judgments of possibility or practicability are made is one important source of disagreement about what actions are really possible in order to satisfy prima facie rights. The point to bear in mind is that these conditions are not invariable and that we have some freedom and responsibility for which conditions we accept in making our judgments.

A fourth aspect of Cranston's argument that should be criticized is the contrast that he draws between the adequacy of legislation to secure political and civil rights and the inadequacy of legislation to secure economic and social rights. This is clearly not a hard and fast distinction, for we already pointed out the need for a human rights system to see to the protection of political and civil rights. The admirable constitutional affirmations of human rights in the Soviet system show the inadequacy of mere paper guarantees for human rights. But it is true that in a country where the rule of law is established and where there is an independent human rights system, the task of defining and guaranteeing political, civil, and personal rights by appropriate constitutional and legal measures is comparatively easy to carry out; whereas the task of satisfying economic and social rights requires the provision of goods and services and has to be related in varying ways to the stage of economic development, to current economic conditions, and to government policies with regard to taxation and welfare. In a modern welfare state, this task usually involves both extensive transfer payments and the labors of an army of bureaucrats, and it cannot be carried on in effective isolation from the shaping of public policy on a wide range of issues. But even though satisfying economic and social rights is a more difficult and complex task than guaranteeing personal and political rights, it does not seem to me that this difference calls for us to regard the one set of claims as inviolable moral demands and the other as utopian ideals. Rather, we should use the notion of human economic and social rights as a guide to determining the morally significant aspects of economic systems and policies, and as a moral norm for assessing their results. But this assessment will have to be more complex than factual determinations about whether or not governments imprison dissidents or torture political opponents.

A fifth point of difficulty in Cranston's argument, though it is less than explicit, is his assumption that the task of satisfying human rights is one that is purely internal to a given society. In an economically interdependent world, what it is practicable for a given society to do to satisfy economic and social rights is likely to depend, at least to some extent, on decisions taken outside the boundaries of that society by various economic and political agents (other nation-states, multinational corporations, international financial institutions, international organizations, and nongovernmental organizations). If there is a universal responsibility to respect and satisfy human rights, then this responsibility bears in a special way on those outside agents who partially determine what it is practicable for others to do to satisfy economic and social rights. The difficulty or even impossibility of satisfying these rights within the limits of the nation-state system and the existing framework of international cooperation does not deprive basic economic and social claims of their status as human rights, but rather points to the need for transforming the existing international order. Here, I suggest, is one place where human rights policy and the debate over the new international economic order can and should overlap. [33]

Despite my disagreement with Cranston's use of the test of practicability to deny universal moral status to economic and social claims, I believe that the test itself is an important and valuable contribution to our understanding of both the theory of rights and the working of human rights policy. For the constraints of the possible and the practicable enter into our determination of what prima facie rights have moral priority and urgency in a given situation and so of what claims should provoke action, even while other claims have to be set aside with regret. The test of practicability can also help us to understand the development of economic and social rights over time. There is a certain tendency on the part of human rights advocates to think of human rights along the lines once used to define the essentials of the Christian faith: quod semper, quod ubique, quod ab omnibus, that is, as what is acknowledged always and everywhere and by all. The root of this tendency is the affirmation that human rights are universal moral rights. Now this tendency can lead in two different directions. One is the imposition of a set of fixed moral demands on all societies; this is easily branded as a form of cultural imperialism or of abstract moral idealism. The other way is to look at the diverse situations and capacities of various societies and then, in order to preserve the universality of human rights, to limit the content of human rights, especially in the economic and social sphere, to what is practicable for the weakest of these societies.

Against this tendency to insist on uniformity of human rights in all societies, I would suggest that we think of economic and social rights as universal at a certain basic level and then as developing from that basic level. Rights to certain kinds of benefits are limited at all stages by what the society in question can provide and so remain under the test of practicability. But, as a society develops its skills and its resources, it is better able to provide goods and services to meet the rights claims of its members. This is not merely a process of bestowing new entitlements on the members of the society by positive law; it is also the recognition of a prior moral claim which previous limitations made it impossible to satisfy. The ways in which the right to work, the right to rest and leisure, the right to health care, the right to education can be satisfied obviously change as the society develops; and so the concrete form which these rights assume in a given society is subject to change. (Something similar holds true for the right to political participation, which is to be satisfied in different ways in different cultures.) The possibility of satisfying these rights at a higher level is one source of the moral urgency of development. But we have to learn to proportion the form and extent of rights claims to the limited capabilities of the society that we are dealing with, while bearing in mind the special urgency of basic human needs, the claims of future generations, and the necessity of wider and more creative forms of international cooperation which can broaden the capabilities of particular societies.

IV. SHOULD THERE BE SOCIAL AND ECONOMIC HUMAN RIGHTS?

The previous sections of this paper have dealt with the notion of human rights as universal moral claims and with some of the theoretical difficulties that have been brought against the inclusion of economic and social claims within the scope of human rights. The effort of the third section, in particular, was to show that the inclusion of social and economic claims was not an incoherent extension of the notion of human rights. But we passed over the task of offering positive arguments for social and economic rights. There are, I believe, a number of ways of doing this. One could appeal to a basic right to equal concern and respect, to the sense of human solidarity, to obligations arising from human need, to the concept of human dignity. [34] One might also try to justify a policy of respect for economic and social rights on grounds of utility or of enlightened self-interest. Here I would like to sketch out a line of thought which draws on recent writers in the liberal tradition and which takes as basic the value of the human individual and his or her freedom and then moves on to claim that regard for economic and social rights is both required by respect for the worth of the individual and compatible with the development of a free society. It seems to me that this line of thought, which focuses on the ground of human rights, is particularly appropriate for a country such as ours, where liberal individualism has played so prominent a part in our system of values and where attempts to meet universal claims based on need are likely to be perceived as threats to freedom and prosperity.

Robert Nozick, in whose political philosophy the notion of rights plays a central part, raises the question of the ground of rights thus: "In virtue of precisely what characteristics of persons are there moral constraints on how they may treat each other or be treated?" [35] In a brief and admittedly inconclusive discussion, Nozick argues against rationality, free will, and moral agency taken separately as answers to this question. But he suggests that taken together with the human being's ability to "regulate and guide its life in accordance with some overall conception it chooses to accept," [36] they are jointly sufficient to serve as the basis both for the agent's possession of human rights and for the agent's ability to strive for a meaningful life.

Feinberg comes to a somewhat similar conclusion. He takes up Gregory Vlastos' argument that "the doctrine of universal equal human rights presupposes a concept of equal and universal human worth that is to be sharply distinguished from the idea of human merits." [37] He then offers his own emotivist account of the concept of human worth.

> The real point of the maxim that all men are equal may be simply that all men equally have a point of view of their own, a unique angle from which they view the world. They are all equally centers of experience, foci of subjectivity. . . . It may follow (causally, not logically) from this way of so regarding them that we come to *respect* them in the sense tied to the idea of 'human worth.' . . . In attributing human worth to everyone we may be ascribing no property or set of qualities, but rather expressing an attitude—the attitude of respect—toward the humanity in each man's person. [38]

Feinberg's position on human worth is an instance of metaethical emotivism in which ethical principles are regarded as expressions of emotions or attitudes; but it has the advantage over Nozick's position of linking human worth not simply to the human agent's capacity for rational action and planning, but also to the agent's capacity for feeling and experiencing the world. It may well be that Nozick's effort to base human rights on the agent's ability to direct the course of his life will fail for people in cultures very different from our own and for deviant persons in our own culture. But it is precisely in the case of such persons that there is likely to be special need for protection of rights, especially in their encounters with a rationalistic and technocratic dominant culture.

Feinberg's approach also makes explicit something that is present in Nozick's use of the notion of human rights, though it is only implicit in his discussion of the basis of human rights, that is, the individualist character of the doctrine. For it is the individual who has a point of view of his or her own, and who is a center of experience and a focus of subjectivity. If human nature, whether described along Nozick's lines or Feinberg's, is in some sense the ground of human rights, it is the actual human individual who is the subject of these rights. The moral claims that are advanced in any doctrine of human rights are claims that are advanced in behalf of individuals and that are to be made good by either the actions or omissions of institutions and of other individuals. If one judges legal, political, economic, and social institutions by the criterion of human rights, one is ultimately asking about the treatment of individuals by these institutions. (This is not to deny that one of the most important human rights that individuals possess is the right to participate in various forms of communal and institutional activity, nor is it to deny the importance of institutional arrangements for enabling people to exercise their rights effectively.) In the last analysis, it is the individual who is tortured or treated with dignity, who is fed or starved, who is enabled or forbidden to express his or her thoughts and to follow his or her conscience. In this sense, human rights, whether they be religious and political or economic and social, are ultimately individual. Corporations and other institutions may by a legal fiction be regarded as persons under law and may be the subject of certain legal rights, but morally their rights are subsidiary to the rights and interests of individual human persons. This is not to say that overriding or violating the rights of institutions and groups is always justifiable or that it does not often involve a violation of the human rights of individuals. Thus, violating the legal rights of a church or religious group may well involve violations of the rights of individuals to free expression and liberty of conscience. Furthermore, the best way to defend human rights in general may well be to establish or to preserve certain institutional arrangements.

Nonetheless, because the ultimate subject of human rights is the human individual, there is a certain individualistic bias in any doctrine of human rights. The positions adopted by Nozick and Feinberg are individualistic in the stronger sense that they involve a positive appraisal of the individual's individuality, that is, her ability to experience things in her own way, to adopt her own plan of life, and to determine at least to some extent the meaning of her life. It is possible to argue for an extensive theory of human rights, which includes economic and social rights as well as the freedoms of classical liberalism, precisely on the grounds that secure possession of these rights enables human persons to cultivate and develop their individual excellences and plans of life. This view would be the deontological equivalent of Mill's utilitarian argument for individuality in Chapter 3 of *On Liberty,* in the course of which he says:

> As it is useful that while mankind are imperfect there should be different opinions, so it is that there should be different experiments of living; that free scope should be given to varieties of character, short of injury to others; and that the worth of different modes of life should be proved practically, when any one thinks fit to try them. It is desirable, in short, that in things which do not primarily concern others, individuality should assert itself. [39]

While equal and universal human rights ensure a minimum level of security, well-being and freedom of all members of society, they can provide the basis for variety and pluralism within society precisely because of the elements of subjectivity and self-determination which are present in the individual person who is the subject of human rights. In this way, the uniformity that might result in a single status society, in which the rights of persons were derived only from their status as human beings, would be avoided. [40]

Adopting the individual human agent, with his subjectivity and his ability to shape his life meaningfully, as the ground of human rights also gives us a way of developing the relation between needs and rights. David Miller in his recent book, *Social Justice,* has argued that ideal rights (as contrasted with positive rights) can be reduced to claims on the bases of needs and deserts. Thus, in considering the economic and social rights enumerated in the Universal Declaration of Human Rights, he comments: "What is actually contained in this section of the Declaration is a list of basic human needs, together with the principal means of satisfying them. Thus what makes this class of human rights relevant to social justice is that they are claims based upon need, and moreover of a universal and urgent kind." [41]

The major difficulty that affects the effort to derive rights claims from statements about needs is the problem of the double variability of the estimates that people have of their needs and of the goals that people have in relation to which their needs are to be determined. [42] No one wants to confine the domain of just claims to those things that a human person needs for subsistence and physical survival; but once one goes beyond these things, how does one distinguish between what people really need and what they may strongly desire, between their real needs and the needs that they think they have? Furthermore, one has to recognize that people need different things in different cultures and different situations. Thus in a remote rural area, a telephone may be necessary for survival; whereas in many other situations it may be a convenience, but not a necessity.

Now Miller, after criticizing the view that needs can be analyzed in terms of wants or psychological states, offers the following account of the notion of need: " 'A needs X' = 'A will suffer harm if he lacks X.' " [43] He maintains that harm has to be understood to include emotional and intellectual damage to a person as well as physical hurt; but he does not think the harm can be understood in simple universal terms so that the same things harm each and every human person. Thus he warns against "the view that the concept of harm can be applied to a person on the basis of general empirical criteria, without reference to the aspirations and ideals of the person concerned." [44] He also argues that using the concepts of harm and need does not require that we reach agreement on "a strong theory of human nature—a definite account of how human beings ought to live and the kind of satisfaction they ought to enjoy." [45] Such an agreement would obviously require a consensus that would be very difficult to achieve in a pluralistic society and that would be unattainable for the world as a whole. In the absence of such consensus, the use of the concepts of harm and need to determine social policy could well be an instrument of an oppressive bureaucratic or theocratic elite which would lay down what constituted real harm and real need. So Miller offers what I would term a pluralistic and ultimately individualistic account of harm and need. He writes:

> Harm, for any given individual, is whatever interferes directly or indirectly with the activities essential to his plan of life; and correspondingly, his needs must be understood to comprise whatever is necessary to allow these activities to be carried out. In order, then, to decide what a person's needs are, we must first identify his plan of life, then establish what activities are essential to that plan, and finally investigate the conditions which enable those activities to be carried out. [46]

Thus, as Miller points out, we can hold that the needs of a European intellectual are different from those of a Russian peasant, without reducing this to the obvious differences in their wants. This variable understanding of needs is obviously less easy to apply to the formulation of social policy than a simple empirical notion of needs, but it does have the great merit of respecting the freedom of individuals to determine their own plans of life. It retains most of the advantages of a simple empirical notion of needs, for there are some things (food, shelter, medical care, elementary education) that all or nearly all persons have need of in order to carry out their plans of life.

Miller's approach also involves us in certain evaluative and moral judgments about plans of life, some of which we would have to reject as unintelligible, dangerous, or irrelevant to problems of justice. Thus Miller holds that we should reject the pyromaniac's plan of life as unintelligible and that what he needs is not matches but psychiatric help. [47] He also holds that in resolving conflicts about justice, we should not consider plans of life that call for superior status. [48] There are, of course, further questions that Miller does not raise about what sorts of plans of life a society should actively promote. But it is clear that his approach takes us well beyond what we earlier laid down as the realm of human rights, that is, those just claims which an individual person makes (or which are made for the individual person) simply on the basis of being a human person. For the claims that are being advanced here for those things which are necessary for the individual's life plan are conceded to be variable and relative to the persons whose life plans are under consideration. These claims are dependent on the individual's preferences and beliefs as well as on those social and personal factors, including his or her own choices, that have brought it about that the individual has these preferences and beliefs.

Now it seems to me that we do not judge that the fact that a person needs some thing in order to carry out a rational plan of life confers on the person a right to that thing. We may grant that a person's wanting something is a good reason for trying to bring it about that he gets it, and that the person's needing the thing is a stronger and better reason. But it becomes clear that when we are dealing with scarce goods, where demand normally exceeds supply, we cannot affirm that a need creates a right, even if the need is related to a rational plan of life. Consider the case of a college student who wishes to study medicine. This may form part of a socially useful and morally laudable plan of life. The student's desire, when joined with ability to complete the necessary studies and to do the work of a physician, does count as a good reason for trying to obtain a medical education for her. If a place in medical school is denied to the student because of morally unacceptable reasons (e.g., because she is a woman or a member of a minority group or the child of parents whose religious or political views are objectionable), she will have good reason to think that her rights have been violated. But this is not because she has a human right or some more specific type of right to a medical education. I would propose that the right that is violated is a human right to fair and nondiscriminatory treatment. What is morally objection-able is not that she does not obtain a scarce good such as a place in medical school, but that the action of denying her that good involves unfairness. We can compare this with a case in which there is agreement to accept a random procedure for distributing places to qualified candi-dates, or with a case in which a candidate with superior qualifications is preferred to one with adequate qualifications. In these cases we may feel regret that a qualified person has failed to obtain an important good or that certain particular good results that might reasonably be expected will be lost. But we do not regard the denial of the good to the unsuccess-ful candidate as a denial of the candidate's rights.

I have been arguing that the fact that a person has a need for something as part of a rational plan of life does not create a right to that thing. But a reply could be made that on the nonabsolutist concept of rights that I proposed earlier, the candidate for medical school actually does have a right to the place in medical school but that for a number of reasons (e.g., scarcity of places, presence of more qualified applicants) it is justifiable to override that right. Now it is true that the concept of human rights does allow for exceptions in certain cases. But it seems less than helpful to broaden the notion of rights to cover cases involving the distribution of scarce resources where overriding rights would then become a routine necessity. Such an extension of the notion of rights would also blur the distinction between what is in one's interest as ration-ally conceived and what one is entitled to as a matter of right. It would also lead to a weakening of the force of rights language, which is a resource that rights theorists should be anxious to conserve. A game in which all cards are trumps is an impossibility; a game in which two or more suits are trumps is likely to be an irritating tangle.

It may also be objected that by denying the general inference from need to right, I am undercutting the position I took earlier in defending social and economic rights against Cranston's criticisms. Here I would appeal to Cranston's own test of paramount importance for determining the scope of rights. Those goods and services which are necessary for subsistence are of paramount importance and can be claimed as a matter of right. I think that same point can also be made with regard to goods necessary for functioning as an agent within society (e.g., basic education). Obviously, these goods will be included within a rational plan of life, but the claims to them have a greater urgency than do claims to other goods also included in rational plans of life. One reason for this is that agents can, given altered circumstances and changes in their own preferences, develop alternative plans of life in which the absence of certain goods will not be a decisive obstacle, though it may be a genuine hardship and may involve harm to the person. But the absence of the goods that are necessary for subsistence and, to a lesser extent, of the goods that are necessary for functioning as an agent in society, cannot be remedied by adopting an alternative plan of life. Goods necessary for subsistence and for functioning as an agent in society have a paramount importance and an urgency which is not captured simply by relying on the notion of the requirements of a rational plan of life.

What, then, remains of value in Miller's approach? First, it directs our attention to determining the needs of persons on the basis of their own conceptions of themselves and their plans for themselves. While not all needs can be the basis of human rights, it is important in a pluralistic society that we recognize the variety of needs that people have as a result of their different social situations and their different histories. When a society has attended to the basic liberties and necessities of its citizens, the claims of persons for goods needed for their rational plans of life have a morally significant place. Neglect of these claims leads to frustration and resentment; if it is not justified by the exigencies of poverty or of national emergency, it is likely to require a comprehensive policy of repression. If one accepts Miller's point that denial of the goods necessary to a rational plan of life involves harm to those that are deprived of these goods, one can then argue on utilitarian grounds or by appealing to a principle of beneficence that harm is to be minimized. [49]

Such considerations have weight even in deontological moral systems, nearly all of which acknowledge some sort of principle of beneficence. The claims that people advance to goods that are necessary for the realization of rational plans of life are worthy of respect and deserve sympathetic consideration, even when they are not to be considered human rights. For they are claims that are bound to be made when people feel a certain measure of security in their personal and civil rights and in their possession of the goods required for subsistence and for functioning as agents in society. Sensitivity to these claims which express the aspirations of individual persons in their communities is, I would suggest, a defining mark of a humane regime or polity. It is an essential part of the public and governmental response to the demands made by groups that have previously been marginalized or discriminated against. For members of such groups are not interested merely in having their basic needs provided for on an administrative basis; they themselves wish to enter into the process of shaping their lives in society in an interesting and satisfying way that expresses their own preferences and aspirations. Carrying on such a process clearly requires an enormous amount of dialogue, reflection, and comparison of situations if policies are to be formulated which both meet the needs of different persons (since the groups involved are far from homogeneous) and also satisfy at least certain general standards for equal treatment of persons.

This should be a characteristic and central concern of a democratic polity which respects human rights, for the pursuit of rational plans of life is an appropriate activity for persons to undertake once their human rights are secured and even when these rights are to some extent unsatisfied. The satisfaction of the claims that people advance with regard to the plans of life that they wish to pursue is, in terms of moral urgency, secondary to the observance of human rights; but, in terms of historical development, it often precedes the establishment of human rights for all. This is particularly likely to be true in bourgeois societies, where the demands for justice by articulate and organized groups are generally concerned not with what is needed for subsistence nor with basic liberties, but with things desired because of their usefulness to individuals in carrying out their plans of life. Those who advance these claims are not totally mistaken in thinking that the issues they raise are matters of justice and involve rights of various sorts; but they frequently lose sight of the moral priority of claims to goods necessary for subsistence and of other human rights.

This neglect of the difference in moral urgency between claims for goods necessary for subsistence and claims for goods necessary for rational plans of life shows up in John Rawls's notion of primary goods as "things that every rational man is presumed to want." Rawls goes on to say: "These goods normally have a use whatever a person's rational plan of life. For simplicity, assume that the chief primary goods at the disposition of society are rights and liberties, powers and opportunities, income and wealth." [50] Rawls here expresses in rather abstract and general terms a view shared by most political philosophers, including those in the Catholic and Marxist traditions, that it is reasonable and appropriate to ascribe desires for certain general classes of goods to everyone and to propose both principles of justice and social policies on that basis. But the generality of the approach obscures the priority of certain items within the class of primary goods, namely, those which are necessary for subsistence as well as those which are necessary for functioning as an agent in society. From the standpoint of a theory of justice which aims at comprehensive principles applying to all claims, the failure to make this distinction is intelligible; from the standpoint of a theory of human rights, the failure to make it leaves us in a situation of moral and practical confusion.

When recognition of the moral priority of claims for essential goods (those necessary for subsistence and for functioning as an agent in society) is given effective form in social policy, individuals are liberated and enabled to pursue their own plans of life. In a liberal society, they are free to do so in a variety of competitive and cooperative ways. Recognition of the social and economic rights of others constrains the free pursuit of interest and of one's own plans on the part of some. But against this we can set some important advantages. First, this constraint is a moral constraint which serves to prevent the realization of one's plan of life from degenerating into the purely selfish pursuit of interest. Second, it enables more people to achieve some measure of human fulfillment and excellence by pursuing their plans of life. It thus makes the values of life in a free society more generally available and more widely shared. Third, it creates the basis of a comprehensive and nonexclusive form of community. For to acknowledge the rights of others is to enter into a form of community with them, a community which is both presupposed and realized by the common task of satisfying those claims that we recognize as universal moral rights. Our common humanity leads us to acknowledge and respect each other's human rights; satisfying these rights requires us to live as a community in deed and not merely in word. Acknowledging the needs, the liberty, and the worth of other individuals in this view is not a retreat into selfishness but a step to a just ordering of the world.

NOTES TO CHAPTER 4

1. Max Stackhouse, p. 147 in this volume.
2. Ronald Dworkin, *Taking Rights Seriously* (Cambridge, Mass.: Harvard University Press, 1977), p. xi.
3. See John Rawls, *A Theory of Justice* (Cambridge, Mass.: Harvard University Press, 1971), pp. 201–205, for a brief account of conflicts of liberties and the need for limitations if liberties are to be made effective.
4. For a discussion of some of the ambiguities present in the notion of absolute rights and for a review of some of the considerations that limit the number of exceptionless rights, see Joel Feinberg, *Social Philosophy* (Englewood Cliffs, N.J.: Prentice-Hall, 1973), pp. 83–88, 95–97.
5. See David Miller, *Social Justice* (Oxford: Clarendon Press, 1976), pp. 76–77. In his discussion of situations where meeting rights claims can lead to morally unsatisfactory results, Miller has positive (i.e., socially acknowledged) rights in mind; but his conclusions apply also to ideal rights.
6. Feinberg, p. 86.
7. See W. D. Ross, *The Right and the Good* (Oxford: Clarendon Press, 1930), pp. 18–33, for an elucidation of the notion of prima facie duty.
8. Feinberg, p. 88.
9. Universal Declaration of Human Rights, Article 25.
10. Feinberg, p. 88.

11. Maurice Cranston, *What Are Human Rights?* (New York: Basic Books, 1962), p. 38.

12. *Ibid.,* p. 37.

13. Richard Pierre Claude, "The Western Tradition of Human Rights in Comparative Perspective," in *Comparative Judicial Review* 14 (1977), pp. 8, 10.

14. Feinberg, p. 95.

15. *Ibid.,* pp. 66–67.

16. Rawls, p. 527.

17. Aquinas, *Summa Theologiae* I-II, 90, 2. More explicit consideration of the relevance of Thomas's notion of common good to the theme of human rights can be found in Chap. 3 of this volume. The notion of common good has also been interpreted so as to lend support to national security ideology. See Chap. 3 of companion volume, *Human Rights and Basic Needs.*

18. Jacques Maritain, *The Rights of Man and Natural Law,* tr. Doris C. Anson (New York: Scribner's, 1945).

19. See Chap. 5 of this volume.

20. A somewhat different reading of the possibilities in the Catholic approach to human rights can be found in the priority principles proposed by David Hollenbach in *Claims in Conflict: Retrieving and Renewing the Catholic Human Rights Tradition* (New York: Paulist Press, 1979), pp. 203–207.

21. Rawls, p. 114. There is an important treatment of this issue in Alan Gewirth, *Reason and Morality* (Chicago: University of Chicago Press, 1978), pp. 217–230. Gewirth concludes (p. 229) that "the moral duties . . . include positive actions to defend other persons' right to basic goods when the actions are necessary for such defense without bringing comparable harm to their agents."

22. Rawls, p. 114.

23. *Ibid.,* p. 115.

24. Cranston, p. 34.

25. *Ibid.,* p. 35.

26. *Ibid.,* p. 41.

27. *Ibid.,* p. 37.

28. *Ibid.,* p. 39.

29. For a standard account of the distinction between teleogical and deontological theories in moral philosophy, see William Frankena, *Ethics,* 2nd ed. (Englewood Cliffs, N.J.: Prentice-Hall, 1973), pp. 14–17.

30. Some of these projects of the powerful in Latin America are considered in the essays of the companion volume, *Human Rights and Basic Needs.*

31. Cranston, p. 37.

32. *Ibid.*

33. In *Human Rights and Basic Needs,* the essays by Richard Feinberg, John Willoughby, John Weeks, and Elizabeth Dore clearly illustrate the connection between commitment to a basic needs strategy as a means of

implementing human rights and arguments for changes in policy by international financial institutions and governments.

34. See the role of principles of decency and dignity in the determination of a moral minimum of welfare, as treated by Drew Christiansen, "Basic Needs: Criterion for the Legitimacy of Development," pp. 23–25.

35. Nozick, p. 48.

36. *Ibid.,* p. 49.

37. Feinberg, p. 93.

38. *Ibid.,* pp. 93–94.

39. John Stuart Mill, *On Liberty,* in *Essays on Politics and Society,* ed. J. M. Robson, Collected Works, XVII (Toronto: University of Toronto Press, 1977), pp. 260–261.

40. Feinberg, pp. 88–89.

41. Miller, p. 79.

42. For another treatment of the issues here, but one which is also concerned with preserving the distinction between basic and nonbasic needs while allowing some modification of standards of need to fit different social conditions, see Christiansen, pp. 43–49.

43. Miller, p. 130.

44. *Ibid.,* p. 131.

45. *Ibid.,* p. 132.

46. *Ibid.,* p. 134.

47. *Ibid.,* p. 135.

48. *Ibid.,* pp. 139–141.

49. See Frankena, pp. 45–48, for a discussion of the content of this principle.

50. Rawls, p. 62.

JOHN C. HAUGHEY, S.J.

5. *Individualism and Rights in Karl Marx*

If this chapter were to address itself to the issue of human rights in Karl Marx, it would be quite brief, for Marx seldom addresses himself explicitly to human rights. But looked at another way, the entire body of his writings is one long analysis of what violates human dignity and human rights, as we are conceiving them in this project, and what must be done to enhance respect for them. Before getting to this material, however, we must begin with those notions of Marx that will enable us to understand where human rights and dignity fit into his grid of ideas.

I. THE RELATIONSHIP BETWEEN BEING HUMAN AND "THE BEING OF NATURE"

Marx has usually been labeled a materialist. Are human beings, in Marx's mind, of the same substance as the material universe? If they are, in what does their dignity consist? If they are not, how are they different? Should he be called a materialist?

Marx's analyses did not juxtapose "man" and nature as if they were separable. Rather, nature was a totality which had two parts to it. One part was conscious, active, sensate, capable of modifying matter—this part was the human species. The second part was inorganic, insensate, inactive, and external to the human species—what most other philosophers would call nature. For Marx, there were two ways of participating in the "being of nature." [1] One way was as a human; the other way was infrahumanly. For Hegel, to whom Marx was so indebted, "nature was alienated mind." [2] But for Marx, being human meant that one was inalienably part of matter, was inseparable from matter, and was inexplicable apart from the material universe. Human dignity did not consist in some kind of ability to escape or transcend or be over against matter, but rather consisted in the capacity to act on matter in the pursuit of human needs. Marx rejected all forms of idealism, whether philosophical or religious, that attempted to conceive of human dignity as transcending matter. [3] Furthermore, he roots dignity in human activity rather than in some ontological status that "human nature" enjoys at rest, so to speak. [4] Typically, Marx made this point in a conscious contrast to scripture. "In the beginning was the deed." [5] All human activity furthermore, aims at meeting needs. Insensate nature contains what human beings need to complete themselves. Hence, the eternal interdependence between matter and man. It is sheer fantasy to conceive of any realization of human dignity that comes about a-historically or immaterially or spiritually.

Most of these ideas come from Marx's *Manuscripts of 1844*. This corpus contains what some have referred to as Marx's anthropological insights. [6] At that early stage of his career, he was looking at the human condition as "man making objects and perpetuating himself through these objectifications." [7] In his next stage, the anthropologist turned into a political scientist. At this second stage the insight which governed his work was: "The human essence . . . is an ensemble of social relations." [8] But these social relations are formed by the modes of production. As in the first stage, so here common human dignity is realized only through human activity. The foremost activity for achieving and asserting human dignity in this second stage of Marx's development is revolutionary praxis. [9] If, in the first period, he had focused on productive labor modifying insensate nature, in the second period he was more conscious of how the modifiers of insensate nature were being modified by the objects produced by their labor. It is in this period that he is most critical of those who thought you could first change consciousness and after that, the world. He sees the best minds of the world, all through history, duped by that false assumption. [10]

Without repudiating either of the two previous stages, in the third or last stage of Marx's writings (which include the *Grundrisse* and *Kapital*) the political radical becomes an economist.

Nature in this last stage contains an endless reservoir of dumb material for economic man. It is a "primitive toolhouse" and totally instrumental for the activities of economic man. [11] Productivity and the conquest of economic want are now more important to Marx than the interdependence between mind and matter, although he never repudiates his initial materialism or naturalism. His naturalistic anthropocentrism, as I believe it should be called, has so developed by this last stage that man is now master of nature; nature "supplements man's own bodily organs adding a cubit and more to his stature, scripture notwithstanding." [12]

Furthermore, Marx would emphasize one activity which makes the human species stand out from the rest of nature. That is the activity of consciousness. This feature of human capacities can create finalities which in turn can recreate the human condition, and at the same time we can be conscious of our consciousness. In this we are a special kind of being while still remaining part of the being of nature.

II. HUMAN DIGNITY AND HUMAN NEEDS

If human dignity is achieved by activity expended in meeting our needs, what analysis does Marx give of human needs? In many ways it is quite standard. Some of our needs are common to all biological organisms struggling to survive, and some are peculiar to the human species. But whether they are about the business of meeting their survival needs or needs beyond survival, it is the way human beings go about this activity that makes them different from creatures in the animal kingdom. This peculiarity consists in the free and teleological nature of human activity. "An animal only produces what it immediately needs for itself or its young. It produces one-sidedly, while man produces universally. It produces only under the dominion of immediate physical need, while man produces even when he is free from physical need and only truly produces in freedom therefrom." [13]

Marx's unique contribution to an understanding of human needs lies in his analysis of capitalist society. In capitalist society Marx sees individuals relating to each other not directly, but rather through the products of their respective labors. An exchange comes about between people because each has different needs. So different products are needed to satisfy their needs. In some ways this is good. "The fact that this need on the part of one can be satisfied by the product of the other, and vice versa, and that the one is capable of producing the object of the need of the other, and that each confronts the other as owner of the object of the other's need, this proves that each of them reaches beyond his own particular need as a human being and that they relate to one another as human beings." [14] An interdependence has been created; a social bonding is expressed in this product exchange which has mutual needs as its impetus.

But in some ways, this is the beginning of the problem for Marx. The two persons relate to one another, not immediately, but only in terms of their objectifications. The relations are not between persons, but between things. In a word, according to Marx, "individual A serves the need of individual B by means of the commodity 'a' only insofar as, and because individual B serves the need of individual A by means of commodity 'b' and vice versa. Each serves the other in order to serve himself; each makes use of the other, reciprocally, as his means." [15]

This analyzes capitalism in simple interpersonal dimensions. But the problem of needs grows more complex from this point on. Marx sees capitalism as inducing a plethora of needs which are not authentic human needs but rather the effects of "capital's need to valorize itself." [16] It does this, in part, by producing objects that are actually unnecessary. But these products come into demand nonetheless, because need for them has been successfully induced, especially among the workers. The inducer is the capitalist. But in the long run, even the needs of the capitalist derive from capital's own need to proliferate. What is being satisfied by the workers in the process of capitalism are the needs of "an essentially alien force." [17]

Capitalism isn't all bad, however. While workers are being submitted to the indignity of being used as means for this "alien force's" ends, radical needs are germinating in the workers. Radical needs, for Marx, are whatever is required for a person's own realization. [18] No matter how oppressed a worker is by the capitalist mode of production, his radical needs cannot be totally eradicated. The radical needs of human beings who are being dehumanized, although these needs are largely below the surface of their consciousness in capitalism, are for Marx the seeds in the present society which contain the future promise.

The carriers of radical needs are the members of the working class. The working class is "a class with radical chains, a class in civil society that is not *of* civil society . . . a sphere of society having a universal character because of its universal suffering and claiming no particular right because no particular wrong but unqualified wrong is perpetrated on it." [19] This class will bring about the revolution. That revolution will be freeing for all of humanity, not only the working class. This class has been reduced to triviality through the pursuit of paltry needs but, at the same time, radical needs have germinated within it. Marx foresees that "a deep ongoing revolution can only be a revolution in basic needs." [20]

The radical needs of Marx, which he never clearly defines, are not needs directed toward greater possessions nor toward higher wages nor toward a better standard of living. Radical needs are perceived from a situation of alienation, i.e., when there is a recognition that one's social relations are being mediated through things. Radical needs come down to the human need one has to express oneself freely according to one's unique sense of self. There are further needs: to care for others and to exercise all of one's capacities, and finally, the need for more "free time," as Marx calls it. He contends that the wealth of society, in the future, will be measured by the degree of free time enjoyed by its citizenry. [21]

It should be obvious, by now, that need in Marx is not merely an economic category, but is closer to a criterion for value. "He tends to treat concepts of need as non-economic categories, as historical-philsophical, that is, an anthropological value-categories and therefore, as not subject to definition within the economic system." [22]

A final insight into Marx's understanding of needs can be gained by seeing how individuals will experience needs in the future society which Marx projects. In this projected society, a "higher level" of needs will be met than were met in capitalist society. [23] In this future society, trivial objects of need will not appear on the market, thus generating demand. Rather at that time needs will generate "higher activities," such as the arts. These needs will only be satisfied by relationships between people who are now ends in themselves, not means to ends. The needs and the system of needs in the future society will be a matter of relational quality rather than of quantitative possessions. In this society, persons will have been freed from the domination of things. In this future system, the criterion will be "the need for the development of the individual." [24] The radical needs which lay below the surface during capitalism will have surfaced and will be met in this future society.

In the present economy, on the other hand, we are saddled with a society which has devised a "science of renunciation, of privation and of saving . . . its moral ideal is the worker who takes his wages to the savings bank . . . its principal thesis is the renunciation of life and of human needs." [25] He goes on in the same passage to point up the paradox of the situation. "The less you eat, drink, buy books, go to the theater, or go to the public house and the less you think, love, theorize, sing, paint, fence, etc., the more you will be able to save and the greater will become your treasure which neither moth nor rust will corrupt—your capital. The less you are, the less you express your life. The more you have, the greater is your alienated life, and the greater is the saving of your alienated being." [26]

His imaginings had him conjure up a fully constituted society in the future which will produce "the wealthy man." This wealthy man is one whose "own self-realization exists as an inner necessity, a need." [27] One would have to conclude that Marx foresees a future as a time when the needs of human beings will not be primarily for things but for one another. What other meaning could one attach to the following observation? "Not only the wealth but also the poverty of men acquires, in a socialist perspective, a human and thus a social meaning. Poverty is the passive bond which leads man to experience a need for the greatest wealth, the other person." [28]

So far in this brief introduction to Marx's thought his emphasis has been on grounding human dignity in activity undertaken to meet human needs. But not all human activity leads to the betterment of the human condition. Hence, the third area of our question.

III. POWER AND SOCIETY

There are almost as many references to power in Marx as there are to "man". These references to power cover an enormous range of subjects. Rather than dealing with all the ways that Marx uses the concept of power, we will narrow the topic down to one of them. Where does power come from in society? What are the powers that build society?

Societies come into being, for Marx, by "the relations of production" which obtain within their populations. [29] All power, according to his perspective, comes from the interactions which develop out of these relations of production. In turn, the sum total of these relations of production constitute the base on which all legal, political and ideological superstructures of any society are built. [30] It should be obvious, therefore, that relations of production are a key concept for Marx. Relations of production involve ownership and nonownership. For Marx, the ideal was communal ownership, but the reality was private ownership of the forces of production. The private ownership of most or all of the forces of production in turn created a ruling class, the capitalists. By the same token it created a dominated class, the workers. The act of exchange in which the worker acquiesces, the act whereby the value of his labor is recompensed by an unequal wage contract, is the radical mistake which destabilizes the power base on which society is built. The owning class extracts a surplus value from the labor of the laborer. [31] One of the consequences of this arrangement is that the owning class relates to the working class as if it were merely a part of the forces of production. Hence owners use the things they own and use the people they hire as if they were of equal value. [32]

There are a number of parasites in the economic structure who do not bring about any notable change in the power structure since they do not own any significant productive force or usable natural resources or productive labor power. [33] Marx would put in this group: lawyers, soldiers, priests, salesmen, entertainers, judges, and bureaucrats, among others. The importance of these groups is that they protect the economic base of capitalism by the roles they play in the superstructure. They benefit from the form of society they are in and have an interest in continuing that form. They are revenue receivers, not power generators. They are structure-protecting groups who play an ideological role whether they know it or not. [34]

This last observation leads to the important connection in Marx's thought between the power base and the apparently dominant superstructure. The state, which for Marx is the main feature in the superstructure in the present capitalist era, contains all the legal and political devices and processes necessary in order to maintain social "order". [35] The state or superstructure represents the *de jure* organization of "the general interest." [36] It is built upon the base of the economic structure. While it appears to regulate it, the state is in fact shaped by and manipulated into sustaining it. The power of capitalism's economic base and the constraints it exerts on the superstructure are concealed and unacknowledged. What is out in the open, on the other hand, are all the components of the superstructure. While talking the language of equality, rights, and personal dignity, the state is in fact determined by and beholden to the underlying economic interests of the owning class. Underneath the *de jure* social order exists the *de facto* organization of its power in the present era. The *de jure* order is accessible to inquiry; the *de facto* order is virtually inaccessible.

Any conflict in the present era between the actual economic powers on which the superstructure rests and the purported rights of persons or groups articulated by this superstructure will always be resolved in favor of the owning class. "The bourgeois state is nothing but a mutual insurance pact of the bourgeois class both against its members taken individually and against the exploited class." [37] Rather than a mechanism adjudicating what is good for the members of the society, the state in fact continues to adjudicate on behalf of the interests of the owner class and leaves untouched the economic contradictions that undergird capitalist society. The reason why the state is not unmasked is because it so adroitly retains a pretext of sanctity and postures as exercising its powers out of a concern for the common good. If any change at the level of power is to take place, it should not be expected from the state and all it uses to keep "order." The legal and political superstructure must be unmasked so that the pretense under which it operates is exposed. The only class that can change power's distribution in capitalist society is the working class.

In brief, the source of power for Marx is the relations of production, which are more foundational than any of the legal or political relations which are found in society. This is why he was more interested in power and its distribution than in rights and their observance.

IV. HUMAN DIGNITY AND HUMAN RIGHTS

What is Marx's conception of human rights? He seldom theorizes about the subject. His most explicit observations about human rights are expressed in the judgments he makes about eighteenth and nineteenth century history, especially the history of the French Revolution and its subsequent developments. [38] He saw that revolution as a revolution fomented by one class, the bourgeoisie. An essential part of that revolution was the notion of the equality of individuals. The expectation of that revolution was that equal individuals would have dignity henceforth and forever, because they had won their "natural rights." Their natural rights, in turn, would be ensured henceforth and forever through law. [39]

Marx's problem with this rationale was twofold. The revolution advanced the interests of one class, not the interests of everyone. The interests of that one class did not bring about social equality but, in fact, spawned a whole new unwelcome development: modern individualism. In modern society, Marx saw "an individual separated from the community, withdrawn into himself, wholly preoccupied with his private interests and acting in accordance with his private caprice." [40] Equal rights, in Marx's mind (and he had eighteenth and nineteenth century evidence to prove it to his satisfaction), means unequal opportunity for the appropriation of wealth. This was because the doctrine of equal rights was inserted into a social context of inequality. As a result, the inequities resident in the social context became more and more inveterate. Marx's problem with equal rights, like his problem with democracy, was that from the opening gun some were more equal than others and the less equal could never catch up.

The ideological leaders of bourgeois societies, furthermore, conceived of rights inhering in individuals and abstractly, as if they existed apart from social conditions, he complained. [41] Society then attempted to decide justice claims on the basis of these abstractions. For Marx, this was a fatal flaw both in philosophy and in political theory. Rather than providing a basis for human dignity, this way of conceiving society prolonged the violence of some toward others. Marx's hostility to the human rights doctrine of these societies stems from his judgment that it was a rationalization that obstructed the attainment of the human dignity that human beings could actually achieve. [42]

More specifically, Marx took apart the French Constitution of 1793 and underscored all aspects of its individualism. Its concept of liberation, first of all, gives everyone "the right to do everything which harms no one else. The borders in which every man can move harmlessly are determined by the law, just as the border between two fields is determined by a fence. The concern is with the freedom of man as an isolated monad, withdrawing into itself. The human right of freedom is not based on the connection of man with man, but rather on the separation of man from man. It is the right of separation, the right of the limited individual, limited unto himself . . ." [43] Secondly, "man's right of private property is the right to enjoy one's property and to dispose of it independently, not arbitrarily, without considering other men. It is the right of self-interest." Security, thirdly, "is the highest social conception of civil society, the conception held by the police that all of society exists only in order to guarantee to each of its members the preservation of his person, his rights and his property. . . . Civil society does not, through the concept of security, raise itself above its egoism. Security is rather the guarantee of egoism." Marx concludes his negative assessment of the conception of human rights in the French Constitution: "None of these so-called rights of man goes beyond the egoistic man, beyond man as a member of civil society, as a man severed from the common social life and withdrawn into his private interests and private caprice."

Marx looked upon the societies contemporaneous with himself as blighted by individualism. "Present civil society is the accomplished principle of individualism: Individual existence is the final end, while activity, labor, content, etc. are merely means." [44]

While the actual treatment of rights in Marx is brief, the implications of his brief treatment are complex. It would be too simple, for instance, to say that for him rights inhered only in communities. What is true to say, however, is that he always located the dignity of the individual in concrete social reality. By contrast, he always traced the sources of indignity to individuals and groups of individuals whose interests put them at odds with the community because of their ownership of the forces of production. Indignity comes from egoism and its consequences, for example, the vested interests of a class which inured it against the community's good.

A further reason for the complexity of Marx's attitude to rights is the evolving and dialectical character of his perceptions. There were different dragons to slay at different stages of his career. At each of these stages it is not treatises on the subject of rights that he elaborates, but analyses of the relations that obtain between persons laboring to meet their own needs. As we have already noted, he calls these relations of production. [45] The rights thread, which is a minor element in the body of his works if one looks for explicit references to it, should be located within this broader pattern. The anthropology, so to speak, of relations of production is his more frequent and more favored theme.

V. PRECAPITALIST MODES OF PRODUCTION

So far we have examined the orientation Marx would have taken to the basic concepts of our project. In order to be truer to Marx's own grid of understanding, however, we have to go about the matter in a different way. Our questions are not his. For example, if we asked our question in terms of what rights an individual should enjoy, Marx would object that there is an epistemological flaw in the very question. We would be trying to answer our question by abstraction of the individual from the social reality of his or her life. Abstractions for Marx are mental cuts into living aggregates which pose as insights into reality and miss its wholeness. Marx also presumes that the person asking such a question is in a capitalist society where alienation inevitably causes the would-be perceivers to misfocus. Capitalist society appears to use neutral categories whereas in fact its categories are refractions coming from systemic disorder. These categories become part of the problem rather than a source of enlightenment, because they purport to come from an accurate perception of reality and do not.

One of the ways that Marx suggests perception can be made more accurate is to become aware of what we are leaving out by focusing on something which is only part of the reality perceived. Since "man" is always "an ensemble of social relations," any attempted perception of reality must include the particular relations in which the data being analyzed are ensconced. But perception must also include the acts of production in which the members of "the ensemble" engage with one another. In brief, persons-acting-together-to-produce is the irreducible minimum unit of intelligibility in Marx's epistemology.

For concepts to be true, they must represent "real, transitory, historical, social relations." [46] For there to be any truth value to one's perceptions, they have to be perceptions of a "living aggregate." [47] In scholastic terms. Marx's criterion of truth would be an "adequatio *relationis* cum intellectu" (a perfect correspondence between the intellect and this relationship). Knowing for a more traditional mind, on the other hand, is an "adequatio *rei* cum intellectu" [48] (a perfect correspondence between the thing and the intellect). This latter definition means that what is in the mind conforms with the particular quiddity in the world. These preliminary remarks are necessary for understanding Marx's peculiar kind of epistemology. He loads concepts with more than seems logical or warranted as his way of compensating for the possible misperception of the reality he is trying to apprehend.

We are now in a position to understand that Marx saw human nature and its history in terms of the modes of production. His modes-of-production insight into anthropology makes the conditions of production and the forces of production and the means of production all an intrinsic part of anthropology. We are what we do and produce and reproduce. [49] Each generation inherits from its predecessors "a mass of productive powers, of capital and circumstances, which on the one side the new generation modifies, but which on the other side dictates its conditions of life and gives it a specific development, a special character. The circumstances make men just as much as men make circumstances." [50] In the course of producing, people make life and are made by the circumstances by which they produce. Marx's concepts of the mode of production and of the relations of production must be kept together.

His concept of the mode of production is dialectical. It describes the processes and materials whereby a society reproduces itself, even while it simultaneously contains an ingredient that contradicts the extant mode of production of the society. This latter, in turn, will lead to the revolution which produces the next mode of production.

Marx began his historical study of the modes of production in earnest in the 1850s. His most complete treatment of precapitalist societies or modes of production appears in his *Grundrisse,* which was written between 1857 and 1859. His interest in exploring the nature of these precapitalist communities was not to develop a metaphysics of community, but to see how different social structures based on different property relations than those of capitalist society operated.

In history there were five major modes of production, according to him. The main precapitalist modes of production were oriental, classical, and feudal. These were followed by the main object of his analysis, which is the capitalist mode of production and that which follows it, namely, the socialist mode of production. While economics is basic to the existence of each of these five modes of production, it is only in the fourth, or capitalist mode of production, that the economic is the main determinant of the base which effects the rest of the relations and superstructural components of society. [51]

After primitive communism, the most ancient of these precapitalist societies were found in China and India. What interested him most in these societies was the absence of private property. The individuals in the groups in these societies possessed the land that they worked but did not own it. The land was owned by the despot or the sovereign. (It would be better to call the sovereign or the despot the proprietor of the land rather than the owner, since the land was not private in our sense but a possession which made the community a community because of its common use of the land.)

The thousands upon thousands of little villages that were like so many "disconnected atoms" were notable for the static character of their existence, according to Marx. Very little social change went on because of the absence of private landed property from which a more rapid evolution in relations would have taken place. Social change was rare in the productive forces and conditions because there was a high degree of communal self-sufficiency. This was due, in part, to the fact that the peasants' mode of subsistence was primarily agricultural. [52]

Marx next analyzes the ancient classical mode of production. He sees this mode of production as pivoting on a primary relation of production: slavery. The city-state is the ordinary political form within which the ancient classical relations of production develop. The city-state is the overall proprietor of the land. It sets aside part of the land as common land for everyone's needs and distributes the rest to individual families as theirs. This is the beginning of a kind of private property. So state property and private property coexist. No sooner does this happen than social classes begin to take shape and society begins to come apart, with some growing rich and others poor.[53] Eventually, there are the patricians and the plebeians.

This form of society and its mode of production developed much more rapidly than the Asiatic mode of production. Two of the reasons for this were the density of the European population and the proximity of one city-state community to another. The accumulation of wealth, as such, was not a driving force with the Greeks and Romans. Gandy notes: "They use a large part of the surplus product for unproductive expenditure on art, religious works and public works."[54] The number of a man's slaves was the measure of a man's wealth. Slave labor provided those who were becoming wealthy with the leisure to pursue civilization. The very fact of the slave "makes labor dishonorable for free men." And yet man is inherently a laborer. "This contradiction spells the doom of all production based on slavery and of all communities based on it."[55]

The feudal mode of production is the last precapitalist form of community that Marx analyzes. This is largely a western European development, according to Marx. One of its defining relations of production is serfdom. This is a relation of personal dependency that binds people to the land as serfs. The other relation of production that defines feudalism, of course, is lordship. The lord's power came from the fact that he had the land, usually from his father. The serfs that he inherited he received just as he received the soil itself. In Europe the foundation of feudal ownership of land was the fief. The "landlord" distributed these fiefs to his vassals or serfs in return for their loyalty and service. Personal dependency characterizes the social relations of production in this moment of history.[56] Religion and the sacredness of tradition helped to hold these social relations of production together for centuries.

A number of generalizations are possible on the basis of Marx's reading of the dynamics of these precapitalist communities. He observes, "The further back we go into history, the more the individual, and therefore, the producing individual, seems to depend on and constitute a part of a larger whole; at first it is quite naturally the family and the clan which is but an enlarged family; later on it is the community growing up in its different forms out of the clash and the amalgamation of clans."[57] In the Asiatic form of society, individualism does not arise because private property is unknown. Unfortunately, people are themselves the property of the oriental despot. In the ancient classical mode of production, on the other hand, individualization begins to develop in the cities because property begins to be "mine or yours."[58]

One begins to see the way Marx read the data of precapitalist society. He saw the communities which constituted its several moments as relatively self-sufficient. [59] They were organic totalities which were relatively stable because the individuals who constituted these communities accepted the definition of themselves from the communities into which they were born. There was a harmony between the individual, the community, and nature. Individuals as producers were bound to the materials of production—primarily the soil. They were also bound to the community's mode of production. There was a direct relationship between what they produced and what they exchanged or consumed. Because of the immediate unity between their laboring and the natural conditions of production, both the mode of production and the relations between individuals could be called natural in the sense that they were prearranged and written into the nature of things. [60]

Property was held in relationship to and by virtue of membership in the respective communities. The aim of production in the precapitalist forms of society was not wealth but ultimately the reproduction of the same kinds of individuals, whose relationship to the community would remain the same. [61] Relations within these organic communities are described by Marx as internal. Internal relations obtain when "individuals enter into connection with one another only as individuals imprisoned within a certain definition, as feudal lord and vassal, landlord and serf, etc., or as members of a caste . . . or as members of an estate. . . ." [62] Internal relations have an advantage over the external relations which will obtain in the next or capitalist period of history insofar as internal relations are defined in terms of the relationship between the individual and the community. The disadvantage of these internal relations is that one is not free in the precapitalist mode of production to be anything other than who the person is defined to be by his or her community. The mode of production predetermines individuality.

Property for Marx, both in precapitalist society and in capitalism, is not so much a thing as it is a relation. It does not refer directly to owning objects, but rather to the relations that are involved in the appropriation of the means of production and the conditions whereby production comes about. [63] In the course of using the material resources and all that goes into the mode of production, relationships are generated and taken for granted. These, in the precapitalist mode of production, are relations of domination because the master, whether he be feudal lord or despot or slaveowner, determines the actions and the whole mode of existence of those who are under him, since he controls the conditions of the individual's and the group's subsistence.

The important thing about all of this, for our purpose, is that individuality and private property are inexplicable without one another.

Insofar as individuals were defined by their relationship to the whole (as is generally true in these precapitalist societies), the conception of the rights of individuals does not emerge. The beginnings of a change can be seen in the ancient classical society, where the acquisition of property by some puts those who do not own their own property in a relationship of servitude to those who do. But this means that for Marx the emergence of the individual is a negative thing historically. Individuality is necessarily individualistic and egoistic and negative in his mind.

In feudal society, a premodern form of individuality and of rights begins to emerge. The serfs and the peasants have a kind of inherited right to till the soil owned by the lord. They also have a kind of right to be protected from outside force by their lords. But the clearer preliminary conception of rights develops between lords. Marx, for example, noted that in just one country, France, by the fourteenth century, there were 100,000 tiny fiefs, each with a lord and his subjects. Their very number made disputes inevitable. The disputes were settled sometimes by force, sometimes by agreement. The agreements led to customs and in turn to codification of ways of resolving disputes about the respective claims of both parties. What is important here, of course, is that rights have to do with property and with the communities that are in dispute with one another, rather than with persons or the rights of individuals as individuals. It would be true, then, to say that for Marx the notion of rights historically emerged both from the fact of private property and also from the relationship between communities and their interactions with one another, rather than directly from relationships between individuals. [64]

VI. THE CAPITALIST MODE OF PRODUCTION

Capitalism's mode of production has several distinguishing characteristics. First, capitalism produces its goods and services as commodities. A commodity is distinguished from a simple product in Marx's mind by reason of the fact that it gets to the consumer (or in the case of services, to those served), not immediately or via its producer, but through an impersonal third party. The mode of production in the capitalist stage of history, therefore, is largely an impersonal one in comparison to the relatively personal mode of production in the previous epochs when producers themselves ordinarily exchanged their products directly with one another. The fact that the products produced by labor in the capitalist era are exchanged and distributed as commodities rather than as products is a major reason for the alienation of the laborer and the depersonalization of capitalist culture. Central to Marx's understanding of the process of commodity exchange is that not only labor power but the laborers themselves can be purchased. In effect, persons become part of the commodity exchange process in capitalism. [65]

The notion of surplus value is equally critical for understanding the capitalist mode of production, according to Marx. "The whole capitalist production rests here: that labor is purchased directly, and in the process of production a portion of this labor is appropriated without compensation, but is then sold in the product. This is the ground of existence, the idea of capital." [66] The inequity between the value of the wage to the laborer and the value of the laborer's work to the employer is either hidden from the laborer or acquiesced in by him. The difference between the value of the work done and the wage received creates a surplus. This surplus value generates capital and capitalism. The "fair wage" that the worker receives for his labor is radically unfair, according to Marx. The illusion upon which capitalism rests is that the worker is being fairly paid for the value of his work. [67]

Notice that Marx does not allow the question of wages to be considered in abstraction from the question of the mode of life that individuals create for themselves. "The mode in which men produce their life depends, first of all, on the conditions of the means of life which they find before them and which are to be reproduced. The mode of production . . . is a defined kind of activity of individuals, a definite way of externalizing their life, a definite mode of life." [68] How one allows his powers to be used begins to dictate who one is.

There are several paradoxes to the human relations which exist in capitalist society. First of all, the social relations in this period are free. They are free in the sense that the worker is free to put himself under contract to the owner so that the skills that he has and products which he is capable of producing will redound to him in the form of a wage. He is free to sell his capacity to labor for money. This is a degree of independence that the serf and all precapitalist individuals did not enjoy. It is a superficial kind of freedom, however, since the individual really has no alternative to selling his capacity to labor.

There were a host of factors which created the transition from feudalism to capitalism, not the least of which was the rapid growth of trade and the growth of means whereby products could be distributed with increasing efficiency. The chief precondition for the existence of capitalist society, however, was workers who were not tied to land or to property. The unity between producer and community, and therefore, in turn, between the community and the soil that was being worked, began to dissolve. Once they were separated from the soil which was the source of their livelihood, the workers' ability to work becomes the only means

for their subsistence, the only property they own. Once the worker becomes dependent on money as the medium of exchange which he has
agreed upon as the relative value of himself, relations in capitalism become external. That is to say, individuals are now in relationship to other
individuals through something, or through things. These mediated or
intercepted relations are called external by Marx. In exchanging his capacity to work for a wage, the worker has disunited himself from other
individals to whom he inevitably grows indifferent. Yet the laborer can
not be totally independent of others since he, like them, has need for the
work of others' hands. But it is their products, not their persons, that each
needs from the other. Their products are therefore another source of the
externality of relationships. [69] While human beings were the purpose
behind both the use of material resources and the activity of production
in precapitalist stages of history, in the capitalist stage of history it is for
wealth, not for people, that the mode of production begins to exist.

Another paradox of social relations in capitalism is that these relations of production are in some sense relations of equality. One can look
at the equality of these relations under the rubric of needs, rights, and
power. First of all, needs. Both parties, the capitalist owner and the
laborer, have needs. The owner needs to purchase labor power so as to
produce the commodities that are necessary for him to continue in existence as owner. The need in the laborer, on the other hand, is simpler. It
is the need to subsist, a need he cannot satisfy unless he sells his capacity
for laboring. "In the concept of the free laborer, it is already implicit that
he is a pauper, or virtually a pauper. According to his economic conditions he is pure living capacity, which, since it is endowed with living
requirements yet deprived of the means to satisfy them, is in itself not a
good or form of property but indigence from all points of view." [70]

The bogus kind of equality which these kinds of social relations
entail can also be seen, according to Marx, under the rubric of rights. It
seems that there is an equality of rights on both sides. But upon closer
inspection, it is obvious that the rights that are being spoken of are the
rights which attach to property rather than to persons.

> At first the rights of property seemed to be based on a man's own
> labor. At least some such assumption was necessary since only com-
> modity owners with equal rights confronted each other, and the sole
> means by which a man could become possessed of the commodities
> of others was by alienating his own commodity; and these could be
> replaced by labor alone. Now, however, property turns out to be
> the right on the part of the capitalist to appropriate the unpaid
> labor of others or its product and to be the impossibility on the part

of the laborer of appropriating his own product. The separation of property from labor has become the necessary consequence of a law that apparently originated in their identity." [71]

The separation of property from labor begins to ascribe dignity to property rather than to persons. Persons with property begin to gain legal protection which conceals the actual condition of the rest, which Marx calls "emancipated slavery." [72] The notion of human rights is a juridical veneer which proves unsatisfactory because it communicates a semblance of equality and freedom rather than their substance. The fact that they have not received an equivalent for their labor power begins to make workers more unequal to owners than they were before the exchange. The laborer has in fact not only acquiesced in but has added to the voracious dynamism of surplus value. Marx's analysis of the result is worth noting. "By a peculiar logic, the right of property undergoes a dialectical inversion, so that on the side of capital it becomes the right of an alien product or the rights of product over alien labor, the right to appropriate alien labor without an equivalent. And on the side of labor capacity, it becomes a duty to relate to one's own labor or to one's own product as to an alien product." [73] Marx continues in the same paragraph:

> The right of property is inverted to become on the one side the right to appropriate labor power and on the other the duty of respecting the product of one's own labor and one's own labor itself as values belonging to others. The exchange of equivalence, however, which appeared in the original operation, an operation to which the right of property gives legal expression, has become turned around in such a way that the exchange by one side is now only illusory . . . the relation of exchange has thus dropped away entirely." [74]

The result is that there is a complete separation between "wealth and labor which now appears as a consequence of the law which began with their identity." [75]

The law that Marx is referring to here is the law of exchange of equivalents, which is in his view referred to with equal appropriateness as "the law of the stronger." The law of the stronger is what had created relations of domination in the precapitalist era. In the present capitalist era the law of the stronger is now laundered through the process of juridical rights. The juridical beginnings of the rights tradition, as has already been mentioned, were to be found in the declarations of freedom of the French and American Revolutions, according to Marx. He was impressed by the partialness of the victory won for human dignity in that era because after the guns grew quiet, property was still dictating to people who were entrapped in "the narrow horizon of bourgeois rights." [76]

Some of the moral outrage that burst from this nineteenth century analyst about the "spiritual" condition to which the capitalistic way of conceiving needs, rights, and power has reduced modern people, is worth noting here. "Private property has made us so stupid and partial that an object is only ours when we have it, when it exists for us as capital or when it is directly eaten, drunk, worn, inhabited, etc., in short, utilized in some way." [77] In brief, "a sense of having" has become paramount to modern people.

In a masterly stroke Marx goes on in the same passage to expose the schizophrenia and avarice engendered in the hearts of people by the economy they find themselves caught in. The irony can't be missed.

> Everything which you are unable to do, your money can do for you; it can eat, drink, go to the ball and to the theatre. It can acquire art, learning, historical treasures, political power; and it can travel. It can appropriate all these things for you, can purchase everything; it is true opulence. But although it can do all this, it only desires to create itself, and to buy itself, for everything else is subservient to it. . . . Thus all passions and activities must be submerged in avarice. The worker must have just what is necessary for him to want to live, and he must want to live only in order to have this." [78]

The inevitable breakdown of human relationships which are intercepted by needs, actual and induced, is eloquently described by Marx.

> Every man speculates about creating a new need in another in order to force him to a new sacrifice, to place him in a new dependence, and to entice him into a new kind of pleasure and thereby into economic ruin. (Everyone tries to establish over others an alien power in order to find there the satisfaction of his own egoistic need). With the mass of objects, therefore, there also increases the realm of alien entities to which man is subjected. Every new product is a new potentiality of mutual deceit and robbery. Man becomes increasingly poor as a man; he has increasing need of money in order to take possession of the hostile being. The power of his money diminishes directly with the growth of the quantity of production, i.e., his need increases with the increasing power of money. The need for money is therefore the real need created by the modern economy, and the only need which it creates. The quantity of money becomes increasingly its only quality. [79]

As if he were anticipating our present inflationary condition and the crude consumerism which is coincident with it. Marx continues on in the same passage:

> Excess and immoderation become its true standard. The expansion of production and of needs becomes an ingenious and always calculating subservience to inhuman, depraved, unnatural, and imaginary appetites. Private property does not know how to change crude need into human need. No eunuch flatters his tyrant more shamefully or seeks by more infamous means to stimulate his jaded appetite, in order to gain some favor, than does the eunuch of industry, the entrepreneur, in order to acquire a few silver coins or to charm the gold from the purse of his dearly beloved neighbor. (Every product is a bait by means of which the individual tries to entice the essence of the other person, his money. Every want is an opportunity for approaching one's neighbor with an air of friendship and saying, "Dear friend, I will give you what you need, but you know the *conditio sine qua non.* You know what ink you must use in signing yourself over to me. I shall swindle you while providing your enjoyment.") [80]

In the final analysis, the dynamisms at work in the capitalist economy are so forceful that Marx sees people turning into things under the pressure. People are transformed into commodities.

> It cannot be otherwise in a mode of production in which the laborer exists to satisfy the need of self-expansion of existing values, instead of on the contrary, material wealth existing to satisfy the needs of development on the part of the laborer. As in religion, man is governed by the products of his own hands. [81]

VII. RIGHTS AND THE INDIVIDUAL

In the first part of this essay, we pursued our project's questions, seeking to find out how Marx would deal with them. In the middle section, we attempted to lay out Marx's own categories more fully while trying to be more faithful to his grid of understanding. Having sketched his world view, we are now in a better position to return to our questions about needs, rights, and power. One of the central issues in this project and in the whole rights debate is the question of how to settle individual claims over against the community's claims and vice versa. How would Marx go about answering this specific question? His answer requires us to concentrate on how he saw the individual. We have already heard his lamentations about individualism. What kind of individuality would he be happy with? What kind of individuality is adverse to the realization of human dignity? How would a "redeemed" individual behave, so to speak, according to Marx?

We have already seen how the young Marx was indebted to Feuerbach for convincingly situating the meaning of the human person within material nature. This philosopher had convinced Marx and many others that to be human means that one must see himself as organic with nature. Marx soon became critical of Feuerbach, however, for focusing on human reality theoretically and in individualistic cameos. He complained that Feuerbach, in his analyses, "remains in the realm of theory and conceives of men not in our given social connections, not under their existing conditions of life, which made them what they are. He never arrives at the really existing active men, but stops at the abstraction man." [82] Marx complains that the only social relationships Feuerbach ever concentrated on were "human relationships of love and friendship," but even these he idealized. [83]

The way Marx used Feuerbach's concept "species-being" is a clue to Marx's own philosophical view of the individual. In his earlier life, Marx was fond of the term because it summed up and communicated all the things that being human meant for him. Unlike the animal world, the human species was capable of self-consciousness and, more importantly, each member of the species was capable of a consciousness of the whole species. Each individual also had qualities in common with all other individuals and the whole species itself had a history. Many of Marx's references to species-being are also exhortations to his readers to retrieve a wholeness which human beings in some prehistorical epoch had once known. In other words, there is a Marxian protology, although it is not a very developed theme in Marx. (By protology, I mean a mythical, prehistorical understanding of how it all began or what we used to be.)

Later, Marx stopped using the term species-being. One of the reasons for doing so was methodological. We can see, for example, in his 1845 *Theses on Feuerbach* that he repudiated the kind of essence-thinking that this term represents and concentrated his attention on the much less abstract social situations for which he had data. Marx was convinced that the best Feuerbach or any other philosopher could ever accomplish would be to have their devotees learn to contemplate reality the way the master did. Marx, however, was anxious not to contemplate reality but to affect it and to change it. An additional reason why he dropped the abstraction species-being was that it summed up Feuerbachian humanism, which

Marx feared "amounted to nothing but a secular substitute for traditional religion, replacing the worship of God with the worship of man as such." [84]

He had the same problem with Hegel and his methodology. According to Marx, we tend to create abstract notions which we then treat as if they have a life independent of mind; we tend to hypostatize them. Like Hegel, we work from these abstractions and attempt to derive the concrete from them rather than from actual social relations and circumstances. Marx replaced species-being with a different perception of the individual. "The human essence is no abstraction inherent in each single individual. In its reality, it is the ensemble of social relations." [85] From this moment on, Marx prided himself on analyzing human beings concretely, meaning not only in their sociality but also in their productive context. For him, social relations are class relations and class relations are determined by the mode of production of the society in which the individuals find themselves. People, according to Marx, are the products of the society in which they find themselves. But they are also producing or are capable of producing society. Human beings create their social reality and human beings can change the social realities in which they find themselves through their praxis, their revolutionary praxis in particular. Revolutionary praxis can transform the mode of production which determines class and social relations.

In further developing his thought about individuality, Marx concludes that there are two kinds of individuals in this world. Moving from seeing humans as being merely real to being really true is a way of encapsulating the full thrust of the Marxist ethic. The real individual, for Marx, is the bourgeois individual who lives in contemporary society pursuing his private purposes. He is deeply affected by the alienation between himself and others, between the products which his hands have made and the society which uses them. "The real man is the private man of the modern state system . . .," whose consciousness is formed by the social reality he helps generate. [86] The true man, on the other hand, is an ideal type of man. He is a man with a vision of what could and should be, and therefore of what should not be. His vision leaves him discontent with being a merely real man. There is a radical enmity between the real and the true man. The real man takes the given as the inevitable. The true man takes what is as the raw material for what must be. Since the true man is not content with the contemporary mode of production, the most important labor or praxis for him is revolutionary praxis. [87] His idealism and altruism are focused on this kind of activity. "Social revolution concentrates on the whole because it is . . . a protest of man against dehumanized life . . . a protest of the individual against his isolation from the community which is the true community of men, that is, the essence of man."[88] While the real man is withdrawn into himself, wholly pre-occupied with his private interests, the true man has his eye on making whole that which has been splintered into a thousand competing, private agendas.

One can grasp the struggle of Marx, who so eschewed abstraction, to bring together community and communality with individuality. Note, for example, one of his attempts: "Though man is a unique individual—a really individual communal being—he is equally the whole, the ideal whole, the subjective existence of society as felt and experienced."[89]

This passage is much less clear than its source in Feuerbach, who so ably assisted Marx in his understanding of the relationship of "man" to nature. According to Feuerbach, "The human individual as such does not contain the essence of man either in himself as a moral being or as a thinking being. The essence of man is only contained in the community, the unity of man with man . . ."[90] Marx commented enthusiastically on this particular insight, as indeed he did on the entire work from which it was taken, *The Philosophy of the Future and the Essence of Religion*. He noted that it was primarily this book that created the philosophical foundation of socialism. Marx wrote to Feuerbach:

> In these studies you've created (I do not know whether this was your purpose) the philosophical foundation of socialism, and this is how the Communists had immediately understood your works. Men's unity with men, based on their actual differences, the notion of the human species brought from the heaven of abstraction to the earth of reality—what else is this if not the notion of society?[91]

False (or "real") individuality flourished in capitalism. Capitalism generated a consciousness which divided individual from individual. An alienated consciousness made communality and community impossible. How does alienation develop? For Marx, consciousness always reifies in the act of labor. The projections of interiority always become "flesh." Whatever value there is in the world, it has been put there by labor. Value is objectified labor.[92] This process of interiority becoming flesh in the material world is endemic to the human condition. It is neither good nor bad. In and of itself, it is not alienating. The material world begins to be shaped by the ideas and purposes and intentions of producers. The work of human hands creates whatever beauty there is in the world. Human beings are both the formal and efficient causes of all that is en-nobling in the universe they have created.

In the capitalist mode of production and under the tyranny of the ownership of the means of production by the few, a fissure develops be-tween laborers and the work of their hands. The objects which they have shaped stand further and further apart from those who shaped them. Value begins to be assigned by one and all to the objects produced rather than to those who have produced them. Those who produced the objects do not relate to or perceive those objects as their own. The laborer makes things which he neither owns nor distributes. An estrangement between the laborer and the work of his hands comes about partly because the laborer ceases to recognize the fact that the objects which he has brought into existence are in fact his own. What was once his glory, his capacity for labor, turns into his nemesis.

The problem does not stop there. "A direct consequence of the alienation of man from the product of his labor, from his life activity and from his species life is that man is alienated from other men." [93] Individuals begin to exist for their own sake. Being a member of "species-being" no longer has any reality to it because the being of others becomes, for the alienated person, "a means for his individual existence. Alienated labor alienates man from his own body, external nature, his mental life and his human life." [94]

An alienated individual is separated from his work, from his own products, from the material world around him, and from others. All the things that could enhance the human condition and make for human dignity disappear and what is left is an individual who has been isolated from the social whole within which his or her humanness was to be realized. The individual begins to abstract himself or herself from the whole with a consciousness of self vis-à-vis others. Abstraction and alienation are two sides of the same coin.

In other words, then, a person can operate from a consciousness generated by capitalism and be incapable of transcending its parameters. Or persons can break through the conditioning of their consciousness and begin to live as members of a conscious communality and pursue the interests of the community. The former kind of individual is "real," alienated, and conditioned. The latter individual is "true," universal, and transformation-minded.

Marx pointed up all the instances of this false consciousness he could detect. Most of the literary figures of his day manifested it, he thought. For example, fictional characters like Robinson Crusoe were created and retrojected into a more glorious primitive state of human existence. The significant thing to Marx was that this figment of capitalist imagination was strong and solitary. It was an attractive image for readers in a capitalist society since they too were in an alienated situation in which they had to try to grow strong over against one another. The fallacy in this kind of individuality is traceable to the fact that "man is in the most literal sense of the word," for Marx, "not only a social animal, but an animal which can develop into an individual only in society." [95]

But if there was anything golden about human prehistory, it was not the individuality of a Robinson Crusoe, it was the fact that individuals identified with and saw themselves as part of their communities. "Man is only individualized through the process of history, he originally appears as a generic being, a tribal being." [96]

Marx doesn't treat the rights of the individual in part, because an alienated consciousness has to undergo a conversion to a social consciousness. It is the whole which gives dignity to the parts, in his mind. In order to stand for human dignity, individuals must undergo a transformation whereby they come into seeing themselves as *pars pro toto*. An individual must move away from being merely real to being true. One becomes true if one's praxis is undertaken with a view to the whole. Recall: to be human is not enough for Marx; one has to do humanly.

A further specification of what this means, as well as a glimpse into Marx's brand of eschatology, can be found in the *Grundrisse*. Here we find true individuals referred to as social individuals. Social individuals are those who do not withdraw from the network of relationships in which they find themselves but, in concert with others, freely choose and determine their lives with those whom they see as an inalienable part of their own existence. [97] Social individuals come to realize and attain substantial equality with one another only superficially in the capitalist era. The achievement of this kind of equality with one another lies largely in the future.

In this projected form of sociality, each member of the community will stand on equal footing with others because all will be equally owners of the means of production. Their equality, furthermore, will be concretely realized by the manner in which the decisions of the community are reached. For social individuals, labor will always be a social act and its product communal.

In the socialist world that is dawning the mode of production, and also the primary form of human interaction, will change from one that is determined by economics to one that is determined by persons in concert. The need of social individuals will be for realization of their personhood through one another. This is their primordial right. The community's mode of production will express and project a quality of reciprocity and mutuality in the relationships that obtain within the community. Production will flow from that mutuality and lead to a distribution of the fruits of the productive process according to the needs of each member. [98] Each of the products of the community will be stamped by the unique contribution made by each of the persons to the productive process. The individual will not be treated as a means to ends devised by an impersonal collectivity, but each will be treated as an end in himself. Relationships between individuals will cease to be mediated through and determined by external objects. The individual will be seen as having legitimate personal purposes as well as social ones. The full development of the potentiality of human species will come about through the development of the potential of each member of that species. [99] The result of this will be a population whose skill differences are unlimited because the unique capacities of each member of the community have been called forth and affirmed. [100]

In brief, then, Marx conjures up a social kind of individual as the locus of human dignity. It is also the kind of individual his system attempts to call into existence. What this social individual has to do is also a description of where the *humanum* has to go. According to a recent philosophical observation, "The fully universal, social individual in Marx may be seen as a teleological concept, like Aristotle's notion of actuality, namely, it is the fully realized form of human development or its telos." [101]

It is not until late in life, with *Capital,* that Marx gives a further specification to what constitutes human dignity. In a felicitous phrase, McMurtry calls this "projective consciousness." [102] Marx notes:

A spider conducts operations that resemble those of a weaver and a bee puts to shame many an architect in the construction of her cells. But what distinguishes the worst of architects from the best of bees is this: that the architect raises his structure in imagination before he erects it in reality. At the end of every labor process, we get a result that already existed in the imagination of the laborer at its commencement. He not only affects a change of form on the material on which he works, but he also realizes a purpose of his own. [103]

The later Marx stresses that the distinctiveness of being human relates to purposefulness. The older Marx gets, the more teleological and eschatological he gets.

Projective consciousness can either be the individual's consciousness or a collective consciousness. The projective consciousness of the collectivity is one in which each of the workers contributes to the dream whose structure comes from their imaginations before it is realized in the material universe.

It would be fair to ask the role of Marx's own imagination in the collectivity's projection. As with everything else in Marx, the answer is not simple. On the one hand, he scorns utopians for their futuristic visions. On the other, he sketches a vision of the future which has enough concrete details for the faithful to steer themselves toward it. His problem with utopian visionaries and their visions is that these remove the eyes of people from what is transpiring before them and sets their faces on "fancy pictures of the future structure of society." Instead of a revolution founded on "a materialistic basis which demands serious objective study from anyone who tries to use it," there is substituted a "mythology with its goddesses of justice, freedom, equality and fraternity." [104]

The idea of communism itself shows how Marx both employs an ideal picture of the future and at the same time denies that he is being utopian in doing so. This can be seen in his famous definition of communism, which combines a projection into the future with a reversion into the past.

> Communism is the positive abolition of private property, of human self-alienation, and thus the real appropriation of human nature through and for man. It is, therefore, the return of man himself as a social, i.e., really human being, a complete and conscious return which assimilates all the wealth of previous development. Communism as a fully developed naturalism is humanism and . . . is the solution of the riddle of history and knows itself to be this solution. [105]

We can see the effects of Hegel's dialectic on Marx's understanding of the meaning of communism. For Marx, it is "not a stable state which is to be established, an ideal to which reality will have to adjust itself. We call communism the real movement which abolishes the present state of things. The conditions of this movement result from the premises now in existence." [106] In other words, the future will be arrived at primarily by dealing with the contradictions residing in the present social relations and modes of production. As an ideal to be striven for, communism is not to be conceived of as extrinsic to the matter of the social relations already existing.

One of the better explanations of this use of ideals articulated by Marx is given by the Yugoslav philosopher, Ljubomir Tadic. For him, Marx's ideals are meant to be derived from attunement to and immersion in the immanent historical process rather than from notions that come to that process from beyond or outside it. The more sensitive one is to the actual social relations affecting people, the more clearly one will be able to see the kind of future that is coming to birth in the present elements of social interaction. [107] But one could complain that Marx wants it both ways. He does not want the workers to approach social change furnished with a series of notions about what ought to be. He wants them to see what ought to be emerging from a combination of what really is and of what their enlightened imaginations will project from what they see. But what they see, they must be taught. Every word of Marx aims at teaching the would-be seer what to see, and this includes the future.

VIII. THE AGENDA

Marx would have "the faithful" see three things. He would have them see the nature of society in terms of class and class struggle. Second, he would have those who belong to the proletariat see that they must begin to take responsibility for themselves. And third, he would have the proletariat see that the state plays a role that deceives and degrades them. Marx's understanding of class, the role of the proletariat, and the need to overthrow the state can all be seen in terms of needs, rights, and power.

It is not until the *Communist Manifesto* (1848) that Marx is able to bring his theory of alienation into line with his theory on the class nature of society. One has to piece together, however, what he means by class. [108] Class involves a certain consciousness on the part of a number of people; the consciousness involves seeing that they have common interests as well as a common culture and way of life. It also means that they agree upon who the enemy is; they discover it is not themselves. Although class struggle existed in the precapitalist period, it is not until the mode of production is capitalistic that class antagonisms break out into universal polarizations. "Society, as a whole, is more and more splitting up into two great hostile camps, into two great classes directly facing each other: the bourgeoisie and the proletariat." [109] The socioeconomic facts of capitalism are driving all intermediate lesser classes into one or the other of these two major classes.

The ruling class, the bourgeoisie, is the result of a long history which had its beginning in the medieval towns and gained momentum with the beginnings of capitalism. This class is the ruling class, and yet it cannot continue to exist without constantly changing the instruments of production and therefore the relations of production. It is, nevertheless, doomed, "like the sorcerer who is no longer able to control the powers of the netherworld which he has called up by his spells." [110] Property is the basic power of the ruling class. Inherent in this kind of power are the problems of surplus value, diminishing resources, chronic overproduction, the need for expanding markets, and so forth. Much more proximate, however, is the fact that power exists in the persons who labor. The consciousness of the laborers will eventually develop to the point where they will see what their real needs are and what is being denied them. The ruling class exists because the ruled do not know the power that they have given to their masters. Once they do, the game will be over for the bourgeoisie.

The proletariat is created by the laborer's need to subsist and by the corresponding wage system. Its occasion for development is the industrialization of society. But industry begins to concentrate workers in centers, which depresses the wages but improves the means of communications between workers. Gradually there dawns an awareness of the basic opposition between their own interests and those of the ruling, owning class. To Marx, the proletariat has no hope of growing out of its condition of servitude by a gradual improvement of living conditions. Its only salvation is to take over the means of production, that is to say, private property. For the sake of the rest, the proletariat must come to self-consciousness. "The movement of the proletariat is the self-conscious, independent move of the immense majority in the interests of the immense majority." [111]

Certain members of the proletariat are more advanced than others, the most advanced being called communists. These "have over the great mass of the proletariat the advantage of clearly understanding the line of march, the conditions, and the ultimate general results of the proletarian movement." [112] The purpose of the communists is to unite the rest of the members of the class by a strong class-consciousness in order to throw off their chains. The communist party must uncover the rationalizations of human greed that the laws of industrial society conceal, as well as all the rights that are being violated by that law.

The proletarian revolution will take place in three stages. First of all, the proletariat must become the dominant class. Second, it must change all the conditions of production, primarily and radically the condition of ownership. Third, after these two steps have been taken through the 'dictatorship of the proletariat,' this very instrumentality must be dismantled, resulting in a society that consists of associations of free producers "in which the free development of each is the condition of the free development of all." [113]

For the first step to be taken, the state itself must be unmasked. The state in capitalist society maintains the order that keeps the inherent contradictions from being unearthed and scrutinized, thereby preserving "an illusory communal life." [114] The state is the organization of power on the part of one class that keeps the oppressed class from seeking, or even from knowing, their radical needs.

One particular population within the state draws particular scorn from Marx. It is the executive branch or, as he calls it, the bureaucracy. The bureaucracy thinks of itself as entrusted with mediating between society and state and with maintaining the unity of the society. Marx scorns the apparent universality in the way bureaucrats go about adjudicating the issues put before them. Although they have, in fact, a universal responsibility, or a responsibility for the whole people, bureaucrats end up constituting an intractable separate subgroup whose interests feed off society in an especially heinous way. It is a closed society within the state which thinks of itself as executing the aims of the state. It becomes an end in itself rather than a means to achieve the social purposes of the state. To quote Marx, "bureaucracy is a circle from which none escapes. Its hierarchy is a hierarchy of knowledge. The apex entrusts the lower echelon with insight into the individual while the lower echelon leaves insight into the universal to the apex, and so each deceives the other." Marx goes on: "bureaucracy constitutes an imaginary state alongside the real state . . . it holds in its possession the essence of the state—the spiritual essence of society; the state is its private property." Rather than the people and more universal concerns being the concern of the bureaucrats, "bureaucracy turns into a crass materialism, the materialism of passive obedience, faith in authority, the mechanism of fixed and formal behavior, fixed principles, attitudes, traditions. As far as the individual bureaucrat is concerned, the aim of the state becomes his private aim, in the form of competition for higher posts—careerism." [115]

If "the state *is* its private property" and has no power apart from the private property it is protecting, then the state must be overthrown. "What then is the power of the political state over private property? Private property's own power, its own essence which is brought to existence. What remains of the political state besides this essence? The illusion that it determines, whereas, in fact, it is determined." [116]

Democracy as a political form is an advance over previous kinds of states. But even the democratic state allows capitalism's odious dualism to continue. A person in these states "has a life both in the political community where he is valued as a communal being, and in civil society where he is active as a private individual, treats other men as means, degrades himself to a means and becomes a tool of forces outside himself." [117]

Recall that, for all practical purposes, the state consolidates and represents the de jure powers of the superstructure in modern society while the de facto sources of power lie concealed at the base. One of the most effective layers of the disguise that conceals the disorder comes from religion in general and Christianity in particular. The latter has been most effective in furnishing modern societies with the rhetoric of reverence for the individual while it has fomented individualism with a vengeance. "Civil society first reaches its completion in the Christian world. Only under the domination of Christianity which made all national, natural, moral and theoretical relationships exterior to man, could civil society separate itself completely from the life of the state, tear asunder all the species-bonds of man, put egoism and selfish need in place of those species-bonds and dissolve man into a world of atomised individuals hostile to one another." [118] Christianity is a special object of Marx's ridicule because it gives rise to "man as he appears uncultivated and unsocial . . . lost to himself, sold, subjected to domination by inhuman conditions and elements—in a word, man who is no longer a real species-being. The fantasy dream and postulate of Christianity, the sovereignty of man—but of man as an alien being separate from actual man. . . ." [119]

IX. REFLECTIONS ON THE PRECEDING SECTIONS

This chapter has concentrated on Marx's own thought insofar as it addresses the dignity of the individual vis-à-vis the community. It has not dealt with the subsequent development of that thought by others. In these few generative ideas of Marx one can already see both the potential and the danger in his perception of social reality. Our contemporary situation testifies to the power and trenchancy of his ideas, as well as to their incompleteness.

For me, a key question is: What is the nature of his contribution? Who is Marx? Is he a prophetic figure who raged at the degrading social conditions of society in order to change the world and its power arrangements so that the human contribution to the establishment of a better world could be given focus? His analyses have had that effect on many. Or is he a philosopher whose analysis of human nature and social reality is only credible to the extent that it can pass muster at the bar of rational consistency? Or is he a scientist whose value stands or falls at the bar of scientific objectivity? Unfortunately, it is much more difficult to answer these questions than to pose them. Marxism itself in its contemporary manifestations—be they political or economic, philosophical or scientific, theoretical or practical—is quite divided about the answers.

Rather than attempting a general answer, I will go back over each section of the preceding essay and indicate briefly my own evaluation of Marx's key insights into the topic of our project.

Being Human and "the Being of Nature."   From the beginning of his intellectual life, Marx was vexed by the philosophical conundrum of the relation between being and doing. He never satisfactorily resolved it. While insisting on not being abstract, Marx nevertheless develops an abstract philosophy of human nature, one that is built on human activity —activity as praxis or activity as consciousness. This inevitably means that he judges life by what human beings do or fail to do. In effect, then, the norm of human dignity becomes: we are what we do. But this also implies other theses: we are nothing if we are not doing something. Alternatively: outside of what is done there can be no norm by which we can take the measure of our meaning. Marx does not make these theses explicit himself; rather they follow from his view of truth as non-abstract, historical, and nontranscendent.

But not just any human activity or consciousness is to be counted as good for Marx. It must be oriented to a goal and a future condition of existence which he describes in detail. Marx is quite explicit in locating the dignity of human activity in its teleology and in describing the shape, so to speak, of the telos. But he is unclear about the basis for establishing the ideal end. Equally unclear is the basis on which he develops his understanding of the human good that would make this unique consummation something we should strive for. If we are so one with nature and are wrongheaded to aspire to anything that transcends it, why should we strive to realize the future condition of happiness to which "the communal future" beckons us?

After looking over his analysis of capitalism, in particular, one can see the weakness of an anthropology built on activity. The activity of laboring which follows contractual acts of unequal exchange between owner and laborer becomes the basis on which Marx judges capitalism harshly. But with the activity of laboring still in the forefront of his attention, he proceeds to sketch the shape of the revolutionary dreams he entertained about "the communal future." The result is a very implausible reduction of the rich complexity of human existence. It leaves out "where people live," which is on hopes and myths that transcend their laboring.

Human Dignity and Needs.   Marx accurately assesses needs. He has little use for a culture whose adherents pursue only "paltry" ones and equal disdain for an economic system that induces unnecessary ones. Why? Because human beings are so much more estimable than the capitalistic system enables them to be. And they are worthy of higher pursuits than their constant scrambling to survive would lead them to believe.

But what this "more" is, is very unclear in Marx, and the basis on which this "more" is constructed he left indefinite. The radical needs, insofar as he gives these any content, seem to be the need to be free to find oneself and the leisure to relate to others without being instrumentalized or reduced to a means by them. This is unassailable. But for a person who wants to find out more about where these radical needs come from, what they are for and what they point to, as well as why we ought to uproot present society in order to realize them, his treatment of these needs is quite inadequate. Not the least of reasons for saying so is that he asserts the worth of the individual person without establishing it.

He relies on a tradition which has given that worth a basis without acknowledging it; in fact, he derides it in its religious expressions.

Power and Society.   There seems to be plenty of evidence for the validity of Marx's contentions about base, superstructure, and power in the societies of which he had first-hand experience. He went far beyond these, however, to construct an analysis of power that he claimed would be true of any capitalist society because ex hypothesi the generative factors such as the nature of capital, surplus value, worker acquiescence, owner egoism, competition, the division of labor and classes would all be operative in each of these. Capitalism for Marx had an intractable nature and any economy which was built on it would be antihuman.

There has been considerable economic development since Marx, of course. Noneconomists such as myself are left with three questions after studying his analysis. First, have adjustments been made since Marx in the social, economic, and political processes of capitalist societies which make his social analysis passé for present economies? Second, can the concealed power, the power of. the base, be demonstrated? If it cannot be proven, then an act of faith in his ideology is being required if one is to act on his contention. But this act of faith has its costs, for the simple contention acted upon is socially destructive and creates deep divisions in the societies about which it is alleged. In Marx's own system, his contention about the base is abstract. As such, it could only be valid to the extent that it could be proven in any concrete situation. Third, if it is established that the real determining power in a given society lies in its economic base, must that society inevitably become post-capitalist or socialist to rectify itself?

Human Dignity and Rights.   Since Marx's judgment on rights claims to be historically based, one way of evaluating it is to weigh its historical accuracy. Was his reading of the French and American revolutions as bourgeois an accurate one? As is commonly known, the class character of these societies and of their interactions is the subject of much dispute. Interpretations vary widely. [120] Marx was not greatly informed about nor particularly interested in the American Revolution in comparison with the French. Painting the two different social realities in the same colors says more about Marx's ideology than it does about the thoroughness of his methods of social analysis.

He laments the "egoism" of the bourgeois concept of rights. Inasmuch as the revolutionaries were children of the Enlightenment, he is right in his perception that their emphasis was on the individual. But their emphasis on the individual was also a definite advance over the previous epoch when individual dignity suffered at the hands of the old regimes and their attacks on the religious, economic, and political freedom of their citizenry. Marx is correct, however, in observing that the missing dimension in both of these revolutions was the place of the community and the individual's responsibility vis-à-vis the community.

One is faced with a peculiar kind of paradox in Marx. His whole life and work can be seen as one long fulmination against those who violate and dehumanize human beings. At the same time, the premise that each person has dignity and deserves esteem is neither argued out nor established by him. One result of this lacuna is that Marxist-inspired regimes have been among the most heinous in the twentieth century in their treatment of individuals, even while they act in the name of humanity. Though Marx looked at the dehumanization caused by the Industrial Revolution and constructed a system to explain and change it, in our century dehumanization can be traced even more to the totalitarian states which have grown out of Marxist ideology.

Marx sought to redress the injustice of his world by an analysis which was social, a program which was collective, and an anthropology which was communal. This opened the way for a social analysis that became a priori, a movement that became collectivist, and an anthropology that was more concerned with the dignity of communities than of the individuals who comprised them.

Precapitalist Modes of Production.   First, a comment on his epistemology. Since Marx, and partly because of Marx, we have learned much about the flow of subjectivity into the hoped-for objectivity of human perception. Variations on this theme have been many, the most germane to our subject matter being the role of praxis in what we perceive, or the fact that our seeing is permeated with our doing (and our not having done). Notwithstanding his contribution, Marx poses an enormous epistemological problem. Did he see more deeply into the reality he observed by his attempt to include within the act of perceiving all the factors operating in the relations of production, or was he simply reading his prior judgments into situations?

His attempt to posit inner connections between seemingly unlinkable realities is more provocative than convincing, more sensitizing than informing. By the same token he has helped make us aware of the degree to which our thought processes are conditioned by the social circumstances of our lives. Our relations to ownership, production, competition, and all the other factors which circumscribe our lives unmistakably affect what we think about and how much we actually see in what we think we see.

If we want to be philosophical purists, Marx's treatment of perception can be made to look bad. For example, in his anxiety to avoid abstraction (which was the same as his fear of leaving something substantial out of his perceptions), he compensates by a bewildering conceptual overload. If, on the other hand, you share his passion for reordering social relations according to a greater justice and dignity, you make lower demands for philosophical purity, with the result that Marx can raise you to a level of social awareness few other systematic thinkers can match.

Capitalist Mode of Production.   It doesn't require an astute observer to agree with Marx that there are glaring weaknesses in the way a capitalist economy operates and affects culture. Socialist economies and modes of production, by the same token, have manifested no fewer weaknesses.

Two things about Marx's description of capitalism should be noted here. First of all, it does not seem to me that Marx has proven that the wage system of compensation for work done, common to both capitalist and socialist economies, is unfair to the laborer. The need for the employer to make a profit does not of itself establish inequity. The risk taken by the capitalist owner or employer does not seem to have evoked Marx's sympathies, which were understandably with the suffering and exploited laboring class. But there have been an enormous number of economic and political developments since the middle of the nineteenth century which have changed the face of ownership and labor, most especially in the so-called first world. The capitalist mode of production has gone through so profound an evolution that it is difficult to apply a nineteenth century analysis to the twentieth century forms of it.

Second, Marx's observations on surplus value are more persuasive. If Marx has indeed isolated a malevolent core to capitalism, surplus value would seem to be a prime suspect. More work needs to be done on this aspect of Marx's analysis. [121]

Rights and the Individual.   Marx retrojects his notions about individuality back to a mythic prehistorical state when individuals were indistinguishable from generic being. We have already seen his reading of the historical development from communalism to individualization. His projection, finally, of individuality into the future would have individuals undergo a radical transformation so that they can live as true or social individuals. The social conditions which the capitalist mode of production has created are wrong in his view because they are inhumane. By working together toward a communist future, we can make social conditions benign. In the course of stepping away from the present state of degradation to the future state of harmony, people can change from "real" to "true" individuals, from lone to social individuals. Their conversions will take place *"ambulando"* according to Marx, or through praxis. The motivation for the revolutionary praxis undertaken together will have come from common suffering and commonly experienced degradation.

This seems true so far as it goes, but it opens the door to a whole host of new wrongs since it does not identify what constitutes the dignity of the individual which is being violated by these nineteenth century social conditions. A lacuna at such a critical point makes what has in fact happened inevitable. Those who have seen the light about what is entailed in being true social individuals have not been loath to create new social conditions for the majority who do not know what's best for society. Human dignity collectivized has degraded human beings no less effectively than all the ills that flow from bourgeois individualism. An imposed collective ideal can be just as destructive as a social condition in which all are propelled by greed.

CONCLUSION

This chapter has attempted to present what Marx's own perspective would have been on the question posed by the Woodstock project, based largely on reading Marx himself and commentaries sympathetic to his thought. It has not been concerned either with subsequent developments within the Marxian tradition or with critiques of Marx's own thought. The aim was to let Marx "speak for himself." In the course of this study, I found myself amazed at the number of contemporary issues his analysis takes into account, which clearly explains the attraction his thought has for so many. While I have attempted to be more descriptive than critical, I have indicated my own problems with his thought at a number of junctures; my major misgivings, however, have been largely confined to this final section.

I conclude with two overall judgments about Marx. First, his anthropology, which of course is only implicit throughout his work, is ultimately unsatisfactory because it is contradictory. It is adamantly anthropocentric, disallowing anything that smacks of transcendence while exhorting its adherents to go beyond what they and their history have become in order to be architects of a new heaven and a new earth. How this *novum* will be something other than a rearrangement of the pieces already given, is quite unclear. The Judaeo-Christian symbol of the Kingdom of God combines history and transcendence, and is thus more satisfactory as a way of understanding the fullness humanity seeks.

The other judgment is that though his anthropology is inadequate, his social analysis has proven a greater stimulus for those concerned about justice than any subsequent alternative. In this analysis the violation of rights is only a symptom of an underlying social pathology. The Woodstock research project, aware of this, has attempted to keep needs and power as the other two dimensions of the study. It is a troika Marx would have approved.

NOTES TO CHAPTER 5

1. Karl Marx, *Early Writings* ed. and trans. T. Bottomore (New York: McGraw-Hill, 1963), "Critique of Hegel's Dialectic and General Philosophy," p. 207.

2. Norman Levine, *The Tragic Deception: Marx Contra Engels* (Santa Barbara: Clio Books, 1975), pp. 4, 6–7.

3. *Early Writings,* op. cit., p. 204.

4. *Ibid.,* p. 208.

5. Adam Schaff, *Marxism and the Human Individual* (New York: McGraw-Hill, 1970), p. 171.

6. Levine, op cit., p. 6. In general, the period referred to as anthropological is best represented by Marx's *Economic and Philosophical Manuscripts of 1844* (Moscow: Foreign Language Publishing House, 1961).

7. *Economic and Philosophical Manuscripts of 1844,* p. 112.

8. Marx's Sixth Thesis from *Theses on Feuerbach,* K. Marx *Selected Works,* London, 1948. Vol. 1 (Lawrence and Wishart), p. 472.

9. Karl Marx, *The Early Texts,* ed. D. McLellan (New York: Oxford University Press, 1971), pp. 220–221.

10. "Life is not determined by consciousness, but consciousness by life." Marx, *The German Ideology* ed. R. Pascal (New York: International Publishers, 1947), p. 15.

11. Karl Marx, *Capital,* Vol. 1, trans. Moore and Aveling (Moscow: Progress Publishers, 1965), p. 171.

12. *Ibid.* p. 172.

13. *Economic and Philosophical Manuscripts of 1844,* p. 113.

14. Karl Marx, *Grundrisse: Foundations of the Critique of Political Economy,* trans. M. Nicolaus (New York: Vintage Books, 1973), p. 243.

15. *Ibid.*

16 Agnes Heller, *The Theory of Need in Marx* (London: Allison and Busby, 1976), p. 69. The phrase is Marx's own from *Capital.*

17. *Economic and Philosophical Manuscripts of 1844,* p. 147.

18. The term itself "radical needs" is Heller's favorite; cf. her Chapter 4, "Radical Needs", 74 ff.; according to Marx: "What characterizes the working class is both its reduction to paltry particular needs . . . and the rise of radical needs" (Heller, p. 89).

19. *Theses on Feuerbach,* p. 264.

20. Karl Marx, *Theories of Surplus Value,* Vol. III, quoted by Heller, p. 89.

21. *Grundrisse,* p. 708. "The measure of wealth is no longer labor time but rather disposable time."

22. Heller, p. 27.

23. John McMurty, *The Structure of Marx's World-View* (Princeton, N.J.: Princeton University Press, 1978), p. 31.

24. *Grundrisse,* p. 611.

25. Quoted from Erich Fromm's *Marx's Concept of Man* (New York: Frederick Ungar, 1961), p. 34.

26. *Ibid.,* p. 35.

27. *Economic and Philosophical Manuscripts of 1844,* Third Manuscript, pp. 137–138.

28. *Ibid.*

29. "Relations of production" is a term which appears very frequently in the entire Marxian corpus without ever being defined by him. These are more basic than political relations. One of the better analyses of the term can be found in McMurty, pp. 73 ff.

30. Michael Harrington scolds many scholars for misunderstanding Marx's concept of base-superstructure. His complaints are: the base is economic only in the capitalist mode of production; even there, Marx's paradigm for understanding must not be mechanistically nor deterministically interpreted, i.e., taken as the sole factor in social causality; the base-superstructure connection must not be made in a way that abstracts the other factors which must be taken into account as parts of an organic whole. Cf. Harrington, *The Twilight of Capitalism* (New York: Simon and Schuster, 1976), esp. Chap. 3, pp. 60 ff.

31. I will take up the theme of surplus value in Section VI.

32. It should be noted here that private property itself does not begin with capitalism. It had antecedents, as will be seen in the section on the precapitalist mode of production.

33. McMurty, pp. 88–89.

34. Marx, *Capital,* Vol. 1, p. 446.

35. This order carries on "independently of the will of individuals." Cf. *The German Ideology,* p. 357.

36. *Ibid.,* pp. 45–46.

37. Cited in McMurty, p. 105, *Marx-Engels-Werke VII,* p. 288.

38. Marx, *The Holy Family,* trans. R. Dixon (Moscow: Foreign Langauge Publishing House, 1956), *passim.*

39. Section V shows the historical beginnings of this connection.

40. Quoted from Kamenka's *The Ethical Foundation of Marxism,* (New York: Praeger, 1962), p. 65.

41. I will treat the subject of abstraction more fully later on in this paper.

42. Rights doctrine added to the pretended sanctity on which modern political democracies prided themselves.

43. Marx, cited in Kamenka, p. 64–65.

44. *Economic and Philosophical Manuscripts,* p. 288.

45. Not simply relationships, nor simply the act of producing, but

always the two together. Therefore, "relations of production." Philosophically, this proves an unsatisfactory combination, since the first of these two distinct realities receives no separate analysis.

46. Quoted from Schaff, p. 90.

47. *Ibid.*

48. Knowledge for Marx is not acquired for its own sake. The act of knowing is in function of doing just as certainly as it is affected by the praxis of the would-be seer. What follows from this, among other things, is that philosophy as speculative is ridiculous and as critique is laudable.

49. "In Marx the ontological reality of all entities is their activity. Subject and object have their being insofar as they are active." Norman Livergood, *Activity in Marx's Philosophy* (The Hague: Nijhoff, 1967), p. 44.

50. *The German Ideology,* cited in Harrington, p. 99.

51. This point in Marx must be seen as central, according to Harrington, p. 68 and *passim.*

52. Carol Gould, *Marx's Social Ontology* (Cambridge, Mass.: MIT Press, 1978), pp. 10–13.

53. *Grundrisse,* p. 378.

54. Quoted from Ross Gandy's *Marx and History* (Austin: University of Texas Press, 1979), p. 27.

55. *Grundrisse,* p. 585.

56. Gandy, p. 34.

57. Quoted from Gandy, p. 35.

58. Marx's obscure words on this are: "As a member of the community he participates in the communal property, and has part of it as his possession . . . his property" (*Grundrisse,* p. 490). Also Gould, pp. 133–135.

59. Gould, p. 10.

60. Gould, p. 13.

61. *Ibid.*

62. *Grundrisse,* p. 163.

63. Gould, pp. 138–141.

64. For Marx, private property "develops out of the disintegration of the natural community. With the Romans, the development of private property . . . had no further consequences because their whole mode of production did not alter." Quoted by Gandy, p. 34.

65. McLellan, pp. 344–347.

66. *Capital,* Vol. IV, cited in Harrington, p. 98.

67. Harrington, *passim.*

68. *The German Ideology,* cited in Harrington, p. 98.

69. Gould, esp. pp. 14–16; 38–39; 71–73.

70. Quoted from Fromm, p. 35.

71. *Capital,* Vol. 1, p. 584.

72. One of Marx's sarcastic outbursts about the condition of people as a result of capitalism.

73. *Grundrisse,* p. 458.

74. *Ibid.*

75. *Ibid.*

76. Quoted from Kamenka, p. 65.

77. *Economic and Philosophical Manuscripts,* p. 132.

78. See note 26.

79. *Economic and Philosophical Manuscripts,* p. 140.

80. *Ibid.*

81. Marx, quoted by Heller, p. 24.

82. *The German Ideology,* pp. 37–38.

83. Adam Schaff, *Marxism and the Human Individual,* p. 79.

84. William McBride, *The Philosophy of Marx* (New York: St. Martin's Press, 1977), p. 85.

85. Marx, *Theses on Feuerbach,* p. 535.

86. Marx, "A Contribution to the Critique of Hegel's Philosophy of Right," cited in Schaff, p. 90.

87. *Theses on Feuerbach,* p. 316.

88. Quoted by Schaff.

89. *Economic and Philosophical Manuscripts,* p. 61.

90. Quoted by Schaff, p. 79.

91. *Economic and Philosophical Manuscripts,* p. 425.

92. Gould, p. 79.

93. *Economic and Philosophical Manuscripts,* p. 103.

94. *Ibid.*

95. K. Marx, *A Contribution to the Critique of Political Economy* (Moscow: Progress Publishers, 1970), p. 62.

96. Quoted by Schaff, p. 82.

97. *Grundrisse,* pp. 171–172.

98. K. Marx, *Critique of the Gotha Program* (Moscow: Progress Publishers, 1960), p. 178.

99. Gould, pp. 108–109.

100. *Grundrisse,* p. 488.

101. Gould, p. 35.

102. McMurty, pp. 22–27.

103. *Capital,* Vol. I, p. 179.

104. K. Marx, Selected Writings, cited in *Utopia and Revolution,* by Melvin Lasky (Chicago: University of Chicago Press, 1976), p. 42.

105. *Economic and Philosophical Manuscripts,* p. 127.

106. *The German Ideology,* p. 171.

107. Ljubomir Tadic, "The Marxist and Stalinist Critiques of Right," in *Marxist Humanism and Praxis* (Buffalo: Prometheus Books, 1978), p. 171.

108. Louis Dupré, *The Philosophical Foundations of Marxism* (New York: Harcourt, Brace and World, 1966), especially pp. 188 ff.

109. *The Communist Manifesto* (Moscow: Foreign Language Publishing House, 1969), p. 35.

110. Quoted by McLellan, p. 181.

111. *Ibid.*

112. *Marx-Engels Gesamtausgabe,* Section I, quoted from Dupré, p. 199.

113. *The Communist Manifesto,* p. 51.

114. *The German Ideology,* p. 45.

115. K. Marx, *Early Writings,* p. 69.

116. *Critique of Hegel's Philosophy of the State,* quoted from Dupré p. 104.

117. David McLellan, *Karl Marx: His Life and Thought* (New York: Harper & Row, 1973), p. 82.

118. *Ibid.,* p. 85.

119. *Ibid.,* p. 82.

120. Two valuable studies of this interpretation: Angermann, Frings and Wellenneuther, *New Wine in Old Skins: A Comparative View of Socio-Political Structures and Values Affecting the American Revolution* (Stuttgart: Ernst Klett Verlag, 1976); James Kirby Martin, ed., *Interpreting Colonial America* (New York: Harper & Row, 1978).

121. Some recent studies on surplus value in Marx include:

James Becker, *Marxian Political Economy* (Cambridge: Cambridge University Press, 1977).

Gilbert Abraham-Frois and Edmond Berrebi, *Theory of Value Prices and Accumulation,* trans. by M. P. Kregel-Javoux (Cambridge: Cambridge University Press, 1979).

Arn Bose, *Marx on Exploitation and Inequality* (Delhi: Oxford University Press, 1980).

Michio Morishima and George Catephores, *Value, Exploitation and Growth* (London: McGraw Hill, 1978).

MAX STACKHOUSE

6. A Protestant Perspective on the Woodstock Human Rights Project

I can only begin with a word of gratitude. On my own behalf, and on behalf of the Protestant churches, I wish to express a profound appreciation for being invited to participate in the consultations which led to the present volume. While many obstacles remain in the path of our movement toward a truly evangelical, truly reformed and truly catholic church, the opportunities for interchange on topics such as this one surely suggest that progress is real and of import beyond narrow ecclesiastical circles.

It is difficult, if not impossible, to speak for all of Protestantism on the question of human rights. Protestantism is not "a" view, but a family of traditions. Further, the specific branches of Protestantism have often been formed in protest—against this or that matter of doctrine, practice, or ethical implication held by this or that dominant religious or political body. Hence, it is not always as easy to say what Protestants are *for* as to say what they are *against*. This is no less true in human rights than in other areas of doctrine and morality. Yet, if we draw back from the idiosyncracies of many branches of Protestantism, it is fair to say that certain dominant streams of Reformed Christianity have had as constant a perspective on human rights as on any other topic. Human rights is understood in terms of *theologically based* social ethics.

Most immediately, of course, the question of human rights comes up when there is a fundamental, experiential sense that something basic about humanity is being violated. Human rights questions arise out of the practical, social, ethical situations of life. They are like Protestantism itself, rooted in a specific protest. But the immediate experience never interprets itself. Which protests are proper, which are mere rebellion? Which senses of violation are valid, which spurious?

It is at this point that Protestant voices turn to theology, for we hold that it is only in a theologically shaped and founded perspective that humans are able to interpret the experience of humanity in a fundamental way. [1] Theology can, of course, be understood to be the arid repetition or rearrangement of dry doctrines in the classroom. More profoundly, however, theology is understood to be the continuing task of discerning what God is about, a task constantly rooted in Scripture, in the witness of the faithful over the centuries (tradition), and in reason. It is a task which directs us toward new practical ways of believing, living, and ordering our world.

With these preliminary assumptions in mind, I think I can best identify the salient aspects of a Protestant understanding of human rights and respond to the views presented by others, by setting forth five hypotheses and a statement characteristic of Protestant expressions of conviction on human rights.

I. THE FIRST PROBLEM OF ALL HUMAN RIGHTS IS HOW TO KNOW ONE WHEN ONE IS CLAIMED

Claims to or about human rights appear on all sides. Emotional calls to action on many fronts, on many questions, are peppered with appeals to human rights. They appear when people feel that something is *de*-humanizing. Feelings, however important, are fickle; they change with circumstances; they have to be assessed. If a claim is to be evaluated by a person, a group, a nation, or the church, for possible action, we have to have a criterion of evaluation. The problem is knowing which claims are valid. That is no small task, for the concept "human" implies something that is not rooted in any specific feeling or circumstance. We have to know what is human in order to assess whether a claim that something is dehumanizing *ought* to be the basis for vigorous action.

There are many attempts to state what it is that is inviolably human, from the old Puritan Bill of Rights to the Declaration of the Rights of Man in the French Revolution, to the United Nations Declaration on Human Rights and subsequent covenants of rights drawn up after the struggle against Fascism in World War II. None of these, however, is self-evident in all respects, and none of them supplies the reasons for its particular contents. All were formed by forging ad hoc political consensus in a specific historical circumstance. They are, thus, subject to change. They are not reliable in the long run. Even if we were to assess these statements as basically valid, we would have to have some basis beyond the statements themselves to do so.

In the final analysis, Protestants hold that this can only come from a valid anthropology. There is no reliable base for understanding human rights except a view of humanity that grasps the core of human life and its meaning in its deepest dimension. That requires a theologically informed anthropology. Nothing else will do. That is why Protestant observers rejoiced when Pope John Paul II spoke these words of support for human rights in his opening address at Puebla:

> The truth that we owe to human being is, first and foremost, a truth about themselves. . . . Thanks to the Gospel, the Church possesses the truth about the human being. It is found in an anthropology that the Church never ceases to explore more deeply and to share. [2]

On this sort of basis, Protestants agree that we can found our discussion of and our action for human rights.

II. TODAY, MANY IN THE CHURCHES ARE LOOKING IN THE WRONG PLACE FOR THE FOUNDATIONS, MEANINGS, AND IMPLICATIONS OF HUMAN RIGHTS

I am not sure why it is that contemporary Christian ethicists and theologians seem to focus their attention on modes of thought that are not rooted in biblical and theological materials. Contemporary religious leaders seem to avoid basic questions of theological anthropology. An enormous amount of work by scholars, practice by clergy, and opinion by laity is shaped by nontheological views of humanity. Perhaps it is simply a matter of the pervasive power of the Enlightenment in much of modern life; or perhaps the ways in which Christian language has been employed by many pre-Vatican II Catholics and many Protestant fundamentalists. These uses of profound Christian symbols have distorted the capacity of many to see their potential for the human rights issues. Whatever the reason, much of the discussion seems fascinated with orientations which are very problematic to a theological perspective in the long run.

Two dimensions of this situation appear to me to be due to a hidden legacy from Thomism present in a number of Catholic thinkers who are not overtly Thomists. There is no doubt in my mind that the more profound understandings of Thomas are fertile and suggestive on the topic of human rights, as the contributions of Jacques Maritain and John Courtney Murray witness. Indeed, it would be beneficial to the whole church if a fresh reading of Thomas were undertaken by Protestant scholars. But the perhaps unconscious impact of Thomas on contemporary Catholic scholars might well be challenged on two fronts. Thinking formed in the Thomist tradition often holds that theology and philosophy are at certain critical points detachable, that faith is one thing and reason quite another. Of course, they are to be joined at certain other critical points, but they are two different things. Thomas was able to link the

Augustinian tradition of faith to Aristotelian philosophy. But if we no longer hold to Aristotelian philosophy, so many presume, it may be possible to separate these once more and link, in a new synthesis, the theological tradition with some other philosophical and sociopolitical theory.

A second and frequent dimension of this way of thinking is the view that philosophy is in fact the broadest and most comprehensive way of thinking about general human problems, including those of justice and human rights. Faith represents a second level of meaning that pertains only to confessing members of the religious community; it involves, in one way or another, "privileged" perspectives and particular obligations that do not obtain for those outside that community.

There are many varieties of Protestant thought on these matters, but as I understand the majority report of Protestantism, the basic perspective is different from the Thomist heritage. I personally agree with this majority report and do not believe that theology and philosophy are so detachable. Every philosophy rests not on reason alone, but on fundamental faith assumptions. And every theological doctrine both requires philosophical reason to make itself clear and has implications for the critical branches of philosophy: metaphysics, epistemology, logic, and (especially pertinent to questions of human rights) anthropology and ethics. Further, I do not agree with the Thomists and post-Thomists that philosophy is the more universal mode of discourse. On the contrary, I agree with most Protestants that theology more accurately and more universally grasps the nature of being, existence, knowledge, human nature, and ethics.

For these reasons, it is troubling that so many of the leading intellectuals of the church are today turning either to the liberal philosophical traditions or to Marxist theory in an attempt to forge a new synthesis between classic Christian faith and a substitute for Aristotle. At each juncture where this was attempted in the papers and discussion of this consultation, the decisive insights from theology were absent, obscured, subordinated, or made to be little more than a sprinkling of holy water on a perspective worked out on different presuppositions.

One can understand the attraction of these perspectives: both liberalism and Marxism have aided in the fracturing of feudalistic, paternalistic structures of thought and society; both have challenged misplaced loyalties to the status quo. In modern history, parts of Protestantism too have been involved in alliances with these two modes of thought. But the alliances have been uncomfortable ones, and I suspect that Catholicism will fare no better.

The problem is this: each of these two modes of thought is fatally flawed from the perspective of theological anthropology. The liberal tradition from Locke through Kant to Rawls and Dworkin is laden with an almost unqualified individualist bias, understands the human in terms of a tabula rasa, and sees, finally, human rights as a matter of contract. The revolutionary realist tradition from Machiavelli through the French Revolution to Marx is unqualifiedly collectivist, understands the human as an ensemble of social relationships, and views human rights as an ideology. One has led to an uncritical acceptance of capitalist economic exploitation, the other brings the echoes of the guillotine and the Gulag to modern life. Neither provides us with a satisfactory sense of the inviolability of *persons in relationship and community;* both leave us relying only on the fluxus quo.

III. IF WE BEGIN TO LOOK IN THE RIGHT PLACES, WE WILL FIND THAT THE COVENANTAL MOTIFS OF SCRIPTURE, ESPECIALLY AS WORKED OUT IN SEVERAL MOMENTS OF TRADITION, PROVIDE THE SOURCE AND NORM FOR HUMAN RIGHTS

By "covenant" I mean a structure of relationship between God and humanity, and among humans, which is given by God, and based on nothing less than the righteousness and grace of God. The centerpoint of the biblical account of the Exodus, the formation of a people called to be a witness to all the peoples of the earth and the giving of the land, is covenant. The New Testament also is covenantal in the calling of the disciples, in the Sermon on the Mount, and in the forming of the church after the crucifixion and resurrection. To be sure, there are competing definitions of "covenant" in the Biblical texts, but certain common features can be discerned: a covenant involves the *bonding of persons* to others *under God's law, for God's Kingdom, empowered by God's love.* On this basis, historic communities of solidarity are formed for the liberation, justification, and sanctification of all God's people.

This covenantal tradition has been a minority report in Catholicism, although it has never been utterly obscured. [3] As I have tried to show elsewhere, [4] some of the major breakthroughs toward modern understandings of human rights come from nowhere else than from the conciliarist Catholics prior to the Reformation, culminating, in some ways, at the Council of Constance which deposed Pope John XXIII, the first. Until the Second Vatican Council, called by Pope John XXIII, the second, that stream remained a minority tradition within Catholicism. Nevertheless, it creatively influenced the formation and development of universalistic concepts in such areas as international law.

Parts of the Protestant tradition took basic notions from the conciliarist Catholics, rooted them once again in Scripture, and made them central to Reformed theology and social ethics. We see the legacy of this direction of thought in Dutch, Swiss, English, and New England federalism, and in innumerable Protestant sects. It is from these roots that the basic character of human rights thought and practice has developed in modern Western religious and political life, and not from the majority report of conservative Catholicism, liberalism, the French Revolution, or Marxism. Indeed, these last traditions frequently misunderstand the nature, derivation, and import of human rights, because they are blind to the significance of these movements. They ideologically and unscientifically presume that nothing of general import comes from biblical perspectives. When confronted with the horrors of national socialism in the twentieth century, however, it was to religious traditions that the opponents of the Nazis turned. It is to these traditions, overtly or covertly, that human rights advocates across the world appeal today, often without knowing whence came the presuppositions they hold. It is my contention that we cannot understand the history, character, foundation, or implications of human rights without attention to these traditions. It will not serve the cause of intellectual honesty or practical action to ignore these traditions in an effort to get a more universally "acceptable" or more "scientific" reading of the human situation by bowing and scraping to the cultured despisers of religion. Nor is it helpful to argue that such a perspective is not of widespread usefulness because it derives from a highly particular set of traditions. All sorts of universally true matters derive from particular histories and insights. It is simply a fact that this is *the* tradition which places all of life under a universal principle of justice, equity, dignity, and freedom, and which evokes dedication and religious zeal for making these principles actual, whatever the concrete experiences of life and social conditions are at a given time or place.

IV. THE COVENANTAL PERSPECTIVE SOLVES SEVERAL PROBLEMS FACED BY BOTH PRESENT SCHOLARSHIP AND PRACTICAL ACTIVITY IN THE AREA OF HUMAN RIGHTS

Reliance on a covenantal understanding of universal law given by God, a covenantal conception of the godly purpose of liberation and redemption, and a covenental enactment of loving compassion which binds each to the neighbor and extends the solidarity of community and care to all, would allow us to see human rights in a perspective which is genuinely evangelical, genuinely reformed, and genuinely catholic. Such a view could provide the basis for the convergence of ecumenically open religious traditions, and it could provide the principles to guide selective and temporary cooperation with liberals or Marxists in those moments when they too protest dehumanizing structures or actions. The covenantal heritage, however, moves beyond criticism and negation of oppression to a constructive vision of the human as created in the image of God and calls us to act sacrificially for the neighbor's rights, as well as those of ourselves or our groups, for the sake of God.

A renewal of covenantal orientations provides also a solution to the tension which is often felt between individual rights and collective rights. In the covenantal traditions, individualism is overcome because the person is understood to be first of all a relational being—in a *relationship* to God and thus a *member* of God's *humanum*. Collectivism also is overcome because it is clearly recognized that people are called, in history, to participate in the universal *humanum* in and through specific religious, cultural, vocational, and voluntary communities. Hence the covenantal view demands recognition of the rights or "sphere sovereignty" of specific groupings—families, churches, unions, artistic and scientific associations, etc.—to be self-governing (under God), and not to be manipulated or controlled by any dominant party, government, or economic power. [5]

It is in this context that those papers prepared for this consultation which focused on the "base communities" in contemporary Latin American liberation movements take on heightened significance. And it is this feature which has been anticipated among some conciliarist Catholics and many Protestants for several centuries when they placed a central accent on "freedom of religion" as the decisive human right. At its core, the drive for religious liberty was not an individualist concern to believe anything one wanted, however silly, but a drive to form unmanipulated communities of faith for both worship and mutual care according to the actual needs of the members. From this basis, it was held, communities of faith could criticize arbitrary power—and they had an absolute right to do so. Indeed, some scholars see in liberation movements the "protestant-ization of Catholicism from within," especially when the freedom to relate the Gospel to the particular needs of the people is claimed as a right in the face of political, economic, *and* traditional church authority. Where communities of faith are free to form, to speak freely about God's law, purpose, and love, and to act on this basis for the redemption of the people in response to concrete needs, the theological understanding of human nature is renewed and human rights can be extended in political, economic, intellectual, and material directions. Where such freedom of religion is denied, the rights of people to speak of their real needs for jobs, for bread, for homes, and for the power to decide their own destinies are soon also subverted. In one sense, the open proclamation of truth and the communion sharing of bread and drink is a paradigm of what is required of all society.

Patricia W. Fagen, after surveying contemporary developments in

Latin America, confirms this view when she concludes that human rights advocacy "can only occur where there exists some institutional umbrella that can protect human rights advocates and offer both political and material support for human rights activities . . . almost everywhere, the churches play the most critical role. Religious groups, when internally strong, are the least vulnerable institutions." [6] The fact that many churches have not used their hard-won freedom in genuinely covenantal ways to speak the truth about oppression and denials of human rights only indicates the constant need for covenant renewal today no less than in the prophetic periods of biblical history.

V. POWER IS TEMPORAL; HUMAN RIGHTS ARE ETERNAL; THE TEMPORAL DEPENDS ON THE ETERNAL

All human rights depend, for their effectiveness and realization, on enforcement. Enforcement requires power. No person and no human community is sufficiently beyond the power of sin that human rights can be actualized without the presence of coercion. Hence every struggle for human rights is likely to involve force at some point or other.

But power cannot create or sustain itself. In cannot even direct itself. The exercise of power is always in the service of a purpose beyond the power itself. The question is the ethical legitimacy of the purpose. Further, orders have to be obeyed to be powerful. Again, the question is the legitimacy of the order. Every power that comes into being tries to claim that its existence and exercise is legitimate. The point, however, is that power is never self-legitimating. Human rights derived from a godly covenant offer the criteria by which such claims may be adjudicated. When power is exercised against human dignity, in violation of community, to subvert the religious bonding (which cuts to the core of what it means to be human), it must be judged as illegitimate and must be resisted. But when power is exercised under the absolute and eternal provisions of the covenant which God offers to all humanity and by which loving, purposeful, and righteous existence is created and sustained, it can be an instrument of redemption. The criteria by which we know the difference between legitimate and illegitimate power involve not only political discernment and social action, but, more importantly, theological discernment and the formation of active, involved, participatory faith communities.

In brief, the most revolutionary principle with regard to the social and political realization of human rights was not enunciated by any ancient philosopher who spoke of the achievements of human excellence on the basis of natural reason, nor by any liberal who argues for this or that version of a social contract, nor by any Marxist who focuses on the material needs and historical conditions which beset humanity, but by Peter when he said "we must obey God rather than man" (Acts 5:29). When the heirs of Peter forget that point, both the Gospel and human rights are in peril.

In conclusion, I wish to submit to this volume a statement recently passed by the General Synod of my denomination, the United Church of Christ. This statement sums up and cogently presents, I believe, a variety of Protestant thinking about human rights which is widely shared among Christians of many communions. I offer it, thus, as a supplement to my five theses and as a contribution to the continuing dialogue between Roman Catholics and Protestants on this very important topic.

A Pronouncement on Human Rights

The Eleventh General Synod in its Resolution on Human Rights directed the Office for Church in Society "to draft a major pronouncement on human rights for the Twelfth General Synod." The Office for Church in Society appointed a national advisory committee, including representatives from other national agencies, minority caucuses in the United Church of Christ, seminaries, and ecumenical agencies to aid it in carrying out this directive.

I. THE CORE PROBLEM

Human Rights are the gift and demand of God. They have their source in what God has done and is doing in creation, in Jesus Christ, and through the Holy Spirit. In every age God calls upon people to proclaim the righteousness and justice in the world. God creates, reconciles and redeems everything that is. Thus human rights are universal demands. No person, no group, no society is excused from recognizing the claim that other human beings must be treated justly and that societies must be ordered on the basis of freedom and equity.

When the church of Jesus Christ has faltered in proclaiming and enacting God's righteousness, other advocates of human rights have stood up throughout the world. They have pointed to a universal moral law to be implemented in all civil orders. Different societies have understood human rights differently and have thus conferred civil rights in different ways. Universal moral law confers human rights that are diversely implemented in the civil orders. Thus, civil rights are subject to legislative acts or political fiat. Human rights, however, are God given and are not alterable by persons, groups or regimes. All persons and all civil orders are under moral obligation to develop policies, programs and politics which recognize basic human rights.

In recent years human rights have become a worldwide concern. The attention stems in large part from increased understanding and recognition of human rights and increased awareness of the widespread violation of human rights. We witness in many locations a growing division between declaration and implementation, recognition and realization, codification and enforcement, rhetoric and establishment of human rights. There is a growing awareness that human rights are decisive not only for the quality of human life but also for the very existence of human life.

We rejoice over what has been accomplished toward creating sound international legal standards since the signing of the Universal Declaration of Human Rights in 1948, but we realize that legal standards alone, however universally declared, are not enough. When we raise the question of human rights today we are also raising the question of the power to realize them and of the powers that prevent their realization. To be committed to human rights means to be committed to the transformation of those values which shore up inhuman systems and the transformation of those systems which spawn inhuman values.

We further realize that standing up for human rights means becoming actively engaged in the struggle for human rights. We have to be willing to sense human misery in its various forms and to be able to suffer with the suffering of others. We have to refuse arguments which set out to rationalize or justify human misery, especially when these causes stem from our own interests and lifestyles. In this way we announce that we are ready to enter into solidarity with all those who struggle for human rights by working for the liberation of persons.

Today there are at least five dimensions of human life in which we hear the cries of those suffering from violations of human rights.

1) In many parts of the world people are crying out from political oppression and yearning for the recognition of their right to determine their own future through participation in the decision-making of the community. They are demanding recognition of the right to the integrity of their person which involves the right to life, dissent and freedom from torture. Under the concept of human rights no civil order may deprive persons or groups of their rights to conscience, to speech, and to assembly by employing reasons of "national security," "true religion," or "political expediency."

2) We hear the cries of those suffering from economic exploitation and pleas for the right of human existence in the face of hunger, unemployment and unjust economic systems. Human beings are demanding

the right to the basic necessities of life: food, shelter, clothing, humanly satisfying work with just remuneration, health care and personal ownership of what is necessary to dignity and freedom. Both developed and developing societies are spawning economic values that determine the allocation of scarce resources in favor of the rich. While the right to property is essential to the well-being and the development of the human person, the principle of ownership can never justify accumulation of wealth by the few that produces poverty for the many.

3) People are crying out from cultural alienation and yearning for the right to maintain and enjoy their cultural identity. Persons suffering from racism, sexism, ageism and prejudice against the handicapped are demanding their right not to be humiliated by the cultural definition of others. In many societies today the most vulnerable people are prevented from claiming their names, their languages, their histories, and their cultural identities by dominating cultural, political, or social forms. People are calling out for a chance to contribute to the community and to develop their capacities for creativity. Human beings have a right to educational opportunity and to cultural forms which express their memories and their hopes. They have a right to the freedom to form and maintain families and to create meaningful relationships.

4) People are crying out together with all creation against the misuses and/or ignorances of technology which are destructive of the relationships between humanity and habitat. The partial realization of our technical utopias has created unimagined possibilities for freeing human beings from disease, hunger, and pain, but it has also created horrifying possibilities for the destruction of nature as well as the manipulation, repression, and dehumanization of our own bodies. Because human beings are part of nature, a violation of the rights of nature is also a violation of human rights. Human rights entail a protection of natural resources and the environment for the sake of future generations.

5) People are crying out from despair and lack of meaning in their lives and yearning for the right to be in open relationships with what they consider to be the source of life. Of primary importance in human rights is the freedom of religion. People have the right to the freedom of faith, the right to public worship and the expression of faith in teaching, criticism, and practice. It is a human right to participate in communities of faith which are free to influence persons to righteousness and to exercise prophetic witness in society. The freedom to relate to what one believes to be the ultimate source of life should prevent the idolatry of society and self.

All of these dimensions of oppression and human rights are interrelated and interdependent. It is quite possible in specific actions to focus on one or another dimension under God's righteousness; however, it is impossible to be concerned about human rights without committing one-self to rights in all of these dimensions. At the same time we concentrate our efforts on specific problems, we must become engaged in relation to the total dimensionality and global context of human rights. There is today no single issue of human rights which is not ultimately global in character.

We acknowledge that there are diverse traditions of human rights which stem from different histories. For example, in the Western in-dividual nations where the struggle has been to limit the powers of rulers, individual freedom has been given primary stress. In the Eastern socialist countries, on the other hand, where the principal struggle has been against poverty, economic welfare rights have been central. These concepts of human rights are not mutually exclusive but are comple-mentary. Both, however, can be used to exercise dominating political power to repress either individual or social rights. In some countries still dominated by hunger and poverty, the proper emphasis is on the right to existence itself. Because human rights questions are in fact global, the struggle for human rights must take all of the diverse perspectives into serious consideration.

As Christians in the United States we affirm our history of struggle for democratic and civil rights of the individual. We may not give up the gains which have been made in this history or the valid emphasis on the rights of the individual and the community over against the state. Our task is to use this democratic tradition to spread civil and individual rights into the economic, cultural, and natural dimensions. We commit ourselves to the best in our tradition.

As Christians we also confess our own failures to achieve a society which fully protects the human rights of all of our citizens. We have been lacking in diligence and commitment to correct the systematic violations of human rights in some of our laws and institutions. We have been deaf to the anguished cries for help by those whose rights are violated because they hold unpopular views, pursue unconventional life-styles, belong to powerless groups, or are deprived of the resources with which to protect themselves. We confess that our lack of passion for human rights has led to economic crises, racial and sexual discrimination, food shortages, waste of resources, pollution of the environment, and inadequate care of and community with the handicapped and the aged. We confess that we have sometimes used the concept of individual rights as a false ideology of individualism to justify the unjust distribution of the necessities of life. Our freedom from the constant struggle for the basic necessities of life has degenerated into a compulsive dependence on exaggerated, destructive patterns of consumption. We have tried to bolster our own economic situation by an unbridled search for markets and raw materials overseas and by massive arms sales and investments in support of regimes which use them to enhance their own privileges and systematically and grossly violate the human rights of their own citizens.

II. BIBLICAL AND THEOLOGICAL FOUNDATIONS OF HUMAN RIGHTS

Human rights are grounded in God's act of creating, reconciling, and redeeming the creation. This act is called God's righteousness and power to make God's creatures alive against the power of death. As creator of everything, God has a claim upon everyone and everything in creation. God comes to human beings in the person of Christ to judge, to forgive, to restore, and to justify us, in other words, to make us alive in the power of God's life or to make us righteous in God's sight. Human rights are promises and commands of God to make and keep God's creatures abundantly alive. Thus human rights are not grounded in static reality, in legal contracts, in the integrity of the individual or state, or in the nature of things. Rather they are grounded in God's faithfulness to man. This relationship of God to creation gives all human beings their inalienable human rights.

This righteousness which God expresses in creation, reconciliation, and redemption is the basis of God's covenant. Human rights are live and realizable in this covenant context. They are alive in actual historical relationships in which God accepts human beings and human beings accept, hope for, and love each other. Rights must be not only declared and codified, but also must be cared for, nurtured, and embodied in covenant relationships between persons, groups, nations, and between human beings and nature.

All human beings have equal human rights by virtue of their being created in the image of God. Because of God's claim upon all God's creatures, human rights have to do with the basic answerability or responsibility of being a human creature. To be created in the image of God means to be called to be God's representative to the creation. It means to be called to care for God's whole creation according to God's intention. Therefore the fundamental human right which gives the human being his or her dignity is also an obligation: to serve and to help in the creation of the conditions for life in the whole creation. The fundamental human right is the right to be responsible to God. Human rights and human duties are two sides of the same coin. "My rights" is an abstraction and in reality nothing without the "rights of my neighbors," which constitute my duty. In view of God's claim upon God's human creatures, rights are given by God as the means for all human beings to fulfill their duties before God's righteousness.

Thus human rights are what people need in order to fulfill their fundamental task of becoming human persons, that is, fulfilling their calling as the image of God. No person, organization, or state has the right to violate the right and dignity of being human in another human being. To do so is a sin against God: it is an attempt to frustrate God's will for the life of God's creation. As a function of God's righteousness human rights shape history. They give structure and form to human relations that serve the systems of life as opposed to the systems of death. They are guides to and forms of the conditions of life. Where they are disregarded, there will be death.

The conditions of life which God is seeking to create through God's own suffering love are freedom, justice, equality, peace, and recognition of God's glory. These are the conditions under which human rights are realized. Human sin, the reality of evil in the world, and the power of death are constantly working against God's creation and producing human suffering. Thus our work for human rights is grounded in God's new creation. God the Holy Spirit is making present the liberating power of the messianic mission of Christ and the new creation of God's future. It is out of the righteousness which God is suffering to create in our midst that we struggle and work for the realization of human rights.

In the struggle for human rights there is no way to avoid conflict between groups, especially between the rich and the poor, the powerful and powerless. The message of reconciliation as the Word of the Cross does not remove these conflicts. It does, however, seek to bring into the midst of the conflicts the fundamental promise of the Gospel that the ultimate goal is the reconciled community within the one family of God.

In the midst of the struggles we will affirm that the power of freedom comes through the free grace of God. God's involvement in the midst of the historical struggle is the reality which prevents despair from failures and overwhelming frustrations in attempts at realizing human rights. At the same time the presence of God's grace keeps us from a compulsive slavery to our self-justification through works.

III. CALL TO STUDY AND ACTION

We have affirmed that our concern for human rights arises from God's grace and the call to be faithful participants in the care of creation and the realization of justice. In response we work in partnership with all persons and communities of good will to articulate, advocate and realize the rights of persons, particularly those without their own voice and power.

Responding then to God's call, the Twelfth General Synod commits itself to the struggle for human rights and

1) Calls upon all members of the United Church of Christ to study and reflect upon the biblical and theological basis for our commitment to human rights.

2) Calls further on the members of the United Church of Christ to advance the cause of human rights through the social and political processes available to them in their vocations as citizens at work in the world.

3) Urges that our churches, church-related agencies, associations, conferences and national agencies be sensitive to the human rights of persons within our own church institutions and their spheres of influence and, where there are violations, to seek to remedy them.

4) Calls upon churches, church-related agencies, associations, conferences, and national agencies of the United Church to devote personnel and financial resources to denominational and ecumenical human rights programs that will enable the United Church of Christ to:

—seek ratification of the Covenant on Economic, Social and Cultural Rights, the Covenant on Civil and Political Rights, and other Human Rights Conventions approved by the United Nations and submitted by the President of the United States to the U.S. Senate for ratification.

—affirm the protection of human life, condemn the needless loss of life including murder and the judicial death penalty, and encourage the continuing study of the difficult ethical questions in any deliberate termination of life.

—participate in the corporate social responsibility movement to exert pressure on business corporations and government agencies, through a range of shareholder actions and recommendations to public officials, to end U.S. economic complicity in the human rights violations of repressive governments.

—be aware of new developments in the continuing struggle for human rights and to respond appropriately, with special attention given to the rights of future generations in relation to the government.

—participate in ecumenical bodies, coalitions, movements and other organizations which work in behalf of human rights through the world in terms consonant with this Pronouncement.

—bring strategically important aid to victims of human rights violations through its own service agencies and through various ecumenical assistance programs.

—request an agency of the Church to develop a course on human rights for congregations; and

—encourage the closely related seminaries to reflect this pronouncement in their total curricular endeavor.

5) Requests specifically that the United Church Board for Homeland Ministries, the United Church Board for World Ministries, the Commission for Racial Justice, and the Office for Church in Society continue to give priority attention to human rights in their mission programming.

6) Commends to the churches, church-related agencies, associations, conferences and national agencies of the United Church of Christ, the study and consideration of the Petition on Human Rights Violations in the United States to the United Nations Commission on Human Rights and Subcommission on Prevention of Discrimination and Protection of Minorities, submitted by the Commission for Racial Justice of the UCC and others.

IV. CALL TO THE NATION

In accepting its own responsibility for participation in the struggle for human rights and recognizing the responsibility of the people of our nation to become concerned with these critical dimensions of the human rights efforts, the Twelfth General Synod:

1) Calls upon the people of our nation to press our governmental bodies—municipal, state, and federal—to address more vigorously the continuing problems of social, economic and judicial injustice in our own country, affirming the rights of all people to earn a living, correcting those conditions which prevent full equality of opportunity or deny the reality of equal treatment before the law.

2. Calls upon the people of our nation to insist that our federal government

—phase out systematically all existing involvements in the support of foreign governments that objective international investigations have found guilty of gross and systematic violation of the human rights of their own citizens;

—assume its special responsibility for the defense of human rights in dictatorial countries deemed of strategic importance to our military and economic security:

—end both military and economic assistance, and especially programs of intelligence and police training, wherever the regimes in power practice torture, arbitrary detention, and the systematic denial of freedom of religion, speech, press, assembly, and of petition for the redress of grievances, including the right of workers to organize for collective bargaining and to resort when necessary to work stoppages in their quest for fair compensation and working conditions.

3) Calls upon the people of our nation to pursue the efforts to seek ratification of the multilateral United Nations human rights treaties which have been approved by the United Nations, signed by the President of the United States, and submitted to the U.S. Senate for ratification.

4) Calls upon the people of our nation to urge the President of the United States to sign the United Nations Optional Protocol on Civil and Political Rights (provides procedures for petition by individuals) and submit it to the U.S. Senate for ratification.

The Twelfth General Synod of the United Church of Christ requests the President of the Church to communicate this Pronouncement to the President and the Congress of the United States, the Secretary-General of the United Nations, and the National and World Councils of Churches and their respective member communions.

NOTES TO CHAPTER 6

1. See, for example, R. Niebuhr, *The Nature and Destiny of Man* (New York: Scribner's, 1941).

2. John Paul II, "Opening Address at Puebla," trans. John Drury, in *Puebla and Beyond,* ed. John Eagleson and Philip Scharper (Maryknoll, N.Y.: Orbis Books, 1979), p. 63.

3. I have in mind, here, the late medieval work of d'Ailly, Gerson, Zabarella, Andreas Randuf, Dietrich of Niem, Nicolas of Cusa, and, of course, Marsilius of Padua and John of Salisbury.

4. See my forthcoming *Religion and Human Rights.*

5. See Abraham Kuyper, *Lectures on Calvinism* (Grand Rapids, Mich.: Eerdmans, 1931).

6. Patricia Weiss Fagen, "Human Rights in Latin America," *Christianity and Crisis* (December 24, 1979), p. 331.

Monika Hellwig

7. The Quest for Common Ground in Human Rights—A Catholic Reflection

Effective action in defense of human rights for all depends not only on clarity in the understanding of the goals, but also on the breadth and solidity of awareness, consensus, and support in society; hence the paramount importance of the quest for common ground in the understanding of human rights which is the concern of this volume. We live in a society in which plurality of normative traditions is inescapable and appears to be permanent. Even the "melting pot" experience of the United States is not really such; our several traditions do not lose their particularity. Nor can they. When we speak of what is of ultimate importance in our lives, our words fail to say precisely what we mean. We must appeal to a language of poetic imagery, to analogies of shared experiences, to visions of the future that are shaped by the sufferings and the promises of the past, and therefore to a language that is always quite particular to those who share the experiences. It is necessarily a language that is to some extent exclusive or esoteric.

It is at this point that a serious ecumenism among traditions begins. Acknowledging the indissoluble differences among traditions, we can lay solid foundations for human rights work by soberly testing the common ground in honest dialogue. Such dialogue does not aim at eliminating distinctive features of each tradition but at sympathetic mutual understanding. This volume is concerned with Western traditions in three strands: the Christian (and predominantly Catholic), the secular-liberal, and the Marxist. It is understood, of course, that this division, while helpful, is also arbitrary. It is neither inevitable nor exhaustive. For instance, Jewish and Muslim traditions might have been considered, as well as more of the Protestant strands in the Christian tradition. Moreover, these are not fully distinct traditions because they have roots in shared experiences and have already intermingled and exchanged in the courses of their history. The division is nevertheless helpful in focusing sharply on some central sources from which people in the Western world draw their inspiration and values today.

Elsewhere in this volume, Philip Rossi points to three areas of common ground that emerged in the dialogue of the three traditions.[1] He lists the recognition of shared human vulnerabilities, human communion or a common social character of human existence, and the aspiration to self-determination in the shaping of one's own destiny. These factors emerge as convictions held in common. Clearly, they provide a basis for common action. Equally clearly, the basis is not yet adequate without much further specification of the content. The thoughtful reader will have seen that most of the essays in this book are concerned precisely with the unfolding and comparing of this content.

There would seem to be four levels at which there are points of contact and at which such explorations can be conducted. They might be called the prethematic, the historical, the logical, and the ecumenical. Possibly the most promising level is the prethematic. In this volume it is particularly the essays of Clarke, Rossi, and, in part, that of Ellacuría which seem to be concerned with the prethematic level. There are human experiences which we share whether or not we produce a theory about them. They are therefore understood at a depth that is prior to, and independent of, the language and symbols of the tradition. This is certainly so of elemental (survival) human needs and of pain. The idea of human rights is surely first shaped by the sense of violation. It has its origin in an existential scream of pain or deprivation. When we hear the scream we know what it means not because we can explain it but because we can feel it. It is by the capacity for empathy that we know what it means. But we have to hear the scream first. It may be a scream of fear or a scream of rage. It may be the hoarse scream of those who have suffered all their lives or the shrill scream of those suddenly overtaken by acute suffering.

When such screams make themselves heard at this prethematic level, and people feel their "blood curdle," there is a radicalizing moment out of which questions are formulated. The formulation is bound to be culturally conditioned. It is made according to the available language and imagery and worldview of a particular tradition. The cultural context for the formulation of the question also influences the answer that is eventually given. Moreover, the context will in some measure predispose people to hear certain screams rather than others, or to give greater importance to certain screams rather than others. Empathy and imagination are shaped both by actual experiences and by the culturally transmitted interpretations of the experiences, and it is at this point that the traditions grow according to their own dynamic and therefore grow apart. That should not, however, obscure the fact that when we search our several traditions, attempting to go back to the roots, we do eventually meet in the common ground of raw human experience of pain and deprivation through the spine-tingling empathy called forth by the screams of the sufferers. And this is at all times a foundation for dialogue.

The second level at which points of contact are to be found is the historical. The traditions discussed in this volume are in fact intimately intertwined in their history. We are not dealing with three different traditions, but with three distinguishable strands of the Western tradition, largely founded in common political and economic experiences through the ages and sometimes intertwining closely while at other times unraveling and moving in parallel lines. Again, Rossi's essay points out a number of fruitful points of contact and exchange and a number of ways in which the resources of the different strands are complementary and mutually enriching rather than in conflict. The Hennelly essay illustrates this with specific reference to Latin American liberation theology. The Ellacuría essay makes a particularly telling critique of the way part of the common heritage, in this case the notion of "common good" in Aristotle and Thomas Aquinas, has been appropriated, and offers a proposal as to how it might be more constructively appropriated. It may be observed here that the question is not to determine with historical rigor the meaning the term had for Thomas in his cultural context, but rather to explore the expanded meaning Thomas' notion (which is a common inheritance) might have for us in our cultural context.

The third level for possible points of contact might be called the logical. The sheer inner logic of the tradition, pursued relentlessly in the light of human suffering and the questions it raises, may tend with a certain ineluctable progression to conclusions that can be shared by the traditions. The matter is certainly worth exploring; if the several traditions are honest and coherent efforts at construing or interpreting reality (the same reality, though seen from different vantage points), one might hope for the emergence of common conclusions at some points. Although cultural bias is necessarily built into any tradition and is constantly being compounded within it, if inquiry and reflection are carried on with any kind of authenticity, "reality talks back" and theory is corrected in new phases of praxis. It is this cautious expectation that lends sharp interest to the essays of Hollenbach, Langan, and Haughey, which attempt the exploration of the several traditions from within, probing their inner logic, and which certainly provide grounds for the Rossi thesis of the three areas of common concern.

A fourth level would seem to be the properly ecumenical, that is, the level at which the traditions are deliberately brought into dialogue with one another, in order that they may be required to answer not only their own but each other's questions. The third and fourth levels are in practice, of course, heavily interdependent, as in this volume in which the ecumenical intention is what motivates the inquiry into the traditions taken separately. Yet the two are not the same. At the third level each tradition is pushed to answer the questions arising within its own frame of reference. At the fourth, each tradition is pushed to answer questions arising outside its own frame of reference. Both are evidently useful in searching out common ground for human rights action.

Those whose main concern is immediate action in behalf of human rights may well ask whether it is necessary to invoke the traditions at all. It may seem both an unnecessary luxury, time-consuming and complicated, and also counterproductive in that the traditions appear to divide rather than unite for action. Yet it is very difficult to motivate people to action without offering clear reasons for exertion, for sacrifice of self-interest, and for the reshaping of political, economic, and social perceptions. Beyond motivation, most people also look to the traditions for grounded and defensible criteria and values. In order to make a convincing case for action to change the present order of things, it is usually necessary to appeal to principles and convictions that people already take for granted in their lives. Hence the necessity for careful study of the traditions and of the common ground on which they meet. It is, however, more than a matter of historical and systematic research. It will have to be a creative enterprise of discerning the "hot buttons" that touch off the flow of empathy and engagement. It will also have to be a matter of constructing bridges of imagination over which empathy can be called forth and extended where communication had failed before.

If imagination is to be used to mediate a more ample understanding and engagement, the particularities of the traditions are of the greatest importance, because they contain the code of symbols out of which the bridges can be built. It is not possible to create instant symbols and expect them to move people to generous action. The education of the imagination is a delicate and a slow process; but the traditions have been engaged in it for a long time and have attained a certain coherence, flexibility, depth, and public consent. For these reasons, though the task may be rather slow and apparently remote from the arena of practical action for human rights, the exploration and harnessing of the resources of the traditions would seem to be of paramount importance not only for academics but also for those engaged in action of the most concrete type.

Another type of question concerning the present endeavor has been raised by the Stackhouse contribution. It is a question concerning the ultimate warrant for the claiming of a human right. Stackhouse suggests that the attempt to find common ground with liberal and Marxist traditions may be a chase after a will-o'-the-wisp, at least if we are concerned with foundational studies on which to ground convictions and strategies for action. His point is important and worthy of careful consideration. He takes issue with an assumption made in ecumenical human rights discussions such as this one—an assumption which he sees as arising out of the Thomistic legacy within Catholic thought. It is the assumption that "theology and philosophy are at certain critical points detachable." [2] Such an assumption allows us to suppose that beyond or beneath the particularities of the faith traditions lies a philosophical realm in which we can all meet on the common ground of right reason and in which we will see the same things and speak the same language. According to this assumption, then, the foundations for the determination and the defense of human rights must necessarily lie in this realm, because by the very definition of human rights they are rooted in the nature of things and persons which we share.

Stackhouse questions this assumption, showing with reference to the liberal and the revolutionary realist tradition that one cannot assume a common grounding of human rights but only common cause made at certain points on practical issues, and then perhaps as a matter of compromise. [3] It is a telling point and, if valid, of considerable importance for the present study. Stackhouse proposes as the one valid foundation for human rights the biblical understanding of covenant. By way of a Catholic rejoinder to his position, one might suggest that the biblical notion of covenant is not necessarily in opposition to an ethic, an ecumenism, a human rights position based on the natural law tradition which tries to find common ground with all persons of good will. The covenant, after all, consists not primarily in that we covenant with God or with one another, but rather that God first establishes the covenant with us.

In the traditions of Israel which we as Christians inherit, there is in the ultimate analysis only one covenant of God with men. Yet there are different ways of sharing the same covenant, even perhaps different degrees of intimacy in which a person or people can be involved or committed. Thus Israel perceives three covenants set within one another. The Sinai covenant, or Abrahamic covenant of circumcision, therefore, while it calls Israel to be the elect of God, a witness people covenanted to God in a special task by means of special observances, nevertheless rests upon the covenant relationship with God that is universal. This universal realization of the divine covenant is in the first place the Noachic covenant, or covenant of the rainbow, in which God guarantees the good order and ultimate meaningfulness of a life lived in terms of moral responsibility and of a society structured according to the demands found in the consciences of men. But this Noachic covenant in turn would make no sense if it were not founded in the covenant of creation, in the very order of things and the very being of persons and human societies, where the God of creation has expressed his eternal wisdom in the harmony and pattern of the way things are. In other words, the God of creation and of all men's consciences and of the special historical vocation of Israel is one God. His name is powerful compassion, for he orders all things wisely and, in spite of the gift of human freedom, he does not contradict himself.

It would seem to be precisely this biblical notion of the divine covenant that is taken over in the Catholic natural law tradition. The God of revelation, the God of Our Lord Jesus Christ, is seen as necessarily in harmony with the vestiges of primitive self-revelation and the many currents of self-revelation to be found in human persons made in the image of God and in human societies and cultural traditions in which that image is expressed and elaborated. It is for this reason that it seems to Catholic Christians quite congruous with passionate commitment to the divine covenant in Jesus Christ to search not only for common ground but even for the foundations of moral commitment to human rights in partnership with those of other traditions. It is understood that if they are persons "of good faith," that is, persons genuinely committed to the search for what is right, the God of creation, conscience, and salvation will not be leading them astray because his covenant holds at the deepest levels of the experience of being human.

This relates to a further question more commonly asked by churchmen and conservative Christians. It is the question whether the attempt to find common ground, and the enterprise of dialogue and common action and strategy with "unbelievers" is not dangerous for committed Christians and indeed counterproductive in relation to the goals of a just society and a truly moral stance in public life. The question assumes that we have in our own tradition all the truth and insight that we need, or that, if we do not yet have it, it is at least accessible exclusively through the resources of our own tradition. This is questionable in fact and on theological grounds. The resources we need to understand and rightly appropriate the issues are, on the one hand, in the vision of ultimate goals which we draw from our faith, but on the other hand, in human experience deeply lived and honestly reflected upon. A faith tradition cannot preempt the truth of human experience or the need to reflect on the whole of it, as lived by all human persons and societies, not only ourselves or our own society. This has been the strength in our times of liberation theology, and this has been the reason for its close dialogue with Marxists and others—a dialogue that has constantly made it suspect to those who have not experienced it from within and therefore have not been party to the renewal of gospel faith and Christian commitment which liberation theology has sparked.

No doubt there is "danger" in a close dialogue and collaboration with the Marxist and liberal traditions, in the sense that these may appear to a Christian participant more coherent than Christianity as he has so far understood and appropriated it. That risk is surely taken simply by living in a pluralistic society and is constantly being taken by those who, though Christian, have no problems with the existing order of their societies and who collaborate in the established political and economic order without questioning. What is perhaps little recognized by Christians today is that collaboration with the liberal tradition, as it exists all around us in the northern countries of the Western world today, is from a Christian theological point of view certainly more "dangerous" than collaboration with the revolutionary traditions such as the Marxist. The latter confesses with Christians, though in different language, that the world is permeated by sin, that its structures and values and expectations betray us by their pervasive sinfulness, and that we are therefore in utter and urgent need of redemption. The quest to explore the human dimensions of deprivation and pain in which that need of redemption manifests itself must necessarily be a common cause with all who have uttered or heard the screams and therefore know the suffering in existential ways.

The question concerning the covenantal basis for human rights also relates to the question of legitimate strategies. The obviously effective strategy is one that moves from the immediate perception of self-interest to action for others or for the common good of the society. The general strategy for the protection of human rights, whether economic or legal-political, would seem to be as follows. First, the agent of change must find ways to awaken a deeply rooted and widely based awareness of self-interest at stake in the matter. Then there has to be a process of expanding the imagination to see complex links and patterns, to recognize further implications, to situate the particular problem within the larger social structure and setting, to glimpse possibilities for successful action. Thirdly, there has to be a challenge to engagement for the common cause, the common good, and even, in the particular case, engagement for the good of the other.

Clearly, in this process of expanding imagination and growing commitment to commensurate action, the values, convictions, and symbols of the traditions can be very effectively used. The question arises whether this is a kind of prostitution of religious faith and of the language of the religious tradition. This question becomes all the more insistent with the realization that the process must necessarily rest so heavily on self-interest as the starting point and motivating factor. It would seem that the covenantal notion as we inherit it from Israel holds the key to the answer; God is a God of wisdom who does all things well and harmoniously, not a God of the absurd. His covenant with human persons means precisely that action for the other is in one's own interest, at least ultimately, and that the radical practice of community and common cause spells personal freedom, at least ultimately, because God covenants with us first and His covenant promises hold at the deepest levels of human experience and forever.

NOTES TO CHAPTER 7

1. Philip Rossi, "Moral Community, Imagination and Human Rights," Chap. 8 of this volume, section III.
2. Max L. Stackhouse, "A Protestant Perspective on the Woodstock Human Rights Project," Chap. 6 of this volume, section I.
3. *Ibid.*

PHILIP ROSSI, S.J.

8. Moral Community, Imagination, and Human Rights: Philosophical Considerations on Uniting Traditions

Three traditions of political, social, and moral thought and practice—liberalism, Marxism, and Catholicism—provided the initial focus for the foundational aspect of the Woodstock Theological Center's project on human rights. Each of these traditions has a different understanding of human rights: what they are, how they can be justified, how they are placed in proper order of priority, and how they are to function in the establishment and working of social institutions. One of the objectives of our foundational work has been to explore the possibility of constructing, on the basis of convergences among these traditions, a normative theory of human rights which could then serve as the basis for common action to secure and to defend human rights. The objective was a bold one, and there is no shame in admitting that it has not been reached.

This essay is a reaction to and reflection on the expositions of the traditions previously drafted by other members of the foundational group. Its main thesis is that differences in the way these traditions understand human rights (what they are, how they are justified, etc.) rest upon different ways each tradition has of picturing human communality—what makes me like to you—and of picturing human community—how we are to live with each other.

In offering this thesis, I hope to provide a useful focus for future efforts to construct a normative rights theory unifying these various traditions. This focus is different from the ones offered in most of the other essays in this foundational inquiry.[1] Its focus is upon the function of the imaginative resources of each tradition, in particular its picture of human communality and human community.

Some of the procedures needed to gain this focus will be conceptual;

others will be historical; still others, and these may be the most important, will be practical; i.e., found in activities and ways of living which para-digmatically manifest a tradition's picture of these matters. The proce-dures used in this essay, limited to conceptual ones, are confessedly tentative and partial; they are also "critical" in a loosely Kantian sense: they spell out the limits which these pictures of human communality and human community place upon each tradition's way of manifesting concern for human rights. It is my hope that, limited though these pro-cedures may be, they will be effective enough to lay bare the roots which convictions about human rights have in what I term "moral imagination": our capacity to envision how we are like to one another, particularly in our vulnerability, and how we are to live with one another in awareness of our common vulnerability. [2]

I. IMAGINATION AND THE FOUNDATION FOR HUMAN RIGHTS

There is an imaginative exercise basic to moral thinking and moral practice: seeing the world from the perspective of another. Fundamental to this exercise is the capacity to envision another "like me" and to en-vision myself "like her." We frequently speak of our most general ways of envisioning our likeness to one another in terms of our being "hu-man." I shall therefore use the term "human communality" to designate features which we might envision to make up our most basic likeness to one another: human communality is a basic feature in virtue of which a person can recognize, and be recognized by, another as "likewise human."

There are different ways of envisioning human communality. The ways important for moral thinking and practice and, thus, for understand-ing human rights are the ones we take to be of consequence for what we do and for the shape we give to social institutions and practices. Each of the three traditions which have been principal *foci* for the founda-tional essays employs particular images and conceptualizations of human communality, which give shape to the moral concerns expressed in the understanding of human rights it offers. As the essays make clear, none of these traditions can be considered monolithic in its understanding of human rights. [3] Yet even though there is room for a variety of under-standings of human rights within the particular traditions, and room for expansion of each in directions which include the concerns of the other two, important differences will remain. These differences rest, as we shall see, upon differences in the images of human communality and human community which express the tutelary insights each tradition has into the bases for human dignity.

This kind of difference can be found by examining the uses to which each tradition puts particular conceptualizations of human communality in its efforts to provide a foundation for human rights. For instance, the form of the liberal tradition elaborated in John Langan's chapter employs a carefully limited conceptualization of this communality as one of human personal "nature": human rights are grounded upon a common (though not fully specific) status each of us has as a human person. [4] This status is conceived to be of "nature" insofar as it is not dependent upon legal conventions, nor upon its actual acknowledgment in particular societies. This conceptualization of nature is quite austere and formal. The problem which Langan's essay addresses, however—the inclusion of social and economic rights within the ambit of the liberal tradition's understanding of human rights—arises in large measure because a particular image of human communality has often guided the use to which the liberal tradition has put even this formal conceptualization of human personal nature.

This guiding image of human communality is that of the individual exercising autonomous choice. This image is expressive of a tutelary insight of the liberal tradition that was given its most powerful expression in the work of Kant: what makes me like to you, and what is fundamental to the status each has as a person, is autonomy, the rational self-determination of our choices. [5] We acknowledge our common status as persons insofar as we acknowledge one another's self-determination.

The liberal tradition has been able to mark out clearly and directly a route from the common status we share as autonomous persons to certain rights: those of political and civic self-determination. This is so because its guide for the route has been human communality imaged as the autonomy of choice each of us seeks to exercise in pursuit of our interests; this image provides guidance to paths which lead to protection of the exercise of autonomy of choice. The liberal tradition has been notably less successful in marking out a route from the common status we share as autonomous persons to social and economic rights. Langan's essay marks out one path to those rights which remains faithful to the guiding liberal insight; it argues that it is appropriate to conceive of the securing of these rights as serving fundamental interests of autonomy, insofar as the items to which these rights entitle us are necessary for proper self-respect and the development of individual excellences and life plans. Langan's essay consequently moves the liberal tradition in a direction which would enable it to share with Marxist and Catholic traditions a central concern for securing social and economic rights. Even so, insofar as this concern could be assimilated as one proper to the liberal tradition, it would, nonetheless, rest upon a picture of human communality which these latter traditions would judge to truncate what each considers to constitute humans in their status (or "nature") as persons. For these latter traditions, what makes me like to you, and you like to me, is far more than the capacity each of us has for the self-determination of our choices, even those choices which are as encompassing as our life plans. Our communality is that, but it is also a history we share and a future we can share; it is feeling, hope, and common endeavor; it is vulnerability and the possibility of failure; it is many things, not just freedom.

We consequently find in the latter two traditions conceptualizations of our status as human persons which are far less austere than those characteristic of the liberal tradition. These traditions thus appear more willing to found and, conversely, to limit rights upon bases of human communality other than and, to their ways of thinking and practice, also wider than that of human freedom. Among the more important images of human communality which shape both Marxist and Catholic conceptualizations of the status of persons and so provide a foundation for their rights, are images focusing on the past and pointing to the future. For both these traditions there is a communality of human history, and there is a communality of human destiny. Each tradition judges both to be of central importance for what we are to do and for the shape we are to give to social institutions and practices.

In the communality of human history and of human destiny we tap into fundamental imaginative resources of both the Catholic and the Marxist traditions. These resources have not always been utilized for marking out a route from those traditions' understanding of our status as human persons to the establishment and securing of rights. In fact, they have not infrequently been invoked to block such a route—both the eternal destiny of a beatific vision and the inexorable determinism of historical struggle have been used far too often precisely in order to override claims issuing from present human vulnerabilities. To this extent, the far thinner imaginative resources of the liberal tradition have been much more adequately deployed for basing claims of rights upon a conceptualization of the communality which constitutes us in our status as persons. The chief resource is the guiding image of a human agent's autonomous choice: the capability each of us has for such choice is the communality which delimits our status as human persons. The claims most firmly secured upon this status are, not surprisingly, those which fit best the guiding image of autonomy: claims for the satisfaction of conditions under which individual self-determination becomes possible. The burden for such satisfaction, moreover, is placed most notably upon institutions of civic and political life. They are taken to be of primary service for the protection of the autonomy of human choice as the proper and most effective instruments for public delimitation, expansion, and protection of the ambits of choice for each individual and group in society.

The imaginative resources of the liberal tradition get strained, however, when claims are pressed, as they have been for social and economic rights, not so much in behalf of conditions of self-determination, but in virtue of need. Claims pressed this way appeal to a different way of recognizing and acknowledging another as "like to me"—not on the basis of a communality of autonomy, but on one of vulnerability. The imaginative resources of traditions, such as the Marxist and the Catholic, which more explicitly represent human communality as one of history and destiny, seem better suited to shape conceptualizations of human personal status which can support claims pressed in virtue of our human vulnerabilities.

A perspective upon human communality of particular significance for understanding human rights is opened up by these imaginative resources of Marxist and Catholic traditions. For both traditions, past and future are fundamental to what makes me like to you and you like to me. As a result, we can conceive of our status as human persons, upon which rights are grounded, to be constituted in history and for the moral future; memory and hope can serve as modes of recognition and acknowledgment of what makes me like to you and you like to me. Central to this perspective is what I would consider the imaginative counterweight to the images of autonomy which have been tutelary to the liberal tradition; from this perspective we can start to discern images of human interdependence and shared vulnerability which also provide a foundation in our status as human persons for claims to human rights.

II. MORAL COMMUNITY AND THE FOUNDATION FOR HUMAN RIGHTS

Recognition that another is like to me and that I am like to him or her only starts us on the path to securing human rights. We can recognize another to be like to us and still think that to be of no account for anything we do. The liberal tradition has to confront this possibility in a most acute form because it takes freedom to be that which most fundamentally makes us like to each other: I can recognize another to be like me in his or her freedom, but what reason does that give for taking that freedom into account for anything I do? One way in which the liberal tradition has dealt with this possibility is framed in terms of "interests." The interest which I have in possessing and exercising freedom in my own person can become also an interest in the possession and exercise of freedom by each and all. When my interest in my own freedom is transformed this way, we have moved along the path which the liberal tradition marks off for securing human rights.

Resistance is one engine for such transformation: when my freedom collides with your freedom, it may eventually force us to explore possibilities for establishing practices mutually serving the interest each of us has in exercising our own freedom. While the Hobbesian portrayal of the state of nature provides the most somber image of such a transforming interest and its outcome, other forms of the contractarian tradition have elaborated more generous possibilities for the transformation of my interest in the exercise of my own freedom into a common interest in freedom for each and all in a society. [6] An important feature of these more generous possibilities, of which Kant's image of an "ethical commonwealth" provides one paradigm, is the connection they make between reciprocal acknowledgments of freedom and a sense of human dignity. [7] This connection offers a way for enriching the liberal tradition's fundamental image of the human communality found in freedom: recognition of another's dignity in virtue of his or her freedom requires that I begin to see that freedom has weight for shaping action and practice beyond merely its power of resistance to my freedom. It requires that I see in freedom, both yours and mine, a basis for worth which we can acknowledge one another to have for a common shaping of action; this worth thus serves to bring us into relations which exhibit possibilities for mutual human interaction transcending the mere exercise of freedom's resistance to the power of another's freedom.

Such an enrichment of the communality of freedom makes it possible to assign to images and conceptualizations of human community an important function in the foundation of human rights. Such images mark out an element of our status as human persons which is as fundamental as autonomy for understanding the character and function of human rights. We may speak of this element as mutuality: in making me like to you, and you like to me, the freedom which perhaps we first grudgingly acknowledged while standing in resistance to one another also makes it possible for us to stand with one another. Freedom's completion is found in mutuality.

The liberal tradition has not always clearly perceived the possibility of this enrichment. Its image of freedom as the exercise of an individual's autonomy links freedom closely to consciousness of one's individuality and to patterns of conduct which evoke such consciousness; the dignity which accrues to each in virtue of freedom often remains framed within this image of individual autonomy, rather than being expanded into a basis for the common shaping of action. As a result, the liberal tradition can readily sketch out procedural constraints—such as the traditional civil liberties of a liberal democratic polity—upon actions,

practices, and institutions, which serve the liberal tradition's most fundamental conception of human dignity: the autonomy of individual choice.
This interest is served by securing conditions which enable the exercise
of autonomy by each and all. It is, however, much more difficult for the
liberal tradition to portray the shape that can be given to institutions and
practices, e.g., family, school, church, which serve freedom's interest in
human mutuality, acquired in virtue of shared acknowledgment of dignity as a basis for a common shaping of action.

The traditions of Marxism and Catholicism, on the other hand,
have made extensive use of the possibilities we have for standing with
each other. These possibilities have been framed in images of human community—e.g., a classless society, the people of God—which express for
each tradition ways of understanding how our status as human persons
finds its completion. These possibilities for standing with each other, and
the images of community which represent their completion, then provide
a frame for each tradition's conceptualizations of the elements which constitute us as persons.

These traditions need not trace back to the autonomy of human
personal existence the possibilities we have for standing with each other.
They may, in fact, take the possibility of standing with each other to be
more fundamental than the autonomy of individual choice in constituting
us as persons. [8] Here they may diverge most sharply from the liberal
tradition by allowing the fostering of human mutuality to take priority
over the exercise of human autonomy as the primary concern for shaping
actions, practices, and social institutions. This possibility is given expression in a tutelary insight these traditions have into the communality which
makes us persons: solidarity, be it as for Catholicism, solidarity in our
origin as God's creation and in our need for redemption from sin, or,
as for Marxism, solidarity in the activity of productive labor. Fundamental
to Marxism and Catholicism are images such as these, whose function is
to remind us that not only are we like to each other, but that what touches
you touches me as well.

The priority which these traditions give to human solidarity has
often been conceived to be in opposition to the liberal tradition's emphasis on individual civil and personal rights. [9] Such priority offers a
basis for speaking of, and enforcing, a community's "right" over against
the rights of individuals. For instance, the Marxist tradition requires that
there be social practices and institutions which bring about consciousness
of solidarity as the fundamental basis for human dignity. While such
consciousness is brought about unwittingly in a capitalist society through
its form of social and economic oppression, a socialist society must consciously form practices and institutions to foster such awareness of solidarity. [10] This effectively provides such a society with a "right" to coerce

individuals and groups in ways which are expected to bring about this consciousness of solidarity.

The Catholic tradition, in its turn, has provided a basis for according a society rights over against individuals in virtue of considerations of a solidarity founded upon human dignity. This tradition's understanding of the human solidarity established in virtue of human dignity has often been fashioned in terms of organic images and functions: dignity, inherent and proper to each individual, flourishes in proportion to the acceptance and discharge of the responsibilities of the state of life to which one is called; these states of life, and the particular roles for individuals and groups within them, are ordered to the attainment of good for each, through their functioning properly for the overall good of all elements of society. Within this organic understanding of human solidarity, the Catholic tradition had, until fairly recently, most frequently taken hierarchical models of human political and social organization to provide appropriate institutional forms and practices both for the protection and flourishing of human dignity. [11]

In accord with this organic and hierarchical framework of understanding, the primary responsibility of the institutions governing society has been interpreted to be that of securing conditions for the proper functioning of each element of society for the attainment of good for all the elements in concert. This responsibility is conceptualized as the "common good" to which each and all have title. This common good, which is attained for all elements of society in concert, is not thereby to be separated from the attainment of an individual's proper and unique good. [12] Such separation does take place in appeals, often glibly formulated, to "common good" offered in justification of policies which have the effect of stifling efforts of individuals and groups in their efforts to locate themselves with proper dignity in the human community. [13] Hierarchical models of the institutional forms for the protection of human dignity and the attainment of common good are liable to such separation if they provide little room for participatory procedures in judgments about the concrete content of the common good.

Talks of the "common good" in the Catholic tradition does, therefore, offer a way of understanding the character even of an individual's proper and unique good which is different from the liberal tradition's understanding of the character of that good. It does not thereby deny or undermine the moral weight of that good. The notion of common good makes it possible to understand that the exercise of individual self-determination is ordered to the attainment of good which, though assuredly one's own, is not merely one's own; it is to serve also to foster the good of others to whom one is bound at various levels of mutuality.

Presupposed in this ordering of individual self-determination to the attainment of a common good is an awareness, effective for shaping practice, of human interdependence. Securing common good, therefore, requires practices which foster awareness of this interdependence and actions whereby it is acknowledged. It should be clear, moreover, that such practices can function to restrain the full exercise of the autonomy of each and all. Paul did as much in exhorting the Corinthians to act out of consideration for the consciences of those Christians who had scruples about eating meat which had been obtained from pagan sacrifices. [14]

For the Catholic tradition, therefore, limiting the value accorded to individual self-determination and placing constraints upon its exercise need not undermine human dignity; such limits may be placed out of consideration for our human mutuality and interdependence. Similar limits are possible within the Marxist tradition. In accord with both traditions it is therefore possible to make relative, both in theory and in practice, the value of that human communality, autonomy, which the liberal tradition takes to be fundamental to our status as persons and, thus, to human rights.

This relativizing takes place, however, in virtue of a human communality—the ties of solidarity and interdependence manifest in history, society, and our hopes for the future—which under various images and conceptualizations, both traditions take to be at least as fundamental as autonomy for constituting us in our status as persons. For these traditions, therefore, the human good which is constituted by the exercise of freedom is not simply that of full individual self-determination. Self-determination takes place in historical and social conditions of interdependence which are as fundamental as freedom in constituting human persons. As a result, freedom exercised in these conditions must serve in the attainment of that human good which these conditions point to as their completion: that good is one we conceptualize and image as community.

III. HUMAN VULNERABILITY, COMMUNITY, AND THE MORAL FUTURE

It is the exercise of imagination in response to the puzzle of "What makes me like to you, and you like to me?" which first gives our thought and practice its moral energy. It is the exercise of imagination in response to the puzzle of "How are we to live well with one another?" which gives long-term direction to the expenditure of that moral energy. We have already noted some of the different possibilities which the traditions of liberalism, Marxism, and Catholicism envision as satisfactory resolutions of the first puzzle. There are differences as well in the possibilities they envision in response to the second puzzle; these differences are also important for the ways in which each of these traditions understands human rights.

The path from the human communality, envisioned in response to the first puzzle, to the human community, envisioned in response to the second puzzle, is not straightforward in any of these traditions. The human communalities of freedom, of solidarity in the productive activity of labor, of origin as God's creation, and of destiny to redemption provide a promise and a basis for community, but they do not by themselves constitute the whole account of the shape which human community takes. Although each tradition marks off a different path from human communality to human community, the establishment and protection of rights serves the same important function for each: rights are established to protect the promise and basis for community first envisioned, however fitfully, in the response given to the question "What makes me like to you, and you to me?"

Differences in the rights each tradition emphasizes, therefore, rest, at least in part, upon differences in the shape of the community which each tradition envisions its characteristic form of human communality to promise. It should be noted, however, that even with these differences the concept of human dignity has an essential function in each tradition's interpretation of the significance of the community promised in our communality: for each the community promised is one in which we are to find the conditions which secure human dignity in its fullness. For the liberal tradition, the community which secures human dignity is one of full autonomy for each individual; for the Marxist tradition, it is one in which human productive sociality is fully expressed, even and especially in the exercise of individual human self-determination; for the Catholic tradition, it is one in which human dignity's source in God's creative and redemptive love is acknowledged in all the expressions of our sociality and of our autonomy.

Various connections can be drawn between the way each tradition envisions human communality, human community, and the particular understanding it offers of human dignity. Here we once more find the Marxist and Catholic traditions diverging from the liberal tradition by providing a more extensive base for human dignity in social and historical considerations. This more extensive base is important in the search for procedures to unify the diverse concerns each tradition has for rights; it provides a way of making our likeness in vulnerability an important feature of the status of human persons upon which we can build a foundation for human rights.

Each tradition's image of human communality is offered in the hope that it has the power to affect conduct. Once I acknowledge you as like to me, and myself as like to you, I cannot pass you by as I might have done before such acknowledgment; nor can I deal with you without now taking into account our likeness. Consistent failure of such acknowledgments of human likeness to affect conduct makes for amorality.

Each tradition's image of human community is also offered in the hope that it has the power to affect our conduct. These images provide ways for us to go on together from the acknowledgment of our human likeness, ways to venture together into the moral future. The images of human community which each tradition provides can thus function as ideals, for human community is the abiding condition of human existence which our thinking and conduct seek to bring about.

Utopian literature provides many instances of sustained efforts at envisioning a moral future. Whatever we may think of particular forms of utopia, the effort to imagine them is important for understanding how each tradition's images of community provide a foundation for practices to secure human rights: how we conduct ourselves now can be illuminated and, perhaps, even improved, by imagining what we can, will, or should be. This imagining of what we can be in the future must nonetheless have an anchor in what we are now and what we have been in the past. The way each tradition envisions the moral future serves to place in bold perspective what it takes to be the fundamental elements of human existence, and hence its particular form of concern for human rights.

In the liberal tradition, for instance, freedom, imaged most often as the exercise of individual self-determination, is fundamental for constituting the human dignity which is to be secured by the protection of rights. Given the liberal tradition's prevailing image of freedom, it is by no means surprising that the practices it takes to secure such protection focus upon the exercise of choice. The liberal tradition will therefore offer protection to practices and institutions which offer areas for the exercise of choice: e.g., democratic polity, the competitive market. It will justify placing constraints on such practices when they begin to limit, or fail to enhance, the range of choice: thus the liberal tradition can be moved to act against monopoly in the market place and disenfranchisement in the polity, and to establish the institution of the welfare state.

When the liberal tradition envisions the moral future, however, a thinness in its picture of what we are and have been becomes apparent. This thinness is most notable in a failure to provide an adequate picture of the intrinsic relation between freedom and the social character and context of human life. It offers no positive characterization of the moral import of the human good served by practices expressive of the social character of human life—e.g., family, education, art, religion—beyond their instrumentality for purposes of more extensive individual self-determination. The liberal tradition acknowledges that the social context and character of human life is needed (in most cases) for the attainment of the particular goods which an individual seeks in his or her self-determination. This requires freedom to take on a social character which, at least in the more austere forms of the liberal tradition's moral theory, it does not intrinsically possess. The liberal tradition can, as a result, find itself boxed into a form of moral Cartesianism: human community cannot be taken as a given feature at the foundation of moral living; it must be argued to, and argued to on the basis of its service of the interest of freedom in individual self-determination.

For the Catholic and Marxist traditions, a social character does not merely accrue to the elements of human existence which constitute human dignity; it is fundamental to the establishment of that dignity. This becomes clear, for instance, in the Catholic tradition's understanding of the past which makes us what we are and promises what we are to be. According to that account, dignity is ours in virtue of our creation in God's image and likeness. The social character of that image and likeness and the dignity it founds can be marked out in at least two reflective considerations, in the spirit of Catholic theology, upon this story of human origins: God's inner life, communicated as image and likeness, is one which the revelation of God as Trinity affirms to be intrinsically social; the judgment expressed in the words of Genesis 2:18, "It is not good for the man to be alone," can be justifiably given the gloss: "For a man alone fails to be human." [15]

For the Catholic tradition, therefore, human community takes shape from a communality of origin as God's creation in his image and likeness. One strand of Catholic tradition, moreover, takes human freedom as a central element of that likeness; it is thus possible for the Catholic tradition to share the liberal tradition's concern for securing conditions for the exercise of human freedom. Concern for freedom, however, is placed in the context of another human communality which the Catholic tradition also takes to be fundamental to the constitution of human dignity: the destiny of being called to share in a life which is God's own. As a result, the Catholic tradition interprets the conditions for the exercise of human freedom in terms which manifest this concern for human destiny: the conditions which are to be established for the exercise of freedom are those which make it possible for each and all to hear the call to this destiny of life and to go on to it.

The Catholic tradition, ironically enough, has not always made it clear that going on to this human destiny of life is a going on together; it has not always given full weight to the social character of this destiny. In consequence, it has not been particularly clear about the bearing this destiny might have upon the shape which we now can or should give to human social practices and institutions. Insofar as it has allowed its picture of human destiny to become privatized under the impact of the atomizing forces of contemporary culture, it has helped foster practices by which persons can become inured or oblivious to the role which social conditions play in securing the elements of human existence essential for full human dignity.

The Marxist tradition is clear that going on to the human destiny it envisions is a going on together.[16] Human community takes shape from the solidarity of human consciousness both of and in productive labor. As in the Catholic tradition, a social character does not merely accrue to the elements of human existence which constitute human dignity, but is inherent in them. For the Marxist tradition, human dignity is enhanced in proportion to one's consciousness of the social character of its bases. This tradition takes the social bases for human dignity to be so fundamental that it precludes acknowledging and pressing for what may be conceived of as "rights" independent of them. This is the conceptual ground for the Marxist tradition's rejection of the liberal understanding of political rights: these "rights" do not derive from consciousness of the social bases of human dignity: moreover, the practices in which they are exercised serve to block consciousness of our human sociality by enabling us to press claims which are merely individual in the interests they represent.

The Marxist tradition envisions human community taking its shape from the solidarity of human consciousness of and in productive labor. It therefore envisions the moral future as one in which all the products of human labor are given their shape and function in full consciousness of such solidarity. As a result, the fundamental moral categories of the Marxist tradition bear upon the consciousness of such solidarity and the attainment of the future which it promises and shapes. Within these categories, rights may be conceived as claims made in behalf of the achievement of consciousness of solidarity. The content of these claims—the social conditions of human productive labor—differs from the content of claims made on behalf of autonomy—the conditions of individual self-determination—or on behalf of a human destiny to share in God's life—the conditions of hearing and heeding God's call to this destiny.

Although these claims, which make concrete each tradition's particular concern for rights, differ considerably in content, some of the concrete conditions they require for their satisfaction nonetheless overlap. This conclusion, which gives hope to efforts to construct a normative theory of human rights unifying the concerns of the three traditions of liberalism, Marxism, and Catholicism, is one for which we can draw support from the experience of organizations and individuals who, especially since the end of the Second World War, have been promoting the observance of certain human rights claims. Torture, detention apart from public judicial procedures, systematic suppression even of the possibility of voicing grievances—each of these practices destroys conditions essential to securing human dignity, whether we conceive of that dignity as ordered to individual self-determination, to consciousness of solidarity in human productive labor, or to a destiny of sharing in God's life. The mobilization of international public opinion, which these organizations have accomplished in order to promote action to abolish these practices, has, perhaps, tapped into an imaginative resource basic to the normative theory of human rights we aspire to fashion. This resource is one which is present, though not yet fully manifest or articulated in each of the traditions we have been considering. Each tradition, in its own way, has the power to make manifest that human communality which has been basic to these organizations' impact upon our public awareness of human rights: our likeness to each other in vulnerability.

It should be noted that this mobilization of opinion has occurred despite the fact that awareness of our human communality in vulnerability does not always move us to secure rights, particularly the rights of others. We have little doubt of our own susceptibility to harm and hurt; we are often less sure that we individually have the power to reduce or to eliminate particular kinds of susceptibility to harm. Reliance upon one another provides a surer base for power to deal with certain kinds of our vulnerabilities. [17] There are, moreover, times and circumstances when the power which a particular group acquires to reduce or to eliminate its liability to particular kinds of harm appears to require an increased liability to harm for a few within the group or for others outside of it. When power is exercised in accord with this judgment, it fosters beliefs and practices which enable us, even in the face of another's vulnerability, to circumscribe or to sever links of human interdependence. In the United States, for instance, we have developed a network of beliefs and practices which enable us to circumscribe, in a most curious way, the links between economic practices and the forms of our domestic polity which affect the vulnerabilities of those outside the country. On the one hand, we have generally been willing to accept uncritically the belief that maintenance of our domestic political institutions and civil liberties is tied to the continued successful operation of the institutions of free-enterprise capitalism; on the other hand, we have ignored what now appears as the clear possibility that the fitful operation and frequent failure of comparable civil and political institutions in Latin America to secure even minimal protection of rights we take for granted, may be the result of these same economic institutions. [18] Because we are only selectively aware of the dimensions of our human interdependence, we fail to be alert to ways in which conditions which reduce our susceptibility to harm may be sustaining conditions causing harm to others.

We are like to each other in our vulnerability; we should have heightened awareness of this likeness in view of our interdependence. Our communality in vulnerability presents a challenge to moral imagination as it is concretely exercised in the way each of the traditions pictures our human interdependence, particularly in the form of community. In our likeness to one another in vulnerability, imagination must be powerful enough to see a promise of community: even though we are susceptible to harm and to hurt, particularly at one another's hands, it must still be possible to fashion ways to live, and even to live well, with one another. Each tradition's capacity to establish and promote practices which sustain human dignity can be read as a response to this challenge.

The liberal tradition has often been the least sanguine in the promise of community it sees in our vulnerability; at the same time, it has the most circumscribed view of our vulnerabilities. It envisions our principal vulnerability to be the threat of a limitation or loss of freedom. It envisions the moral future in terms which make the way of our living well together the minimal procedural constraints that we need to place, in the interest of freedom, upon the undertaking of action. Though we may hope for more of the moral future than just those fair procedures which will help us resolve the clashes which must inevitably result from allowing the widest possible play to be given to individual self-determination, we must have at least these procedures if there is to be a moral future at all.

One advantage of this slender picture of the moral order is that it emphasizes the present need for placing procedural constraints on the undertaking of action in the interest of freedom. [19] The liberal tradition thus takes human vulnerability which is made manifest in our communality of freedom to hold out a promise of community, in the form of institutions and procedures protective of freedom. The liberal tradition recognizes that these institutions and practices may leave us vulnerable elsewhere, but judges that price worth paying to attain this moral future of a community of freedom.

The Marxist tradition is the most sanguine. It locates our principal vulnerability in our fundamental human sociality. The greatest dangers to the human character of our existence lie in practices which separate us from consciousness of one another, especially in the productive activity of our labor. Loss of this consciousness allows us to promote, ignore, or endure conditions by which we are harmed in more particular vulnerabilities. The vulnerability of our consciousness of sociality, nonetheless, holds out a promise of community; this promise can be redeemed through practices which exhibit the human solidarity fundamental to productive activity. Establishment of these practices is possible through the historical process in which human persons together fashion their true nature, both in individuality and in solidarity, by the conscious transformation of their productive labor. These practices are expected, in the long run, to eliminate the full range of social conditions which make us susceptible to harm. The process of establishing these practices may, nonetheless, inflict harm on those outside or resistant to it; the Marxist tradition judges the price acceptable in order to overcome the denial in practice of human solidarity and to attain the moral future of a community of full human solidarity.

The Catholic tradition is sanguine about redeeming the promise of a community of life promised to our human vulnerability; it is not sanguine about our unassisted power to redeem this promise. In comparison to the Marxist and liberal traditions, moreover, it has a larger stock of imaginative resources with which to characterize our vulnerabilities. It envisions our most fundamental vulnerability as sin, or the loss of that life which is a sharing in God's own life; each of our more particular vulnerabilities stands in a complex relation to this fundamental one, since particular harms to which we may be vulnerable need not make us also vulnerable to the loss of a sharing in God's life. To this extent the Catholic tradition leaves room for the possibility of renouncing one's rights. Recently, the Catholic tradition has seen with increased clarity how the social contexts which make it possible for harm to be inflicted upon our particular vulnerabilities make us more vulnerable as well to the loss of a sharing in God's life. These social contexts foster despair in the possibility of any sharing of life, let alone God's life.

The formulations of Catholic social teaching enunciated in papal and conciliar statements in the past 80 years have increasingly framed a vision of the moral future of a community of life through concepts and images of interdependence. This interdependence is not conceived as a debilitating mark of finitude, nor as a limitation to be overcome with the fulfillment of human destiny. It is envisioned rather as characteristically human, and as a gift from God with an abiding role to play in human existence as it ventures into the future. It is a sign of hope in the possibility of a sharing of life, imaging, indeed, God's own sharing of his life. [20]

The concerns which the liberal, Marxist, and Catholic traditions have for establishing and fostering human dignity are most characteristically expressed in their images of human communality and human community. The path to a unification of these concerns in a normative moral theory of rights, therefore, may well have to be first marked out by imagination. To do so, it will have to fashion images of our human origin, communality, and destiny which will be inclusive of these concerns— freedom, solidarity, and the sharing of life. Such images, were we bold enough to form them, would provide a foundation upon which we could fashion a comprehensive theory of human rights. Of even greater importance is the hope such images could provide to those who are aware, through pain and hurt, of their present vulnerabilities. These images can provide hope for making a deepened sense of our dependence upon one another an engine for action: these images have power to make us bold enough to acknowledge another's vulnerability as our own and to work together to secure conditions which protect us each and all.

NOTES TO CHAPTER 8

1. See, however, the second part of Thomas Clarke's chapter "On the Need to Break Bread Together,", which employs categories of myth and story to explore dimensions of the imaging of human community in the sharing of food and drink.

2. For a more extended account of moral imagination, see my "Moral Imagination and the Narrative Modes of Moral Discourse," *Renascence* 31 (1979), pp. 131–141, and "Moral Imagination and Moral Interest in Kant," *The Modern Schoolman* (forthcoming).

3. See, for instance, Chap. 5, section iv of this volume; David Hollenbach, *Claims in Conflict* (New York: Paulist Press, 1979), pp. 89–100; and the beginning of Chap. 1 and of Chap. 4 of this volume.

4. See beginning of Chap. 4.

5. Immanuel Kant, *Groundwork of the Metaphysic of Morals,* trans. H. J. Paton (New York: Harper & Row Torchbooks, 1964), pp. 104–108. The interpretation one gives to the term "rational" is crucial to the proper understanding of Kant's account of the relation of autonomy to our dignity as persons. I suspect that at the root of the problem which the liberal tradition has in reconciling freedom with the positive shaping of a common good in community is an understanding of "rational" which pays little heed to the communality presupposed in its exercise.

6. John Rawls, *A Theory of Justice,* (Cambridge, Mass.: Harvard University Press, 1971) offers a notable example of a systematic philosophical elaboration of such a transformation of interest.

7. *Religion within the Limits of Reason Alone,* trans. Theodore M. Greene and Hoyt H. Hudson (New York: Harper & Row Torchbooks, 1960), pp. 88–91.

8. See Hollenbach, *Claims in Conflict,* pp. 45–46; Chap. 5, section VII.

9. See Hollenbach, *Claims in Conflict,* pp. 20–24, 45.

10. Chap. 5, section VIII.

11. Hollenbach, *Claims in Conflict,* pp. 92–93.

12. Hollenbach, *Claims in Conflict,* p. 64; in this volume, Chap. 3, section I 3 c.

13. Such an appeal seems basic to the conceptual structure of "national security" ideologies; see Margaret E. Crahan, "National Security Doctrine and Human Rights in Latin America: The Southern Cone," in *Human Rights and Basic Needs in the Americas,* Chap. 3, section I.

14. 1 Cor 8:1–13.

15. See Hollenbach, *Claims in Conflict,* pp. 43, 126–127.

16. See Chap. 5, section II.

17. An important form of the liberal tradition makes this reliance upon one another, rather than our imaging of God, or our solidarity in productive activity, the central motif of its "story" of human communality, mutuality, and community. That story is "social contract."

18. The linkage between the performance of economic practices and institutions in supplying the basic needs of a nation's populace and the ability of that nation's political practices and institutions to secure and protect human rights deserves intensive investigation. Chap. 11 of this volume and Chap. 6 of the companion volume suggest that the failure of international economic practices shaped by market and profit considerations to supply adequately the basic needs of large sectors of the populace in developing countries perpetuates social conditions which hinder the establishment and working of participatory institutions. The "social analysis" characteristic of Latin American theology focuses upon this linkage; see Chaps. 2 and 3 of this volume.

19. Chap. 4 section II indicates concretely how this can function advantageously in fostering practices which secure rights.

20. Hollenbach, *Claims in Conflict,* pp. 95–96.

HERNAN MONTEALEGRE

9. The Security of the State and Human Rights

The prominent position which human rights hold in our modern societies becomes clearly evident during those periods when a severe crisis forces a state to define its own deepest identity in order to surmount the crisis. [1] This is the lesson of the contemporary attempt to understand many Latin American states in the light of a new doctrine, that of national security, [2] which includes the disavowal and violation of fundamental human rights as one of its basic characteristics. The illegitimacy of this practice, along with the strength and particular nature of human rights, becomes obvious when one accepts the challenge of the problem of state security, confronting it directly rather than avoiding it.

In the context of the Americas as well as on a global level, an urgent need has arisen to seek solutions for the opposition which some seek to establish between national or international human rights and state security, and also to make clear their true relationship. In the following pages, an attempt will be made to do this from a legal perspective. However, although this perspective is always necessary in discussing human rights, it cannot be used exclusively, since the development of the legal perspective goes beyond law itself and affects other areas, such as politics, economics, society, morality, and religion. It is, then, a basic and necessary perspective, which can provide a coherent, interdisciplinary approach to the problem.

In Latin America today it is a fact that various governments have instituted states of siege, states of emergency, and other exceptional legislation as a way of controlling their societies. To justify this, they propose arguments based on the security of the state, which is said to be in severe jeopardy. Such a pessimistic analysis has led recent governments to adopt the extraordinary means established by law to confront dangers to public order: declaration of a national state of war, indictment of citizens on the charge of treason, and attribution of the legal status of enemies of the state to certain persons or organizations in the nation. This has resulted in an unprecedented application of traditional provisions of the legal system, which hitherto had only been employed in cases of actual war between states.

Nevertheless, this application of the traditional provisions, which were in fact contained in the Latin American juridical codes, has been hasty and certainly illegal, since the circumstances which led to their implementation are not those foreseen by the codes. Moreover, important new elements of international law have not been utilized, although they were designed for just such circumstances. The continuance of this anomalous situation thus requires a detailed study of the questions it has raised.

The juridical study of state security must include the contributions both of traditional law and modern law. While traditional law represents the existing juridical order in an incomplete manner, the modifications which modern law has introduced can only be understood in relation to the traditional law from which it evolved. Both stages of law, and particularly the basic relationship between them, have received little or no development in our countries, thus giving rise to a vacuum in an area that is vital for Latin America today.

The distinction between a traditional law and a modern law as regards state security is based on the differing perspective from which each one considers the problem. In the cases of war and of insurrection, traditional law interprets state security from the standpoint of the legal concept of external or internal war. In the case of an external attack, the law of nations granted to states an unlimited power to have recourse to war. Once war began, explicit norms regulated the conduct of hostilities by placing limits on the use of force. With regard to internal conflict, the determining factor for law was to establish the objective limits within which, according to the gravity of the situation, exceptional and specific powers were granted to the authorities to overcome the danger to the nation. But the internal conflict itself was considered to be a matter of concern only for the state involved. Moreover, the law benefited established governments, since it allowed them to seek the aid of other countries for a favorable resolution of the internal problems which threatened their stability.

The conditions of the modern world have brought states to a different appraisal of these problems. An international society that is profoundly interdependent and subject to immense risks (which could not have been foreseen through the traditional prism) cannot look upon external wars as matters of interest merely to the contending parties, who would make their own decisions regarding problems of security.

And it cannot fail to take account of the fact that internal conflicts, given certain specific conditions, do have international repercussions. The traditional idea of security as an isolated question that is the exclusive bilateral responsibility of the parties having recourse to force or the sole internal responsibility of the state affected, has been changed in its basic presuppositions and has been replaced by a notion of security that has universal and indivisible characteristics. From this new perspective, any war and any significant recourse to force constitute to some extent a threat against the global system of international security.

In particular, after the experience of the Second World War, law not only opted for the prohibition of war but also laid the foundations for becoming an instrument to eliminate its causes. The Charter of the United Nations, which forms the basis of the modern law of nations, was influenced in its elaboration by the specific causes that led to the Second World War. For the authors and signatories of the Charter, these causes had their roots in totalitarian regimes, whose most distinctive feature was total disregard for the dignity of the human person and his or her fundamental rights. Eliminating collective violations of human rights is, according to the United Nations Charter, a question of prime importance for international security. In this way, also, the new law of nations no longer treats the a priori favoring of established governments as a factor contributing to security; rather, it sees that in certain cases it clearly promotes insecurity. The recognition of a people's right to free determination is another essential element, for it has resulted in a more objective outlook with regard to internal conflicts where traditional law had favored established governments.

This process has resulted in bringing government itself before the law when it becomes a cause of insecurity. The admission of this possibility, now incorporated into law, uncovers a whole new dimension which requires an overall reformulation of state security in the present juridical context.

I. THE PARTICULAR SECURITY OF THE CONSTITUENT ELEMENTS OF THE STATE

A synthesis between traditional law and modern law can be achieved by looking at both from the perspective of the constituent elements of the state, as these are treated by international law.

A state is composed of three constituent elements: its territory, its inhabitants, and its government. Without any one of these elements, the reality of a state does not exist; on the other hand, they suffice for a state to exist. Certainly also, the problem of state security concerns the totality of its constituent elements. Under the law, a state is secure when it relies upon a juridical system which is able to react effectively and coherently against threats to each of its constituent elements.

Threats to these elements can arise from outside or from within the state. The most serious external threat, that of war, is basically directed against the territory of the state. From within, its security is threatened first of all (considering the most serious threat) by insurrection, which breaks out among the inhabitants and is directed against the government. Thus external war and internal insurrection are in fact the two factors which law has traditionally considered to be threats to the security of a state. The modern development of law, however, demonstrates that the internal version of this viewpoint is incomplete and that it must be integrated with the threat which can arise from the other constituent element of the state: the government. It is certainly illogical (and historical events have substantiated this) to suppose that only one of the two active elements which constitute a state, namely, the inhabitants, can threaten the security of the other one, while the government itself cannot become a threat to the inhabitants.

In our time it is clear as a matter of law that a government which systematically violates the human rights of its citizens is a threat to the security of that state. Thus it is necessary to distinguish between the internal threat to a state that comes from its base, that is, an insurrection, and the internal threat that comes from the top, that is, the violation of the human rights of its inhabitants. Both of these constitute a subversion of the state, launched from either one of its internal poles. It is only in this way that we can obtain a complete picture of the problems involved in state security, as well as a proof of the substantial unity which exists between traditional law and modern law.

The security of a state lies in its ability to affirm its fundamental identity in time and in space. To achieve this, the state must juridically protect the basic identity of each of its constituent elements. From this perspective, a state is secure when each one of its constituent elements is secure. For the territory, security consists in its *integrity;* for the government, in its *stability;* for the inhabitants, in the *inviolability* of their fundamental human rights. Thus a state is secure when it can provide juridical protection for the integrity of its territory, for the stability of its government, and for the inviolability of the human rights of its inhabitants; these are threatened respectively by war, by insurrection, and by the violation of human rights.

II. THE GENERAL SECURITY OF THE STATE

The question of the security of the elements of a state taken separately is only the first indispensable level of analysis in this matter. What the law must determine precisely is the synthesis of those particular aspects within a system of general juridical security, a system which will guarantee the state's unity and harmony. To achieve this, the three particular aspects of security must be integrated within a coherent juridical system, that is, one which can coordinate them in the light of the different situations which are possible.

In normal times, when the security of the state is not actually threatened, the legal order must provide preventive means to avoid the threats I have mentioned. In a time of crisis, the state must adopt a posture of active defense in order to reaffirm its integrity, stability, and inviolability. The defense, however, must take place in such a way that the general security, that is, the totality of its constituent elements, is reaffirmed. The partial and isolated defense of one of its aspects, e.g., the stability of the government, can result in the weakening of another, e.g., the inviolability of the human rights of the inhabitants, which results in the introduction of a factor of insecurity for the state. Thus the threat to one element of the state must be faced not from a merely partial perspective but rather from one that takes all the interests of state security into account.

None of the elements of the state can claim to represent it totally, as if the element were defending the general interest of the state by absolutizing itself. This is impossible, since none of the elements by itself exhausts the meaning of the state, while on the other hand none can become a consituent element of the state without being complemented by the others. The attempt of one element to absolutize itself within the state is a subversion of the state, which culminates in either insurrection or the systematic violation of human rights, depending on whether the attempt comes from the base or from the top. Thus the juridical regulation of security must clearly establish the instances of coordination and subordination among the different aspects of state security, so that this may be affirmed in a unified manner.

The coherence of the juridical system of state security becomes especially necessary in a time of crisis, since every direct threat to one of the elements affects the others, at least indirectly. War, which strictly speaking threatens the territory, also introduces a factor of insecurity for the government and the inhabitants. Insurrection, whose objective is to overthrow the government, also threatens the inhabitants and may threaten the territory if it is a secessionist movement. The violation of human rights, which is directed against the inhabitants, becomes a danger for the government's own security, since it incites internal action against the government. Moreover, when the violation is widespread it becomes a threat to international peace and security, and other states that are affected may feel impelled to act against the culpable state. This complex and broad view of the threats to each one of the state's constituent elements emphasizes their character as threats to state security as such. At the same time, it accentuates the need for a general and coherent defense of state security when one of the elements is specifically threatened.

In the case of war, the legal regulation of security grants exceptional powers to states to defend their territorial integrity (which at the same time strengthens the stability of their governments). This is accomplished by means of the internal and international norms of the law of war, which permit the use of force against the enemy and the punishment as traitors of citizens who attack the state's security. Furthermore, human rights are also explicitly protected in war by means of norms which limit the use of force and punish war crimes. Both aspects of the law of war are equally necessary to protect the integral security of states threatened by war.

In the case of insurrection, the government defends its own security and that of the state in general by exercising exceptional constitutional powers and applying sanctions against the rebels. Human rights are also protected, because their suspension is permitted only within boundaries previously established by constitutions and by relevent international agreements. On the other hand, the traditional legal order protects rebelling inhabitants when they fulfill the conditions to be recognized as belligerents, while modern law protects them by means of the norms of international humanitarian law, the right of free determination (when applicable), and human rights.

As regards the violation of human rights, the inhabitants are protected by the juridical order when it condemns such practices as crimes and judges that the government which resorts to them is dangerous to the state. Consequently, it provides the inhabitants with the right to resist the government in the terms used by the Universal Declaration of Human Rights: "It is essential, if man is not to be compelled, as a last resort, to rebellion against tyranny and oppression, that human rights should be protected by the rule of law" (Preamble, Paragraph 3). The international standing which has been given to human rights is an attempt to correct the weak position of the inhabitants vis-à-vis a government that violates their rights. The specific link which law establishes between this situation and international security contributes to the recovery of a just internal order. As a result, it contributes to the strengthening of the security of each element of the state, including the stability of a government which respects the human rights of its citizens.

The interdependence established by the juridical order between internal peace and security and international peace and security has been justly enforced by international organizations such as the United Nations. This implies a rejection of all unilateral state intervention, which would constitute a factor leading to insecurity. It is also an aspect of law which brings into question every extreme use of force, external or internal, so that the general security of states may be enhanced.

III. THE LEGITIMATE DEFENSE OF THE SECURITY OF THE STATE

Aggressive war, insurrection, and the violation of human rights are the most serious instances in which the state can be the victim of an illegitimate attack by force. What ultimately threatens security is such an illegitimate recourse, external or internal, against any of the state's constitutive elements.

The ultimate reaction of the law when confronted with an illegitimate attack by force against the state consists in the right to resort legitimately to the use of force. The recourse to force is illegitimate under law insofar as it consists in aggression, while it is legitimate when used for defense. When facing horizontal aggression (war), ascending aggression (insurrection), or descending aggression (violation of human rights), the state is authorized to respond with force as a last resort. But the defense which the law permits is only "legitimate" defense.

This introduces a structural factor in every legitimate use of force which consists in its *proportionality*. If the defense against aggression involves an action that is clearly disproportionate, this obvious excess in the use of force becomes a form of aggression in its own right. Thus it is not sufficient to call upon a previous aggression in order to justify the use of force on the part of a state; it is necessary to prove that the response is proportional in the present circumstances. The law is categorical both in condemning aggression and in regulating the responses to it in different circumstances. An unlimited right to the use of force does not exist. When the prohibition of initial recourse to force is not observed and force is unleashed, the law steps in to curtail its further development. By performing this function, the legal order becomes an indispensable factor in security, because it protects the state in every direction from which it can be attacked by unjustified violence. In effect, when force surpasses the level of legitimate defense, this excess aggravates the problems of state security.

Wars in which the use of force is absolutized, i.e., "total wars," redound against the security of the states which launch them. Such was the case of Germany in the Second World War, when no peace terms were considered acceptable except those based on its "unconditional surrender." On the other hand, while only the aggressor state commits a crime against peace by launching a war of aggression, the excesses in the use of force during the war itself are judged to be war crimes, whether they are committed by the aggressor state or by the state acting in legitimate self-defense. Governments also do not possess an unlimited right to use force against insurrections (which are ascending aggressions), but rather can only repress them according to the principle of legitimate defense of the state. If, in order to crush an insurrection, the government systematically violates the human rights of any sector of its citizens, it exceeds the boundaries of legitimate defense and becomes for its part a threat to the security of the state. In this way it aggravates the insecurity of the state and places its inhabitants between the double dangers of ascending aggression and descending aggression. It is not legitimate either that the resistance of the inhabitants to some violation of their human rights by the government consist in collective recourse to force, whether or not this is preceded by a rebellion. But recourse to force is justified as a legitimate defense of the state when it is a question of an extensive and systematic violation which affects particularly the rights to life, to personal integrity, and to liberty of the inhabitants. [3]

IV. THE VIOLATION OF HUMAN RIGHTS AS A THREAT TO THE SECURITY OF THE STATE

In those states that have committed themselves by international agreements to respect human rights, it is the government as the international representative of the state that is directly responsible before the community of nations for the observance of human rights. Constitutions, moreover, impose on the authorities the specific duty of insuring such rights for all the inhabitants. Thus, public authorities are the proper subject of the internal and international obligation of insuring the observance of human rights within a state. The position and influence of a government are a distinctive element within a state. Because of this, if a government engages in a systematic violation of human rights, then it not only commits particular crimes against the persons harmed but also attacks the very security of the state itself.

While certain acts of particular individuals can of course affect the human rights of other persons, it is only with respect to crimes of war, genocide, and crimes against humanity that there is a transgression of an international obligation that is specifically related to human rights. On the other hand, the attack on the internal security of the state takes place because of the government's indirect fostering of insurrection. The government alone is in a position to threaten state security specifically by means of the systematic violation of human rights. The violation of human rights is a threat to state security because of the direct effects which it produces and also because of the internal and external response which it provokes.

By its direct effects, the violation of human rights attacks the security of one of the constituent elements of the state, that is, the inhabitants. To take the most serious cases, systematic attacks on the right to life, to the integrity of the person, to residence in one's own country, to freedom of expression and association, to participation in government, mean in effect persons murdered or tortured, prisoners, exiles, and people suffering from general oppression; in other words, it is a picture similar to that produced by a war or insurrection. Furthermore, the systematic violation of human rights entails the destruction of public institutions, if not materially, then certainly with regard to their proper functioning. This is caused by the concentration of public power in the hands of the executive power, which makes any division of powers a merely apparent one that varies according to different circumstances. The inhabitants cannot rely on the basic guarantee of their security, that is, a proper system of checks and balances among the public powers. Both the inhabitants and the constitutional and institutional system in which they express their identity are directly crushed by a government which attacks and controls the state by force through a systematic and massive violation of human rights.

Secondly, the collective violation of human rights threatens the security of the state, insofar as it leads the inhabitants to react against a government whose criminal acts are destructive of national identity. The Universal Declaration of Human Rights recognizes that this situation "compels" the person "to have recourse, as a last resort, to rebellion" (Preamble, Paragraph 3). This means that the violation of human rights introduces into a state a structural factor of "rebellion," which flows over onto the security of the government itself and increases the insecurity of the state.

Thirdly, the violation of human rights in a state is considered by international law to be a threat to international peace and security. This negative international repercussion also affects state security. For other states that feel they are affected by the violation react against the offending state, above all by isolating it morally and politically, which results in the weakening of its international position. [4]

V. INTERNAL POWERS WHICH THREATEN HUMAN RIGHTS

The question of human rights is located within the broad theme of the relations between the individual and society. The purpose of human rights is to achieve the survival and development of the human person in the midst of the powers of society. In their natural functioning, these powers tend to absorb the individual and to manipulate him or her within their abstract mechanisms. They do this without sufficient consideration of the fact that their activity should take into account the sphere in which they operate, that is, the sphere of human persons. Human rights establish that vital area which cannot be invaded by other social actors, so that the person may not be harmed by the social process. From a historical perspective, the most urgent juridical defense which the person has had to undertake vis-à-vis the powers of society has been in relation to the government of a state. But in its full sense there is no doubt that the intent of human rights is the protection of the person faced with the excessive power of any or all of the social actors. In this juridical vindication of the person we must distinguish the following four historical situations, which are identified by the social powers which were felt to be most threatening at the time: kings, governing groups within constitutional states, modern antidemocratic regimes, and the new structural powers of the modern world.

1) The initial historical moment of the legal development which human rights have achieved in the West must be located in the acceptance by medieval monarchs of limitations on their absolute power with regard to specific social groups. This is found in the English Magna Carta of 1215, especially in clause 39, which proclaims the recourse to habeas corpus in the following terms: "No free man will be arrested or detained in prison, or deprived of his goods, proscribed or exiled, or molested in any way; and we will not pass judgment on him or place him in prison, except by a legal judgment of his peers or by the law of the land." From the same period come different civil statutes that were obtained in different parts of Europe from monarchs such as Alfonso IX of León, Andrew II of Hungary, and Peter III of Aragón.

2) The second historical stage is marked by declarations on the rights of man at the end of the eighteenth century and by their general incorporation into state constitutions in the nineteenth and early twentieth centuries. Their purpose was to defend the individual not from the permanent power of the kings but from the transient power of the groups who control the government of the state at any period under the new constitutional systems. Whereas previously the person protected himself from the absolute sovereignty of the king, now the protection was

from the absolute power of the people as invoked by successive governments. The specific human person was reaffirmed as an irreducible end of the political organization of the nation.

3) Regimes have arisen in the twentieth century which destroy constitutional democratic systems and assume extraordinary powers, demanding a radical and total submission of the individual to their designs. Examples of this include the totalitarian and fascist regimes which initiated the Second World War. This type of regime poses the problem of human rights in its most acute form. And it also leads to the conviction that the internal recognition of rights must be accompanied by international recognition as a complementary method for defense of the person confronted with governments that violate fundamental human rights. The person thus acquires an international status and is defended in his or her fundamental rights against the deviations of his or her own state. This problem is posed again in our own day with the appearance of new antidemocratic regimes in various countries, particularly in Latin America.

4) But especially today the person is confronted by social powers different from the state which try to transform him or her into a cog serving their collective interests. Examples include the huge economic and technological consortia, national and international, which form part of the structure of the modern world and which in vital areas are opposed to the enforcement of human rights. In the perspective of the present article, these powers can attack the security of a state not only by affecting the human rights of its inhabitants, but also by becoming agents of insurrection and war.

As has been noted previously, both the internal and the international juridical order have imposed on public authorities the specific responsibility of ensuring the protection of human rights.[5] Since governments are precisely that social power which has been historically identified as the principal threat to human rights, the obligation imposed on them is an indispensable means to control or annul such a threat. The internal and international establishment of this obligation, as well as the prominent place which human rights hold in the juridical order, imply that the attitude which a government takes regarding rights decides its legitimacy within a state. This is all the more true if the state's eventual failure to fulfill the obligation consists not merely in leaving its citizens unprotected, but even in becoming itself the direct and systematic violator of the human rights of the population of the state. Thus the power that is traditionally the greatest threat to the enforcement of human rights now at least has no way of hiding its offense with impunity before the law.

The fact that human rights are the primordial values in a contemporary state is shown by the way they are described when they are incorporated into positive law. They are said to be inviolable, prior to and superior to the state. In fact, no other element of the juridical order receives such an evaluation. Moreover, it is this very preeminence which is often invoked, apart from their importance for peace and security, to justify their international protection. Thus the American Convention on Human Rights declares that they "do not derive from the fact of being a citizen of a definite state but have as their foundation the attributes of the human person, because of which they deserve international protection of a contractual nature to help or complement what is provided by the internal law of the American states" (Preamble, Paragraph 3).

The basic social agreement within a state to make human rights the touchstone for judging the legitimacy of the actions of the public powers (and ultimately of the public powers themselves) conditions all dimensions of the public sphere. Explicitly among these is the government's role in providing general security for the country.

The security of the state lies in its ability to maintain the integrity of those elements which constitute it. In other words, a state is secure when it is capable of affirming and defending its fundamental identity in time and space. Economic, political, and social models can and sometimes must change, without thus changing the "fundamental" identity of the state. Furthermore, a state really sure of itself permits these changes to happen without serious dislocations, since they demonstrate the dynamism and historical vitality of the basic goals of the state. From this point of view, the prominent position which human rights occupy in the internal and international juridical order makes them a key issue for the "fundamental" identity of a contemporary state. This means that a state is secure only to the extent that it is capable of affirming and defending the human rights of its citizens.

A complete concept of security cannot be limited to the objective of territorial defense and even less to that of the stability of the state's government. Territory and government are only part of the elements that make up a state. The other essential element is the population or inhabitants, who today are considered, both internally and internationally, to be entitled to inviolable human rights. As has been mentioned earlier, three concurrent aspects of the security of the state must be distinguished: the integrity of its territory, the stability of its government, and the inviolability of the human rights of all its inhabitants. In the present case, the security of a government cannot be identified with the security of the state; more specifically, a government cannot establish its security at the expense of the human rights of the inhabitants of the state, that is, at the expense of the insecurity of another element of the state. Thus there arises a question of capital importance: internally speaking, state security can be endangered not only by some or all of the inhabitants, but also by the government itself. Subversion from the top must be added to subversion from the base in order to obtain a complete picture of the possible internal threats to the security of a state. Dictatorship, which is the most serious form of this subversion from the top, threatens the security of the state in a way analogous to insurrection and war.

VI. HUMAN RIGHTS IN THE CHARTER OF THE UNITED NATIONS

The Charter of the United Nations is not an academic proclamation elaborated in the abstract, but rather it is a document with a specific origin and historical meaning. It derives from a concrete experience, and is a particular reaction to that experience. Its antecedents do not lie in the question of war in general but rather of the Second World War, which has its own particular physiognomy. The concreteness with which the authors of the Charter faced the exigencies of the peace they were trying to secure led to a profound change in the traditional treatment which the law of nations had given to the problem of war. Up until that time, the question of the causes of war was located outside the field of international law, which had the role of regulating the phenomenon of war only after it had broken out, no matter what its origin had been. In traditional law the state has free access to the *jus ad bellum,* while law governs the *jus in bello.* Such an unqualified option for war ceased to be acceptable and gave way to an idea that was diametrically opposed: the prohibition of war by means of a treaty renouncing war (1928). Nevertheless, in spite of this treaty and while it was in force, there occurred the greatest war known to humanity until that point, the Second World War. Thus it became clear that if law was going to fulfill an effective function in the prevention of wars, its norms would have to take account of the causes which provoked wars. Then it could have its juridical effect as soon as these causes were ascertained, and it would not merely act after violence had become generalized. This new attitude finally located the law on the crucial terrain of the origins of wars and not only of their effects.

When they incorporated this new problem into international law, the authors of the Charter did not accomplish this in the light of an extensive, previously elaborated doctrine, but rather reacted to the concrete experience they had lived through in the course of the Second World War. From this point of view, then, their plan was not so much to prevent war in general as to prevent the repetition of a war with the characteristics and the causes of the one they had recently experienced. Furthermore, the general outlines of the Charter of the United Nations were already elaborated in the course of the war itself and as a direct result of it. The most obvious characteristic of the war was immediately evident, whether one studied its origin or its development. Its origin was due to oppressive and aggressive fascist regimes, and its development was characterized by the extreme cruelty with which these same regimes treated both combatants and civilian populations. Both facts highlighted the same fundamental reality: the disavowal of human dignity by the systematic violation of the fundamental rights and liberties of the person. "The human person and human rights," maintained the French representative in one of the first sessions of the United Nations, "have been the first victims of fascist regimes." [6]

Preventing the repetition of this recent experience demanded the creation of international juridical instruments which imposed respect for basic human rights. This conviction already had its roots in the course of the war, to the extent that the restoration of human rights in the world became the declared *raison d'être* of the allied struggle. Thus a new international order was envisaged, in which respect for human rights would be the condition as well as the guarantee of international peace and security. This concept received its first universal legal embodiment in the Charter of the United Nations on June 26, 1945, but it had already been announced by President Roosevelt in his annual message to the Congress of the United States in 1941. It was also mentioned in allied declarations on the objectives of the war, such as the Atlantic Charter of August 14, 1941, the Declaration of the United Nations on January 1, 1942, the Teheran Declaration on December 1, 1943, and the Yalta Declaration on February 11, 1945. In the Declaration of the United Nations on January 1, 1942, 26 nations proclaim "the conviction that total victory over the enemy is essential for the defense of life, liberty, independence, and religious liberty, as well as to preserve human rights and justice both in our own countries and in other states." [7] "This majestic document," said Churchill, "declared who we were and why we were fighting." [8]

The conviction that respect for human rights is a requirement for international peace had already developed after the First World War. This was true at least with regard to the treatment of European minorities, and the recognition of their elemental human rights was required by different international treaties, such as the one signed by Poland and the allied powers on June 2, 1919. Schwarzenberger notes:

> The most that could happen was just treatment in the new states, which would have been guaranteed by international protection of their *status* as minorities. By insisting on this, the principal allied powers knew that they were doing much more than fulfilling their duty toward these minorities. They were fully aware of the dangers for international peace which could arise from unjust treatment of

the minorities. In his talk to the plenary session of the Peace Conference on May 31, 1919, President Wilson emphasized this argument in favor of the treaties on minorities: "Nothing . . . can with greater probability disturb world peace than the treatment which could be given in specific cases to the minorities. And thus, if the great powers have in some sense to guarantee world peace, is it unjust that they seek to be satisfied that just and necessary guarantees are granted to the minorities?" [9]

In the same way Oppenheim asserts: "The rule of protecting the minorities, despite the interpretation which it received in practice, was justified in a real way as a system of international viligance, both in the interest of the elemental rights of the individual as well as of international peace." [10]

The atrocities of the Nazi regime before and during the Second World War gave a new and decisive impulse to the search for connections between respect for human rights and world peace, while at the same time they raised the problem to a truly universal level. The fact that the new international order was projected as an antithesis to this particular historical experience is recognized in different ways by various authors. Shigeru Oda states:

> The concept of the protection of human rights originally arose in the area of domestic legislation, such as the Magna Carta in England, the Bill of Rights in the Constitution of the United States and the French Declaration on the Rights of Man. This domestic concept was translated into international terms only after the Second World War. The cruelties and oppression of the Nazi regime in Europe created the conviction that the international recognition and protection of the human rights of peoples throughout the world are essential for the maintenance of international peace and order. [11]

According to Moskowitz, "the reaction of the world to the Nazi holocaust during the Second World War prepared the ground for including the resolutions on human rights in the Charter of the United Nations. This gave a global dimension to the struggle for human rights." [12]

In spite of its origin in one concrete historical experience, and in another sense because of it, the new conception proved to be much more far-reaching. The force of the evidence provided an invincible argument for those historical trends which insisted on basing societies on respect for certain inviolable rights. The international society itself and not just individual countries was experiencing the vital necessity of accepting such principles. To achieve this, a largely unexpected but urgent connection was established between the internal juridical order and the international order.

The Charter of the United Nations was not the only document forged under the pressure and stimulus of the recent war. Important treaties and international legal concepts were elaborated which showed the receptivity of the community of nations to the new principles. Thus international law came to ratify and to provide an important complement to the internal aspiration of societies to guarantee fundamental human rights vis-à-vis the state itself. To start with, the Charter excludes the possibility of making human rights a matter reserved to the domestic jurisdiction of a government. On the other hand, on August 8, 1945, the statute of the international military tribunal of Nuremberg introduced into law the notion of crimes against humanity, a notion designed to protect basic human rights, "whether or not they infringed the laws of the country where they were committed." Thus human rights were given a rank superior to the laws of the state. At the same time, the United Nations in its first general assembly issued a resolution declaring that the principles of the international judgment at Nuremberg were a desirable development of the law of nations (Resolution of the General Assembly, 95:I). The precise formulation of the resolution was entrusted to the Commission on International Law, a specialized body of experts which eventually concluded that international law had primacy over internal law in this matter.

Moreover, it was the extermination of millions of people by the Nazi regime and other analogous practices that led to the adoption of the Convention on the prevention and punishment of the crime of genocide on December 9, 1948. The Convention declared genocide to be a crime under international law and included among possible offenders both private persons and public functionaries, including rulers. Genocide is defined as acts executed with intent to destroy, in whole or in part, a national, ethnic, racial, or religious group, by inflicting death or grave mental or physical harm on the members of the group; deliberately imposing on the group conditions of life calculated to produce its total or partial destruction; imposing measures intended to prevent births within the group and forcibly transferring children from one group to another. The Convention orders that its implementation be subject to the jurisdiction of the International Court of Justice and also to the competence of the United Nations, with the result that the crime of genocide ceased to be a matter reserved to the internal jurisdiction of the states. Also, on August 12, 1949, four Conventions were signed in Geneva that were designed to protect the human person from the cruelties of war and that included humanitarian norms in case of an armed conflict without international dimensions. The protection of fundamental human rights within an internal armed conflict already in progress is a means that serves not only to defend the dignity of the human person but also to avoid an aggravation of the crisis, with repercussions for international peace and security.

The basic principle which guides this whole development, that the observance of human rights is a condition for the peace and security of states, is reiterated in the international law that has developed since then. The contemporary international juridical structure bears the indelible mark which it received originally from the experience of the Second World War. Its reiteration demonstrates that it is a question of a deep-rooted conviction and at the same time reveals the necessity in modern times to continue developing the implications of this relationship. The Universal Declaration on Human Rights in 1948 states explicitly that "recognition of the inherent dignity and of the equal and inalienable rights of all members of the human family is the foundation of peace in the world" (Preamble, Paragraph 1). It adds that "disregard and contempt for human rights have resulted in acts of barbarism which have outraged the conscience of mankind" (Preamble, Paragraph 2). At the same time it makes explicit a profound link between human rights and peace and security by stating that when rights are not protected man feels compelled to the ultimate recourse of "rebellion against tyranny and oppression" (Preamble, Paragraph 3).

For its part, the European Convention on Human Rights in 1950 also recognized that rights are "the basis of world peace" (Preamble, Paragraph 3), while the International Pact on Civil and Political Rights (1966) declares that "recognition of the inherent dignity and of the equal and inalienable rights of all members of the human family is the foundation of peace in the world" (Preamble, Paragraph 1). Texts concerning collective security also studied this relationship, such as the Pact on Mutual Assistance of Rio de Janeiro (1947), which proclaimed that "the regional American community affirms as a manifest truth . . . that peace is based . . . on international recognition and protection of the rights and liberties of the human person" (Consideration, Paragraph 6). In their Fifth Consultative Meeting in Santiago, Chile (August 1959), the Ministers of Foreign Relations of the continent issued a Resolution (VIII) in which they say: "In diverse instruments of the Organization of American States, the norm has been established and repeated that . . . peace has as its basis the recognition of the intrinsic dignity and of the equal and inalienable rights of the human person" (Consideration, Paragraph 3). The Final Declaration of the Conference on Security and Cooperation signed in Helsinki (August 1, 1975) by government leaders from Eastern and Western Europe, the Soviet Union, the United States, and Canada, states the following: "The participating States recognize the universal value of human rights and fundamental liberties, whose observance is an essential factor of peace . . . " (A, VII, Paragraph 5).

The impact of the experience of the Second World War on the development of this material can also be shown negatively, for instance, by the fact that the vigorous development which this theme received in the beginning lost its force as the image of war receded. Nevertheless, today a tendency exists to recover such a thrust, and the first necessity is to achieve a detailed and dynamic understanding of its foundations and potentialities. The juridical task par excellence today is to develop the legacy and historic advice of the Charter of the United Nations: If you want to eliminate war, if you want peace and security, respect human rights. In confronting this imperative, one realizes how critical was this foundational moment of our epoch. Thus, with a sense of urgency similar to that of the past, one sees how necessary it is that the irreplaceable link between peace and security and human rights should systematically organize the internal and external life of human society. As we have seen, the bases for this task exist in an impressive framework of international instruments. If, in addition, internal legislation is reformed in accordance with these instruments, and if the obligation to respect human rights is complemented by the creation of effective mechanisms for their international and internal protection, we will have taken the steps which the present moment urgently demands of the law.

Beyond historical reasons, the theoretical importance of this theme for international law is another development. According to Lauterpacht, the relation between human rights and peace is profound and decisive in the system of the law of nations. The protection of human rights, he asserts, along with the preservation of peace "constitute the crucial goal of international law." And he adds this striking remark: "Such tasks are complementary and, in the ultimate analysis, identical." [13] For his part, Fitzmaurice, in an excellent essay in which he examines the place which human rights could hold in traditional international law, points in one of his conclusions to the grounding of such rights on the basis of international peace and security. [14] He begins with a statement of Shigeru Oda that the treatment which a state gives to its citizens, in the absence of international treaties, does not usually pose questions of international law and remains in the sphere of domestic jurisdiction.

Fitzmaurice then explains that, if it is true that there are no customary rules of international law which directly obligate a state to a specific treatment of its citizens, there are general principles of law which are relevant to the matter, even without considering the Charter of the United Nations. Indeed, these principles are the source of such customary law and probably require states to treat their citizens in a manner consistent with humanitarian standards. In this way, he observes, the matter would also cease to be the exclusive domestic competency of a state, because a customary—though indirect—international obligation would exist with regard to it.

Fitzmaurice then refers to instances of the state's direct responsibility for the individual in international law concerned with humanitarian conduct, such as the case of war crimes, which gives the individual the right to demand humanitarian treatment for himself or herself and obliges the state to provide it. He also mentions the doctrine of the abuse of law, which limits the powers which a state can invoke with regard to its subjects, as an example of customary principles which ensure the humanitarian treatment of persons. Finally, Fitzmaurice alludes to the following general principle of law which is of greater interest at this point: *sic utere tuo ut alienum non laedas* ("Exercise your right without harming that of others"). The following passage should be stressed, not only because he locates the relationship under discussion in profound systematic requirements, but also because he highlights the significance of the original juridical work of the Chilean internationalist Alejandro Alvarez on this vital issue:

> Another general principle of law can be invoked at this point: *sic utere tuo ut alienum non laedas*. But in what sense can it be held that the way a state treats its citizens does harm to other states? In one epoch of history, this certainly could not be held. But have modern conditions brought about a change in this? It is not necessary to postulate a juridical principle concerning the interdependence of states which implies legal consequences, such as that on which Judge Alvarez based much of his judicial reasoning. Even without that, there certainly exist grounds to hold that in our day any serious denial by a state of the human rights of its citizens, or of any particular category of them, not only has repercussions by opening the way to international frictions, but also harms other states by provoking tensions and even outbreaks of violence in their territories. This can also be the source of the kind of frictions which lead to war, and there is abundant evidence that this has happened and is still happening. As Judge De Visscher has said, without respect for human rights, the executive power develops "internally into a tryanny and externally into an engine of destruction." How well those who live in this century are aware of that! [15]

VII. HUMAN RIGHTS BEFORE THE INTERNAL ORDER AND THE INTERNATIONAL ORDER

Insufficient attention has been given to the fact that human rights are considered by international law from a double point of view. First of all, the law of nations has introduced a new substantive element into its norms, which is the recognition of the dignity of the person. The result is that the individual is progressively incorporated into a role as a subject of international law and recognition is given to his or her fundamental human rights, which cannot be disavowed by other subjects of international law, especially by states. This way of assimilating human rights is *by extension,* since it means that the norms of international law are expanded to a new area, which is the dignity of the person. Previously, this had not been thematically and directly considered to be a separate juridical object of international law.

Second, human rights have become material for international law because their enforcement or disavowal (especially when they are collective) have repercussions on a juridical object traditionally considered by the law of nations, that is, international peace. Thus, this perspective of interest in human rights is *by inclusion,* since it concerns a matter which today is seen to be included in the traditional concern of the law of nations to maintain peace between states. Therefore, an internal conflict which violates human rights affects two juridical objects of international law: the dignity of the human person and international peace.

For international law, both questions are linked together, because defending the dignity of the individual threatened by the excesses of his or her state impedes the establishment of aggressive regimes. Thus peace is strengthened and an essential function of international law is fulfilled. For the modern law of nations, collective outbursts of violence normally have their origin in a previous violation of human rights in a society. A continuous line is perceived, which begins in the violation or human rights and ends with the employment of force with external repercussions. An oppressive regime is for international law the beginning of an aggressive regime; the enactment of internal violations is the forerunner of external violations. Thus the defense of the dignity of the person turns out to be at the same time a defense of the peace.

The individual, then, has become for international law an essential element in its system: if the law of nations intends to establish peace, there is no other way but by alliance with the human person, which goes beyond its alliance with the states. More profound than the community of nations is the discovery of the universal community of human beings, whose basic rights and their mutual recognition are a primary element of the system.

Moreover, through this conception international law recovers the authentic meaning of a state. Insofar as it is a juridical person, it requires representation. Thus international law, when it regulates the relations between states, in practice lays down norms for the representatives of states. But this certainly does not imply an identification between the states and their representatives, because in international law states also include a territory and a population. In this framework, the problem of the violation of human rights is not that of a state against its citizens, as is commonly held, but, strictly speaking, that of one of the elements of a state (the government) against another of its elements (the population). Consequently, it is the state itself that is affected by the problem. It is not a private matter but essentially a public one, which places in conflict the constitutive elements of the state as such in the same way that insurrection and war affect the state as such.

For the law of nations, it has become clear that it is a principle unanimously accepted by modern states committed to international law that the population of a state submits to being governed by an authority and entrusts its represenation to it only on condition that the authority recognize the population's inalienable rights. This implies that a government loses its legitimacy in a modern state to the extent that it disavows such rights. The relation between government and governed is one which is constituted only on the basis of the observance of such a social pact. In the classic expression of the Declaration of Independence of the United States of America in 1776: "Governments are instituted to guarantee the natural rights of man, deriving their just powers from the consent of the governed . . . and the people has the right to abolish governments when they do not respect that purpose." The same idea is stated in the Declaration of the French Revolutionary Convention on July 24, 1793, and more recently in the Universal Declaration on Human Rights in the paragraph cited earlier. This confronts international law with the problem of a temporal government disavowing nontemporal rights which define the very nature of a modern state, even though it was by virtue of recognizing them that the state was accepted as a member of the community of nations and as a subject of international law.

By granting international recognition to human rights, international law is committed to the restoration of the basic social pact of a nation; thus, it is committed to the objective defense of the basic natural order of a modern state. Furthermore, the international character which is granted to human rights makes their disavowal by a government not merely an internal subversion but also an international subversion, an assault against international society as a whole, which is forced to reestablish the proper order. The restoration of international order necessarily implies the restoration of internal order in this respect, since the same act, the violation of human rights, is today an attack on both orders. International law becomes a permanent counterweight and guarantee against usurpations of inalienable rights, and clearly manifests its fidelity to states rather than to governments.

If it is kept in mind that human rights, which previously existed as constitutional guarantees in different countries, have become established as the result of intense internal social conflicts and that they owe their international recognition to the cruel experience of the Second World War, then the potentially explosive nature of violations can be perceived. By establishing those fundamental rights, the causes of social conflict were eliminated or at least controlled and a relative internal peace was assured. The negation of those rights brings the situation back to conditions that prevailed before their establishment, that is, it necessarily leads to social conflict. Since it is a question of basic rights upon which the totality of the social order is constructed, their disavowal means the destruction of the essential conditions of social living.

Societies pass through stages during which social conflicts achieve a relative historical stabilization. In different periods the struggle is for different forms of rights and in the future it will be for new forms. It is natural that this process achieves success in only a partial and gradual manner. But what cannot be permitted is for a society in a later historical era to violate collectively those basic rights that were established in a previous era. Along with infidelity to past generations, that would involve a retrogression which does violence to the historical development of a country. The different states which today are committed to international law have achieved a kind of evolution in this matter. Thus the defense of already established human rights by international law contributes to the advance of states toward the future and helps to prevent humiliating lapses into more primitive stages.

The opportune and effective involvement of international law helps toward a solution before an eruption of generalized violence. Thus, international law contributes not only to international peace but also to the internal peace of the states. This alliance, then, between international law and the individual can produce nothing but benefits: for the cause of international peace (which is the primary juridical object of international law); for the cause of internal peace (which is the primary juridical object of the states and their internal law); and for the cause of personal dignity (the ultimate juridical object of all law).

The individual, then, has emerged on the international scene as a proper subject, demanding the recognition of fundamental rights from the community of nations. And at the same time that the individual enhances his or her dignity and acquires the universal status that corresponds to the human condition and vocation, he or she has also become an essential factor for international peace and security.

In pursuit of its proper juridical concern of international peace, the law of nations is expanding the number of subjects for whom it recognizes international rights and imposes international duties; they include the state, international organizations, societies, and individuals. International society is no longer merely a community of sovereign states, nor are international relations merely formal and subject to the discretionary criteria of absolute sovereignties. Relations between nations have been given substance, principally through the commitment that has been undertaken to actualize the content of human rights. This changes the structure of international law, making it impossible to escape the transforming impact of the emergence of the individual, who now imposes his or her own conditions on states, societies, and international organizations. The task now is the peaceful development of a complex international society with a plurality of actors, while the old international society of individual states is definitively transcended. The vast scope of such a challenge is not the theme of this article. But in this light one must stress the exceptional importance of human rights both for international and internal law, so that the issue can be situated in the broad perspective that it deserves, while keeping in mind that its development has scarcely begun.

Notes to Chapter 9

1. Dr. Montealegre participated in the conference on human rights that was held at the Woodstock Theological Center on January 20–22, 1980. Afterwards he agreed to submit this essay, which synthesizes major ideas from his recent book, *Le seguridad del Estado y los derechos humanos* (Santiago, Chile: Ed. Academia de Humanismo Christiano, 1979). The translation into English is by Alfred Hennelly, assisted by José Zalaquett.

2. See the antecedents of this doctrine in Chap. 1 of the companion volume, *Human Rights and Basic Needs in the Americas.*

3. The close relationship between violations of these human rights and violations of socioeconomic human rights, which in conjunction foster rebellion, is described by Alfred Hennelly in Chapter 2 of this volume. See also Chapter 11 by Drew Christiansen.

4. The violation of human rights, therefore, threatens in law both the internal and the external security of a state.

5. The European Commission on Human Rights, using the term "state" in its sense of public power, declared in the case of *Ireland,* 1972: "The responsibility of the state under the Convention (of Europe on human rights) can arise from the acts of its organizations, agents, and servants. . . . The system for protecting human rights that the Convention established is designed in the form of obligations which correspond to states. From the point of view of process, the result is that all charges of violation have to be made against the states as defendants. In this sense, they are responsible for any violation within their jurisdictions, through the imputation to them of the acts mentioned previously" (*ECHR Ireland Report,* 1972, 383). Referring to the particular prohibition of torture, the same Commis-

sion states with reference to the case of Greece: "In the first place, the acts prohibited under Article B will become the responsibility of a Contracting Party only if they are committed by persons who exercise public authority. . . . The transgressions of article three are therefore governmental acts. . . ." (*ECHR, The Greek Case* [Strasbourg, 1969], Volume II, Part 1, p. 12, par. 26). As regards torture, it is defined in the 1975 Declaration of the United Nations as an act committed by "a public functionary or other person acting at their instigation."

6. *Journal of the General Assembly* 53 (December 8, 1946), p. 287.

7. Cf. Winston S. Churchill, *La Gran Alianza* (Argentina: Ed. Peuser, 1950), p. 602.

8. *Ibid.*

9. George Schwarzenberger, *La Política del Poder* (Mexico: FCE, 1969), p. 539.

10. L. Oppenheim, *Tratado de Derecho Internacional Público* (translation of the eighth English edition; Barcelona: Ed. Bosch, 1961, Tomo I, Vol. II), p. 289.

11. Shigeru Oda, "The Individual in International Law," in *Manual of International Law* (Ed. M. Sorensen, 1968), p. 497.

12. Moses Moskowitz, *International Concern for Human Rights* (New York: Oceana Publications, 1976), p. 160.

13. Lauterpacht, *International Law,* 428. Pope John Paul II has spoken recently in similar terms. The passage will be cited in full, since it provides invaluable moral support for the greater thesis of this article: "After all, peace comes down to respect for man's inviolable rights, while war springs from the violation of these rights and brings with it still graver violations of them. . . . Indeed, it is a significant fact, repeatedly confirmed by the experiences of history, that violation of the rights of man goes hand in hand with violation of the rights of the nation. . . . The rights of power can only be understood on the basis of respect for the objective and inviolable rights of man. The common good that authority in the state serves is brought to full realization only when all the citizens are sure of their rights. The lack of this leads to the dissolution of society, opposition by citizens to authority, or a situation of oppression . . ." (Encyclical *Redemptor Hominis,* March 4, 1979, no. 17).

14. Sir Gerald Fitzmaurice, "The Older Generation of International Lawyers and the Question of Human Rights," in *Homenaje a don Antonio de Luna* (Madrid, 1967), pp. 320–331.

15. *Ibid.,* p. 329. He adds the following note regarding Alvarez: "Although the positions of Judge Alvarez were too advanced to be of much help to the Court in its specific juridical task, they were a fertile source of new ideas."

Thomas Clarke, S.J.

10. On the Need to Break Bread Together

One clear and significant factor in the discussion of basic human needs and rights is the varied role and influence of organized religion in contemporary public life. The key role of the Ayatollah Khomeini in the upheavals in Iran and the visits of Pope John Paul II to Mexico, Poland, and the United States are a few instances. Less dramatically, religiously based nongovernmental organizations exercise considerable influence on domestic and international issues through lobbying, monitoring, and educating. In Latin America popular religiosity, as well as official church teaching (as at Medellín and Puebla), along with religiously linked liberation movements and basic communities, represent forces for change. And in the United States such neuralgic issues as abortion, women's rights and the ERA, the links between multinational corporations and repressive foreign governments, military spending, and environmental questions are some of the areas where the principals must reckon with religiously committed groups on one side or the other. It is hardly surprising, then, that current concern over the fulfillment of human needs and respect for human rights should be conceived as religious as well as secular in character.

The present theological essay expresses such a concern and seeks to be of service to those, religiously committed or not, who are seeking to promote human rights. To those who share, in whatever degree, in the religious faith of the author, it offers an opportunity to root themselves anew within their own tradition, to reexamine the religious and theological bases of their ethical attitudes, and to find fresh motivation for their persevering engagement. For others, whether engaged in research, communications, advocacy, or policy analysis, it seeks to promote a better appreciation of the less pragmatic dimensions of their concerns, and a chance to come in touch with their own basic horizons, values, assumptions, and motivations.

It seeks these goals by asking: What difference, if any, does it make for the promotion of basic human needs and rights when these are viewed from a religious or quasi-religious horizon in which the notion of human communion is primary?

To bring both the question and the response to a sharper focus, one central instance of basic human need and right has been chosen for reflection: the sharing of food and drink. Even more than my personal attraction toward reflecting on this facet of human experience, its centrality prompts such a choice. It is, first of all, anthropologically central. Immediately related to individual and communal survival and to the heart of family life, it is at the core of the human endeavor. Together with the marriage bed and the altar or shrine of religious worship, the table at which we share our meals is one of the primary symbolic realizations of our humanity. Secondly, it is religiously central. Most religious traditions, particularly the Judeo-Christian ones, in which the Messianic banquet and its anticipation in Passover or Eucharistic ritual are primary symbols, draw upon the human experience of the shared meal for significant doctrinal, disciplinary, and ritual expressions of faith. Thirdly, it is politically and economically central. While it cannot be totally isolated, even for purposes of analysis, from other areas of need and development in an increasingly complex and interdependent world, it is manifestly a crucial *locus* in the needs/rights/power struggle. The production, distribution, and consumption of food is deeply interwoven with other economic and political concerns. Its linkage with the massive population question is almost too obvious to require mention. For all these reasons, then, a focus on the sharing of food and drink seems particularly apt for illustrating the bearing of religious and theological reflection on current concerns over basic needs and rights.

A final preliminary remark has to do with the genre of this essay. More partial than what has traditionally been termed "systematic theology," it is an exercise in religious and theological reflection that may aptly be termed "horizon theology." It is, first, an exercise of *theology,* as distinct from the scientific study of religion, in that the reflection takes place within a community of religious faith, on the basis of the myths, symbols, and creeds distinctive of such a community. But, while it is spoken by a religious believer, it can be listened to and, within limits, evaluated by anyone, religious believer or not. The genre does not preclude intelligibility or even partial convergence of understanding and assent on the part of those who profess other religious faiths or whose basic commitment is to secular values. It is, secondly, *horizon* theology. [1] It is not immediately concerned with ethical principles and norms touching public policy, but rather with questions of "ultimate concern." [2] It deals with those fundamental human meanings and values which go to form basic mindsets, paradigms and ideologies. These, in turn, form the assumptions and the climates within which ethical principles and norms are formulated and policies designed and executed. Further, its primary vehicle is less deductive or pragmatic reason than human imagination. Its operative assumption is that, after wrestling with intractable complexity and confusion, an imaginative interlude may yield fresh energies and new perspectives.

To this end, the first part of the essay offers not an analysis or interpretation of the food and hunger problem but rather a meditation which aims at evoking a *felt* overall appreciation of its complexity, intensity, and depth. This part will be successful to the extent that it begets or confirms in the reader a readiness to let go, provisionally, of efforts to *solve* the food and hunger problem, in order to *wonder* whether what is most needed at the present juncture is not fresh sources of energy and insight for the continuing struggle. The second part proposes one such source, the notion of human communion as this emerges from the Christian myth and is elaborated in Christian theology. The third part returns to the primary question of the essay, and asks briefly what differences might occur in the struggle to promote human needs and rights in the area of food and drink if such a struggle were conducted against the horizon of human communion. [3]

I. IMAGINING THE FOOD CRISIS

A simple image may help provide an initial framework for meditating on the interaction of the very diverse systems that shape the food and hunger problem. The primary focus of concern may be represented by a first circle—a group of people, in family or other situations, sharing a meal. Some distance away is the second important focus—a circle standing for the harvesting of foodstuffs from land, sea, and sky. The image is completed by a curved line between the two circles, which stands for the totality of systems and processes involved in the passage from the second circle to the first. The image is, in effect, another expression for the familiar triad: production, distribution, and consumption.

Now *all* of the systems and types of analyses which will be mentioned here pertain in varying measure to *all* three facets of the image. This is a consideration which must never be lost sight of. But it may still be appropriate to describe certain systems and their analyses in terms of one or other of the facets. A certain arbitrariness will be manifest in the choices made.

Thus the first circle, where people share meals, is touched particularly by systems and analyses having to do with nutrition, health, and culture (including the cultural dimension of religion). Some comments on each of these may indicate the massiveness and complexity of the problem we are dealing with.

Nutrition and the various systems created to understand and foster it (research, analysis, experimentation, policy planning) is not a bad place to begin. It touches most immediately the sheer survival and basic physiological health of persons. It receives a great deal of attention in research, and nutritional statistics and viewpoints are a major factor in shaping food policy. Inevitably, nutritionists have their differences among themselves. How uniform, for example, are nutritional needs within a particular region or culture, and still more among different regions and cultures? What combinations of foods will offer a particular people or class of people a minimal or ideal balanced diet of proteins, minerals, etc.? Difficulties and doubts will increase as nutritional considerations intersect with broader factors such as health, climate, or the aesthetic and social aspects of human eating. Even when, for example, nutritionists have agreed on the nutritional plus or minus of, say, soft drinks, health specialists as well as psychologists and sociologists will come on the scene to suggest that other values must be considered before solid strategies become possible.

One common focus of nutritional concerns is worth noting within this essay: the individual person's nutritional needs. This is legitimate and in fact necessary, given what is being measured by the instruments in this field. The danger, however, is the danger that accompanies all specialization, namely, that a partial perspective may become absolutized, and the food and hunger question may be perceived as consisting merely in protein or vitamin deficiency, while broader dimensions and deeper aspects are neglected. It is not being suggested that nutritionists (or any other group of specialists) should change their methodology or even refrain from urging their viewpoints when there is question of shaping public policy. But at some point (or points) in the synthesizing of diverse analyses, the broader dimensions and deeper aspects need to be attended to. Specifically, so far as this essay is concerned, the fact that persons do not merely consume food but share meals is absolutely central and basic to the food and hunger question, particularly when seen in terms of human dignity and human rights.

Health and the various systems affecting health, its analysis and care, are clearly adjacent to the field of nutrition. The *effective* nutritional value of one or other diet will depend on the state of health of the eater. A nursing mother in Nigeria, a miner afflicted with silicosis in Chile, an obese and sedentary European bureaucrat have quite different dietary and nutritional needs from the viewpoint of health. It is not irrelevant in prescribing an appropriate diet to consider whether one is likely to die from exposure to traditional contagious or infectious diseases or from so-called "diseases of civilization." Factors of emotional and psychic health and sickness will likewise alter the actual need and the actual benefit of available food and drink. Both addictive feasting and addictive fasting (dietary faddism) can nullify what otherwise would foster health. The complexity of the matter is thus further confirmed when one considers the interaction between nutrition and health, and between the specialties and specialists involved in research, provision of the means, actual care, and policy formation in each field.

Culture, which penetrates deeply into every facet of human life, including the processes of harvesting and distributing foodstuffs, is mentioned here, at the circle of consumption, because it is here that cultural values are most powerfully influential. Most commonly people do not eat alone, and most often having to do so is felt as a privation. Even prisoners are permitted, with some risk to institutional order and security, to share meals, and it may be the most oppressive aspect of solitary confinement that one has no companion to break bread with. In the Western world at least, the common table is possibly the most important vehicle for the education of children into society and for the handing on of the cultural heritage. This dimension of the food and hunger question, which is neglected, carries with it many opportunities and problems. Both in societies of plenty and in societies of want, many assumptions (aesthetic, social, cultural, religious) shape meal time and its positive or negative impact on the quality of life. It is here that shared habits which foster or harm sound health—psychic, intellectual, moral or well as physical—are developed and confirmed.

For the typical American middle-class family, for example, what would be a week's menu be like without meat, even without beef? Staples like rice and potatoes nourish far more than bodily cells within traditional cultures; they have become carriers of the heritage, and changes which substantially affect them need to be taken very seriously by anyone concerned for the quality of life. Where and when and in what fashion people eat (quickly or slowly, standing or sitting, indoors or outdoors, alone or with others, at home or in a restaurant) will affect the actual nutritional value of the food, and consequently the health of the eater, as well as basic contentment and commitment. The popularity of McDonald's in Japan, and the prospect that Communist China may within the decade enjoy the thrill of "going to McDonald's" is probably worth at least as much attention as the balance of trade. In culture we are dealing with irreducible factors within human life, which we cannot safely neglect for what can be precisely measured and weighed. To do so would be to act like the alcoholic who lost his house key in a dark alley and who, when asked why he was looking for it a half block away under the lamp post, replied, "Because there's more light here."

This holds as we move now from the circle where people share meals to the circle where they harvest their food. For meditative purposes, however, there are other more pertinent considerations, and perhaps the general rubric of *ecology* is appropriate for this second focus. One might say, perhaps, that ecology is to production what nutrition is to consumption. At no point of our existence, perhaps, do we humans experience ourselves more fully as situated within a cosmos than when we are involved with nature through the labor of drawing our sustenance from it. The tetrad of soil/water/fertilizer/energy crystallizes the several dimensions of the farming experience and the many interweaving problems which afflict it today. There was a time when humans provided for their nutritional needs within the geographical area where they lived. The soil was good or passable or could be improved or was abandoned for better soil. Water was present in abundance or else crops were accommodated to the limitations. Fertilizer for the most part was situated within an organic cycle of taking from the land and giving back to it. Humans and domesticated animals, with the aid of primitive forms of waterpower and other simple technologies, provided energy resources. The richness or paucity of material resources determined abundance or want, prompted migrations, dictated life style, etc. The planet as a whole offered limitless resources that at the same time could not be fully exploited. And, even when they knew of one another's existence, peoples in different parts of the earth fared well or poorly in relative independence of one another.

Today, with modern science and technology, with travel and communications, with population growth placing enormous demands on the planet's resources, and with growing and ever more complex interdependence of peoples and systems on one another, whatever touches food production anywhere in the world in any substantial degree creates ripples or shock waves around the globe. It is important, of course, to acknowledge the universal gains in the satisfaction of basic nutritional needs which we owe to science and technology. But this realization should not blunt our alertness to the grim by-products of such progress. The advancing desert in some sections of Africa, the curtailment of oil production and shipment because of political or economic reasons, prolonged bad weather in some sections of the earth, unexpected outcomes of one or other phase of the "green revolution," all of these put extreme pressures on most facets of the world "system," and on the "system" as a whole. In consequence, somewhere in the world the well-fed and the hungry will eat less well, the ranks of the starving will grow, food prices will rise, and inflation will keep spiraling.

If both the circle of sharing food and drink and the circle of harvesting crops contain immense complexity, the journey between the two circles brings geometric growth in complexity and interdependence, for it is around this passage that the major human systems are concentrated: political, economic, social, ethical, and religious. While *economics* has broader concerns than the distribution of food resources, this belongs surely at the core of its concerns, and is related to just about every one of its other interests. Such standard and basic economic concerns as balance of payments, free or controlled markets, export or domestic concentration in national economies, the impact of food aid on markets and market prices, the advantages and limitations of grain reserves, the ups and downs of inflation and unemployment in relation to each other, the role and practices of multinational corporations, schemes for land ownership and distribution, optimal size of farms from an economic standpoint, growth in GNP, decisions touching the employment of technology and capital intensive methods—these and other areas of economics both as process and as analysis interweave in a fashion too dizzying for the average citizen to come to any confident judgment as to what is crucial and what peripheral, or as to what direction economic policy ought to take. Of special political and ethical importance are differing proposals on the location of decision-making power within the international economic order. Who calls the shots and who merely carries out the call becomes a particularly pressing question when the minimal food needs of millions and their very survival are at stake.

Politics, both theory and practice, complements and competes with economic theory and practice in determining the passage of food from the circle of harvesting to the circle of consumption. One's impression of complexity grows again as even a few political aspects of the food and hunger problem are reviewed: national sovereignty and whatever limitations on it may be accepted in the interest of regional or global community among the nations; the division of the world into nations which, in ideology and actual practice (not always coinciding), are organized along capitalist or socialist lines (with several varieties of each); the phenomenon of military dictatorships and national security states; the political restraints and coercions because of which some citizens are forbidden to migrate or even travel and other citizens are refugees forced out of their homeland; the importance of food policy as an instrument of diplomacy and foreign relations, where strategic advantages of powerful nations help determine who will be fed and who will go hungry; the balance of economic power represented by the presence of food and fuel resources in abundance within certain nations and not in others; the presence within democratic nations of powerful lobbies of capitalists, workers, farmers, consumers, and managers representing conflicting interests in food policy; and the mechanisms devised by political leaders and the political community to deal with such pressures through appropriate regulatory mechanisms. Undoubtedly the most ominous political factor is constituted by the investment of the wealth (most crucially not the financial but the intellectual, scientific, and moral resources) of powerful nations in weapons of destruction, armaments capable of destroying the human race, together with attitudes and relationships of belligerency and distrust which render it possible that in our time a nuclear Armageddon will put definitive closure on worry about food and population.

Our reflection must mention *science and technology* as constituting major elements in the interweaving of complex systems. They have intensified the food and hunger problem and related problems (notably population and health care), even while they seek to alleviate the untoward results of our utilization of them. The quarrel over technology, like technology itself, is here to stay. Some seek in more and improved technology and the scientific rationalization of life the solution of our ills, while others, in moderate or more radical form, name scientism and technologism as the very enemies that produce contemporary malnutrition and starvation. More specifically, the application of science and technology to food production through such sobering experiences as the "green revolution" has led to a greater sensitivity to the need for caution and adaptation within economies and cultures which may be damaged by indiscreet use of sophisticated techniques. Particular success stories are abundant, but most of them appear to have a less bright sequel, in which some material improvement such as a paved road or a new chemical fertilizer has brought either incidental or overall deterioration to the human scene which it was designed to improve.

Food processing is another significant area in which the actual employment of technology has been sometimes baneful, sometimes beneficial. Inanimate machines are in themselves incapable of reverence or irreverence toward the products of the field and toward those for whose benefit they are being prepared. All depends on whether these tools are made by their creators into sensitive or cruel "hands." Almost an industry in itself, food processing adds enormously to the complexity and challenge of the food system.

It is with mention of the *psychosocial* and (again) *cultural* dimensions of the food and hunger problem that we move toward factors which enter most deeply into the very fabric of the human person and of human communities, and which are least susceptible to exact measurement and to deliberate control by the instruments of political society. But they are not beyond the responsible exercise of freedom, and the scientific study of them, together with philosophical and theological reflection, can eventually yield important insights.

Thus reflection on the cultural dimensions of the food and hunger problem should enlarge our view of the scope of human needs. A nutritionally solid diet can be frustrated of its health-serving purpose unless it is accommodated to the psychic needs of individuals and unless it is in harmony with what constitutes for any given group of people healthy social relationships. I know enough personally of "total institutions" in religious life (having lived for a total of 22 years in a community where, three times a day, close to 300 men would share the same dining room) to appreciate how important is this aspect of the struggle to make human life more human. Were I a prison warden, I suspect that my central concern would be the total quality of the sharing of meals and the environment provided for such sharing.

But I have already touched on some cultural aspects of the actual sharing of food and drink. Here it is more pertinent to advert to the way in which psychology, sociology, and cultural anthropology can enlighten the way in which food and drink are marketed and bought. It is here that media advertising, which is a primary constitutive factor in our technological society and its political and economic structures and processes, has its place. Sample illustrations are: the remarkable growth of "dining out" on the part of American families, not least through the media-linked fast food chains, coupled with the psychosocial power of auto travel and tourism; the modification of children's and adults' dietary habits through media appeals directed at children of various ages; the place of cola and other beverages in the symbolic world of children and adults both in developed and underdeveloped countries. What makes the wheels of food distribution turn is ultimately the way that mercantile imagination and the passion for gain persuade—with a strong ingredient of manipulation—the imaginations and appetites of consumers. A final question concerns what happens to the capacity of addicted consumers to make, in other areas of life such as the political and the familial, free decisions based on preferences which are truly human. Freedom grows with exercise and atrophies with disuse. Within as well as among persons, addiction can be contagious.

It is with categories of consciousness and freedom that entry is appropriately made into the field of *ethics* (both philosophical and theological). It is here that we come to the human precisely as human, and to the values which give life its ultimate meaning and direction. In the various ethical discussions of the food crisis, probably the most disheartening proposal is that the method employed in medical triage ought to be adapted to the decision-making processes which determine who will be well fed, adequately fed, or left to starve in today's world. Ethical theorists and policy analysts have also tried to grapple with the concepts of human needs and human rights, and to test and apply various theories of justice to food and hunger questions. From an ethical standpoint, what proportionate place should be given to humanitarian altruism and to pragmatic self-interest, to love and to justice, to human welfare initiatives by private groups, and to the inclusion of the basic human right to eat in the legal and juridical norms of nations and of the world community? To whom does the land belong? What claim does the worker have to the fruit of labor, and how does this compare with the claims of investors, the needy unemployed, and others? Should the concepts of human needs and human rights be contracted or inflated? What are the ethical values at stake in food and hunger questions, and how does one align them in efforts to move from ethical theory to "middle axioms," to policies and programs? [4]

There is finally—to return to the opening paragraph of this essay—the field of *religion* as a major element adding to the complexity of the food and hunger situation. Especially where religious faith has deeply permeated cultures over centuries and even millennia, deeply rooted attitudes and practices touching directly or indirectly the food and hunger problem can offer formidable resistance to change. Religious attitudes touching abortion and birth control and the eating of meat are a few prominent instances. Religion, too, in its prophetic aspect, can serve as catalyst for social change, as developments in the Middle East and in Latin America have shown. In varying measure, governments and politicians must reckon with both official and grassroots convictions of religious groups that are often sharply in conflict with one another. In the United States, the tradition of separation of church and state is no escape from such tensions, but only an alternative way of dealing with them. As pressures on the human psyche from our technological society mount, a whole assortment of religious or quasi-religious movements, sects, and communities is generated. It is no accident that the issues of peace, environment, population, and food have become a major focus of concern and conflict in mainline churches as well as in small but influential groups like the Mennonites and Quakers. Many religious people are convinced that the church bodies of our country have enormous potential for educating citizens and changing institutions in the area of food and drink.

In reflecting back on this meditation, one topic, intimately linked with food and hunger, deserves a final highlighting, even though it has been mentioned several times. It goes by the name of *population*. The love of man and woman and its fruitfulness in children and family life constitute, with the sharing of food and drink, the very heart of human intimacy. Energy, ecology, employment, domestic and international commerce and trade, may be seen as concentric circles around a center where family life is constituted and sustained within a home where meals are shared. All are profoundly affected by and in turn influence developments in population. This is not the place to review political and economic quarrels, for example touching the relationship of development and population, or the ethical issues involved in governmental policies on contraception, sterilization, and abortion. But, as one tries to catch the urgency of the world food and hunger problem, it is no less urgent to listen to the ticking of the population clock.

I would like to bring this meditative part of the essay to a close, first by recalling its purpose, and secondly, by indicating why it has suggested to me the subsequent development.

Not seeing the woods for the trees is a danger for most intellectual enterprises, particularly in an age of specialized interests and techniques. There is need occasionally for a broad gaze, a meditative and contemplative effort to grasp (and be grasped by) the whole picture. When such an effort—which I have been able here only to sketch in broad outline— is attuned to the reality being meditated upon, the fruit is not a cogent or even plausible argument but a set of impressions and insights which, if they are sound, will commend themselves to others, activate similar recognitions and stimulate similar (and dissimilar) suspicions and scenarios. It is for the reader to say how successful this particular effort has been. In any case, here are several observations.

First, an obvious and massive *complexity* characterizes the present food and hunger situation. This reflects, of course, the complexity of whatever is human, and particularly the complexity introduced into human processes by science and technology.

Second, while complexity in itself is an enrichment, not a diminishment, of the human, it seems equally obvious that a burdensome and massive *disorder* characterizes the present world food and hunger situation. To speak, for the moment, only from an ethical standpoint: a planet where millions are overfed (and harm themselves in the overfeeding), while many more millions are underfed (and are damaged in the underfeeding) contains a gross and dangerous disorder which, coalescing with other major disorders (one thinks of armaments, overpopulation, environmental pollution), poses a clearly catastrophic threat not only to human survival, but to what gives survival its meaning and value, human dignity and the human quality of life.

Third, it appears to me that the methodologies and hermeneutics actually being employed are essentially inadequate because they are incapable of integrating within a coherent approach all the dimensions of the food and hunger problem which demand attention.

Fourth, in the presence of the massive disorder I have mentioned this inadequacy leads inevitably to *burden* and *frustration* as seen in the widespread experience of many zealous workers, who so frequently see a particular breakthrough get swallowed up by unforeseen or unmanageable factors. Overall, the global effort to deal with hunger and starvation becomes a matter of *coping,* of "doing the best we can," a massive Sisyphus experience, rather than a steady and progressive movement toward clearly defined and accessible goals.

Fifth, in such a situation some basic human realities, insights, and values inevitably get neglected. Continuing to look near a familiar lamp post for the key that was lost in the dark alley can be an alternative to despair, provided we are stupefied enough to forget where the key was lost. But isn't there somewhere a flashlight that can help us return to the alley with genuine hope?

Sixth, I believe that such a flashlight is at hand, in the truth that to be human is to be not merely a consumer of nutrients but also a sharer of meals, so that policies which do not aim at *this* goal—the human experience of sharing meals in dignity with loved ones—are ultimately beside the point and neither capable nor worthy of evoking deep and lasting commitment.

Seventh, in the face of the objection that we are "doing the best we can," and that setting ourselves a more ambitious goal would break the camel's back, I would respond that, on the contrary, what is most needed at the present juncture is not linear intensification of present efforts but the kind of fresh energy that we humans receive only when we "look away" from the immediacy of problem-solving to possibilities which, in our anxiety and frustration, we have forgotten. There is a paradox here, which is characteristic of the human spirit. It is ambitioning too little, not aspiring to too much, which in the long run hinders practical progress. I am not suggesting that utopian dreaming can substitute for rational understanding and pragmatic planning. But at the point at which these are felt to be unsuccessful, it is far from irrational to look for fresh sources of vision and energy.

Eighth, this is one of the roles that religion can play in our society. Along with other kinds of communities which exercise a special responsibility for the human heritage, religion in general and, in our American society, Judeo-Christian faith, can call attention to neglected facets of the common human heritage which can enrich us all in time of crisis.

Ninth, it needs to be said that I am not offering a Christian and Roman Catholic version of "Ford has a better idea." Though this essay will not explore other traditions, there are, as I will say in conclusion, good grounds for anticipating that the value of human communion embodied in the experience of sharing meals is a heritage for most of the major allegiances, secular as well as religious, which contribute to our national and global enterprises.

II. HUMAN COMMUNION IN THE CHRISTIC MYTH

In the second part of this essay I would like first to delineate the main features of what I will call the Christic myth, that is, the religious story, at once symbolic and historical, which expresses how Christians look at human life in its deepest aspects. Second, I want to sketch out one broad theological articulation of the myth. In view of the purpose of the essay I will highlight especially the theme of communion, and note the place that the metaphor of meal has both in the myth and in my theological reflection. The intended fruit of this part is a broad horizon, a vision of human communion in the sharing of food and drink, which may offer new energies and the stimulus to seek fresh alternatives for those who struggle to satisfy the human hunger for food. [5] The general direction and a few samples of these alternatives will be discussed in the brief third part of the essay.

The power of religion in general, and of Christianity in particular, is most basically the power of myth and symbol to energize persons, communities, and cultures through various ritual, cognitive, normative, and pragmatic mediations. The Christian myth, it has been frequently noted, is singularly rooted in historical events, centrally of course in the preaching, wonderworking, and fate of Jesus of Nazareth. The myth itself admits of an endless variety of narrative and symbolic expositions and rational interpretations. What interests us here is the place it assigns to the motif of communion. Preliminary to the delineation of a theological horizon, a brief laying out of the underlying Christic myth is called for.

Human existence begins, according to the familiar myth, with two people, joined intimately in their origin and called to be the common font of all human life. This primordial communion with God and with one another is soon shattered, however (note the food-sharing symbol: the "forbidden fruit" of Genesis, chapters 2 and 3), and the negative myth of human alienation is begun with blame, estrangement from the earth, the original fratricide, and a subsequent chain of violence and evil culminating in almost total destruction and a fresh beginning. This whole composition story, of course, emerged from the struggle with evil of a particular historical people in the Near East in the centuries prior to the Christian era. As the myth develops, the patriarchal figures of Abraham and Moses replace Adam and Eve and Noah in the energizing return of this people to its roots. Other peoples are considered significant in the story of salvation only in relation to this chosen people. The theme of human communion is thus narrowed, and finds expression in the special covenant of Yahweh, a particular God, with this particular people, Israel. The early stages of this phase of the Judeo-Christian myth accent corporate, not individual, destiny and responsibility. Further, the communion planned by Yahweh for this elect people is one of earthly peace and prosperity, with no indication of a destiny beyond history. Conflicts, especially with enemy peoples, together with recurring cycles of infidelity and repentance, mark the fragile realizations of communion achieved at this stage.

As the story moves toward its climax (from the Christian point of view) in Jesus of Nazareth, it begins to anticipate in several ways some central features of its later history. The individual emerges as responsible agent and subject of destiny in his/her own right. Yahweh, no longer a mere tribal God but the universal creator, is seen to have designs on all the nations, though the chosen people retains a special favor and an exemplary role. Late in the Old Testament, grapplings with the reality of evil and the problems generated by it lead to a clearer incorporation of notions of immortality and resurrection into the myth. Dimensions of interiority become more prominent in the Wisdom literature, without, however, a disavowal of the political dimensions of the covenant. And, finally, the way is variously prepared, once again in response to conflict and evil, for deliverance and fulfillment, extending to all the nations through the mediation of a Messiah, rising from this people, who somehow embodies both divine and human qualities.

This familiar story becomes the matrix of the Christian myth, as the early Christian communities interweave it with the remembered events of the life and death of Jesus of Nazareth, and interpret contemporary history with its help. Certain elements of the traditional myth are clarified, modified, accented. As the community which bears the promise of salvation ceases to be tribal or national, the fully universal and egalitarian character of human solidarity becomes manifest. There are simultaneous affirmations of the uniqueness and responsibility of individual persons, and, on the other side, of the profoundly corporate character of the salvific process. The clear affirmation of resurrection and life in communion beyond death provides a powerful utopian horizon for human aspirations, but at the same time the reality and value of historical existence, and its relatedness to what lies beyond history, find endorsement of various kinds. Corresponding somewhat to the distinction between history and what is beyond history, politics and interiority are both within the ambit of the Christic myth. At the center of it all stands the person of Jesus who is called the Christ, an individual pilgrim of our planet who somehow, through the mission of his Spirit, has become the central and universal force, at once immanent and transcendent, present and absent, which moves history toward its divinely predestined term.

In this Christic stage of the myth, the motif of communion emerges with a certain fullness and clarity. Every human being without exception, and all the nations, are included in the call to salvation, and achieve solidarity in view of that call. The goal of the journey is clearly depicted as communion, solidarity, *agape* (love)—God with humans and humans among themselves. Images of citizenship in a heavenly city, solidarity in a heavenly kingdom, table-fellowship at the eschatological wedding banquet, are central representations of a common human destiny. There is to be one flock and one shepherd. The body of Christ—his own resurrected human body somehow identical with the corporate unity of his disciples—is already real and yet still in the making, toward the day of *pleroma* (fullness) when God will become all in all.

This communion in transcendent destiny is anticipated and prepared in the historical solidarity of believers within the church, which is the body of Christ. Unity, *agape,* reconciliation are both indicative and imperative within that communion. The Lord Jesus himself is poignantly remembered as exhorting his disciples, on the eve of his death, to love one another, and as praying for the oneness of all who will come to believe in him (John 15:12; 17:20). As the heart of the message is that in seeing him we see the Father who is God, so the heart of the message is also that in meeting the neighbor in need, we meet the Lord Christ himself who will, on the last day, judge us on this recognition of his presence in others (Matt 25:31–46; Acts 9:4). Christ's own embrace of solidarity with sinners even to the extent of laying down his life for them becomes both the model which Christians are to follow and the source of the gift par excellence, the life-giving bond of communion (*koinonia*), the Holy Spirit (e.g. Phil 2:1–11; 3:8–11; Acts 2:33). It is this Spirit, immanent in and energizing the human spirit in individual and community, which creates the impossible possibility, the coherence of diverse gifts, integrated through the supreme gift, *agape,* for the building up of the body of Christ toward the *pleroma* or fullness (1 Cor 12–13; Eph 1:10).

The Christic myth makes room for conflict, both which the community and with respect to the surrounding culture. *Agape,* which constitutes the gift to be sought above all other particular gifts, necessarily expresses itself as patience and the will to seek reconciliation with other members of the body. Society in general is often (not always) viewed as dominated by dark and hostile forces whose defeat is certain (in fact, already in some fashion achieved), but which need to be courageously withstood by the Christian community. The communion of believers achievable within history, therefore, is partial, fragile and ambiguous. Only the victorious return of the Lord will bring the fullness of peace in communion.

A final word needs to be said on the place of the Eucharistic meal within the celebration and appropriation of the myth by the Christic community. That place is, obviously, quite central. It is principally within the structure of the ritual banquet that the narrative remembrance of the myth's beginnings takes place. It is precisely in the recollection of the action of Jesus himself in the paschal meal with his disciples on the eve of his death (linked to his ministerial practice of sharing meals with the outcasts of his religious milieu and to the accounts of his feeding the hungry masses), that the Eucharist itself is constituted as the sharing of the very body and blood of the Lord, and that the community is thereby constituted as his body. The ritual showing forth of his death until he comes in glory is thus at the center of the self-understanding of this community of disciplines. It is crucial for that community's being built up in love, as it withstands pressures from the dying world around it and as it deals with those inner conflicts which signal the lingering in its members of previous worldly attitudes which are incompatible with the gift that has been given. It is this incongruity which makes abhorrent the slightest savor of self-interest or elitism in the context of this sacred meal.

This delineation of the myth has already, to some degree, anticipated the broad lines of the theological horizon now to be sketched. In both myth and theological reflection our focus is on the relevances of communion to human needs in the area of food and drink. The following reflection is rooted in the myth and represents one rational interpretation of it. While especially indebted to some particular theological currents, it seeks a language as open as possible to rapprochement with other horizons, Christian and non-Christian, religious and secular, and particularly with liberal and Marxist ideologies.

In the Christic view of things, human life is a call and an orientation to communion, that is, to mutual understanding and love among persons. The divine objective to be realized in the fullness of the kingdom of God is simply this communion of each created person with God and, mediating and expressing that union, of created persons among themselves. Marital and familial communion and the sharing of food and drink—combined in the one central symbol of the wedding banquet, and given political resonance through the images of kingdom and city—these are the intimate and profound human experiences which find expression in Christian language about human destiny. Other terms, such as "vision," "life," "health," "happiness," describe important facets of the goal of life, but they are best seen as clustering around the central motif of the wedding banquet in the kingdom of God.

Even among Christians, not all acknowledge an assured existence of the human person beyond death. Those who do not can still affirm the importance of transcendent communion, functioning as a utopian horizon never to be fully achieved. (This is an important point for any effort at rapprochement with non-Christian religious and secular interpretations of life.) For the mainstream of Christianity, however, the death of the individual person is not an absolute termination, and there lies ahead a qualitative change in the conditions of human life and the definitive fulfillment of the divine plan in a life beyond pilgrimage.

For such a view the question arises of the relationship between history and what lies beyond history. Here opposite tendencies have traditionally been at work, with significant differences between Roman Catholics and Protestants generally (related to basic views on grace and merit, faith and works), and within each of these traditions. While acknowledging recent convergences, we may say that the Roman Catholic tendency has been toward affirming immanence and continuity in the relationship of the historical and the transhistorical, while the Protestant tendency has been toward asserting the purely future character of the kingdom of God along with the discontinuity between it and any possible anticipation of it within the ambiguities of history. There is no intent here to make a detailed argument for either position, or to fix on any particular language as most congruous. Within the Catholic theological tradition I share, however, there is a strong inclination to affirm a genuine, though fragile, partial, and ambiguous anticipatory verification of ultimate communion as taking place whenever and to the degree that humans (not only Christians), through God's gracious gift, find mutual understanding and love in the concreteness of daily life. Such realizations of communion need not be entirely free of sin and selfishness in order to prefigure the perfect communion of the kingdom. Whether or not they should be spoken of as proleptic or partial realizations of the kingdom of God is, while not unimportant, not essential. It suffices for present purposes that such realizations share to some degree and in some fashion in the destined fullness of communion of humans among themselves and with God. The notion of participation, with its rich theological and philosophical connotations, seems apt to describe this relationship between history and what is beyond history.

From such a position there follows an important corollary for a theological understanding of the sharing of food and drink. Without loss to the other multiple levels and virtualities of this human experience, it may be said that every human meal shared is, from a Christian point of view, a partial realization of and participation in the ultimate communion to which humans are called.

For Christians it likewise follows that between the "ordinary" meals which they share and the ritual meal of the Eucharist by which they express their faith and identify themselves as members of Christ, there is an intrinsic link. The Eucharist represents the sacred celebration of what is in some ways the heart of the human historical process, the sharing of food and drink, particularly in a family context.

Particularly within the context of the discussion of human rights, any helpful theological horizon must offer a perspective on the reality of and the response to conflict. It is obvious that without the abiding experience of conflict humans would not be engaged in struggle over rights. A tendency to minimize conflict has been observed as a special danger in Roman Catholic social teaching, particularly where this assumes an ontological, static, and/or hierarchical form. [6] Whatever may be said about the post-Tridentine theologies and their influence on the formulation of social doctrine, this minimizing of conflict is not inevitable within Roman Catholic theology today. Within the present century the reinterpretation of original sin and concupiscence has led to several insights which provide a basis for taking human conflict seriously:

1) while the Council of Trent does insist, against the Reformers, that baptism removes all that has the formal character of sin, it no less strongly affirms the enduring reality of concupiscence, approves speaking of it as "sin," and relates it precisely to struggle and conflict (*"ad agonem"*); [7]

2) the notion of concupiscence, with the connotations of alienation and conflict inherent in it, has been effectively "deprivatized" (or "repoliticized"), and becomes a helpful tool for the theological analysis of social relationships and structures; [8]

3) hence the societal truth contained in Paul's "where sin has increased, grace has abounded yet more" (Rom 5:20), and in Luther's "simul iustus et peccator" (both just and a sinner at the same time) has been retrieved and extended so as to allow for an understanding of the movement of history toward ultimate communion which is far from being bland and simply progressive in character;

4) hence, after a period in Roman Catholic theology in which creational and resurrectional values were recaptured, the centrality of the cross has been freshly appreciated, especially within political and liberation theologies. [9]

The result of these insights would appear to be that such features of the present world situation as conflict, alienation, ambiguity, provisionality, and pluralism are not necessarily negated or minimized by a theological view centered on communion. On the contrary, adherence to the conviction that human beings are called to communion renders the experience of deep conflict anything but trivial or pointless. If that conviction is combined with another strong conviction in the Roman Catholic tradition, namely, that the responsible exercise of human freedom has weight in promoting the coming of the definitive kingdom, and if both of these convictions are joined with an ultimate reliance on the power of God (particularly strong within the Protestant tradition), a readiness to deal with conflict with tranquil courage and realistic expectations can emerge.

In the same view, ultimate communion related to its partial realizations in the midst of conflict is necessarily a process of *reconciliation*. This important theme calls for some comment within the present reflection. Liberation theologians, not without reason, question a too facile recourse to such talk on the part of those whom they perceive to be agents of the oppressive forces at work in society. In this regard Juan Luis Segundo's argument for withholding the limited energies of effective love from those ill disposed to accept them merits sober consideration.[10] When appeals for reconciliation blunt the passion of the struggle against injustice or leave those making the appeal with unquestioned assumptions about what needs to change, they become instruments of further oppression. If the theme of reconciliation is to be part of a horizon theology appropriate for our society today, both its indicative and its imperative mood must be cleansed of whatever hinders responsible efforts to promote genuine communion. Remembrance of the reconciliation already effected in Christ can degenerate, to use Metz's language, into mere nostalgia, leading to acquiescence in an unchanging *status quo*; or it can, on the contrary, take the form of "dangerous memories," letting the historical sufferings of the poor energize us for efficacious hope.[11] Similarly, utopian imagination of a world free from conflict can be evasive fantasy, or it can, in the movement from dream to project, stimulate the taking of responsibility for the conflictual present. Not all that appears to be reconciling—or unreconciling—is truly so. Psychology testifies that healthy human relationships depend on the ability to say "No" (sometimes with anger), as well as "Yes."

All of which points to the need for discretion on the part of Christian communities and the church as a whole in exercising the "ministry of reconciliation" and communicating the "message of reconciliation." One of the basic conditions for this message and ministry being responsibly undertaken is that the reality of conflict within the church be acknowledged and dealt with on the basis of the Christic myth and not on any other basis. It is not by professing to be a paragon of tranquil communion but by dealing with its own vulnerability to alienation and conflict that the church serves the world by addressing to it an authentic message of reconciliation. Being a human community, it will experience no less than secular communities the human realities of doubt, conflict, dissent, and alienation. What distinguishes it is the explicit acknowledgment of the need for daily reconciliation in conflict, and the naming of this need and of the power to satisfy it in terms of the Christic myth of communion. "I believe in the forgiveness of sins," following immediately upon ". . . the holy Catholic Church, the communion of saints," thus becomes an apt confession of the identity of the Church as sign of reconciling human communion.

Here again, given the reference to human needs regarding the sharing of food and drink, it is appropriate to advert to the centrality of Eucharist. Paul's description of the deplorable behavior of some in the Corinthian church during the celebration of the Eucharist becomes a paradigm for the perennial threat of divisiveness and injustice precisely where communion ought most to be holy—the sacred banquet which reconstitutes the church as the community which celebrates both the pasch of Jesus Christ and the ordinary meals of human families. It is not too much to say that, where a local community is living heedlessly or uncommittedly with situations of unjust hunger, the Eucharistic celebrations of that community lose a certain social validity without which the effective presence of Christ in his body is lacking.

Because the present essay focuses on communion as the destiny of persons, it must pay attention to the relationship of person and community, for it is in community that communion finds embodiment. Both individuals and communities have their needs, and in an imperfect world these needs may conflict. Dealing with such conflict effectively presupposes some prior understanding of the relationship itself. Another fact calling for some attention to the person-community relationship is the very different accents which it is given within the liberal and Marxist traditions.

We have seen that in the Old Testament preparation of the Christic myth, sometimes the individual and sometimes the community of Israel was central. Similarly, the New Testament is sometimes more interested in individual destiny, sometimes in the corporate reality of the body of Christ, and sometimes in the relationship of the individual to the corporate body. The Bible as a whole gives us both a sense of the unique dignity of each human being in God's sight and a sense of the value of each human community, prefiguring the ultimate communion of nations and peoples in the marriage feast of the kingdom of heaven.

Some two millennia after Christ, a study of the social teaching of the Roman Catholic Church discloses a distinct integrative tendency with respect to individual person and community. Assertions of the inviolable dignity of each person are characteristically accompanied or followed by insistence on the social character of personhood. Similarly, considerations of the centrality of the common good stand frequently in polarity with accents on individual dignity. [12]

The basic theological affirmation here is that personhood is intrinsically relational in character, and that personal development has as its core an orientation to be in communion with other persons. This affirmation finds support in psychological, sociological, and philosophical literature, for example, with respect to the needs of the very young and the very old for experience of human community.

Between communion and community, as here understood, the relationship is that of the abstract and the concrete. A human community is a concrete embodiment of communion. The range of communities extends from committed friendship through marriage, family, ethnic group, voluntary association, and nation. Wherever mutual understanding and love among persons are verified with a measure of stability, the reality of community is had. As historical embodiments of communion, all communities live under the influence of change, conflict, ambiguity, pluralism, and the like. Further, a community is not just the sum total of its individual members, but is constituted precisely by their positive relationship of mutual understanding and love. There is a distinct reality of the common good, which includes but is not reducible to the individual goods of the members. A community is the objective actualization of communion.

This discussion of the relationship of person and community leads inevitably to the question of the relationship of love and justice, a theme widely explored in both philosophy and theology. [13] In line with the integrative tendency characteristic of the Roman Catholic tradition (shared, however, by such Protestant theologians as Paul Tillich), the understanding of the love/justice relationship here expounded makes the following basic affirmations.

First, love itself is understood both as a unitive tendency and as the actualization of that tendency in realized communion.

Second, when there is question of human (as contrasted with divine) love, benevolence toward the self and toward the other are inseparable dimensions. Both spiritually and psychologically, healthy human love refuses the dilemma of despising either the self or the other. Humans are incapable of more than a relative altruism, but they are, by God's grace, capable of that.

Third, justice, the virtue which renders to each person or community its due, lies within the structure of love. As a social embodiment or form of love, it stands in a reciprocal relationship with love as communion. Because human communion, modelled on divine communion, is frustrated, not realized, in the absorption of one person by another, the dynamic of love contains affirmation and confirmation of the other precisely as other, and this belongs to the virtue of justice. It belongs to the dignity of each person to be acknowledged and respected in his/her uniqueness. Thus, while love as communion regards the other as another *self* (alter *ego*), love in the form of justice regards the other precisely as *other,* and permits and desires that the other be other.

It might be objected that such a close linkage of love and justice leads in both theory and practice to a neglect of the reality of human ambiguity and conflict, and hence to a sentimental softening of the passion for justice. One response might be that the risk is indeed present, but is a reasonable risk at a time when the dichotomizing of love and justice has tended to depoliticize love and depersonalize justice. A stronger response might be that a prudent love conscious of ambiguity and conflict as existential aspects of the human condition will *insist,* for the sake of both lover and beloved, upon appropriate structures of justice, even within the sphere of deepest human intimacy (witness the insistence in Christian tradition on the contractual nature of the marital covenant), and still more as humans move into more public and less personal relationships, where love as communion lacks the vehicles of intimacy for sustaining due regard for the dignity of the other as other. Especially in a fallen world not wholly redeemed, love must be on guard against its own fragility by providing stable safeguards against the dissolution of the balance between altruism and self-regard. The order of justice represents the structuring of such safeguards into human relationships. Both love and justice are to be seen within a religious and theological horizon of communion which in turn has implications for the identification of human needs and rights in the area of food and drink. To these implications I now turn.

III. HUMAN COMMUNION AND HUMAN RIGHTS

One might summarize the preceding reflections in the following proposition: the sharing of food and drink, whatever other levels of meaning it may have, represents a central anticipation of that human communion which is the transcendent horizon giving back meaning and value to all that is human.

What implications might this statement have, in theory and practice, for the theme of the Woodstock human rights project: Needs, Rights, and Power in an Interdependent World? This concluding part of the essay will delineate some possible implications. Most of these will be theoretical in character, or will deal with those changes in perspective and attitude which are needed if new energies are to flow from the notion of human communion into the struggle to satisfy needs and fulfill rights with all the resources available.

First, the notion of *human dignity,* with the promise it contains of evoking a broad consensus within each of the traditions being studied, is illumined by an appreciation of communion as transcendent horizon. Often the dignity and the good of the person is placed in a polar relationship with the common good, as if they were competing values. When, however, human dignity is viewed precisely as a capacity for communion, then every historical realization of the common good becomes at the same time an anticipatory realization of the transcendent good of each person. This remains true even though, at the level of struggle over finite goods in a conflictual world, contradictory claims cannot be simultaneously satisfied. Paradoxical as it may be, the "losing" claimant in a rights dispute remains a beneficiary of the experience, provided—a large proviso indeed—the settlement has been just. For in the measure that justice—inseparable, as we have seen, from the communion of love—has been achieved, the result is to enlarge the presence and power of human solidarity, which benefits *all,* whether "winner" or "loser" from a more narrow perspective. Conversely, the perpetration of injustice violates the human dignity of perpetrator and victim alike. For injustice is essentially and comprehensively alienating, and, by depriving the aggressor of some measure of communion with others, it assaults and weakens his human dignity as well as that of the victim. Thus even from the standpoint of genuine self-interest, injustice is self-destructive by its very nature, by its diminishment of communion. It is not fanciful to see here a secular version of the powerful gospel challenge, "What does it profit anyone to gain the whole world and suffer the loss of one's soul?" (Luke 16:26)

Second, the notion of communion as transcendent horizon for all that is human affords a new perspective for considering the subject of *basic human needs.*[14] If communion is conceived as that which gives meaning and value to all that is human, then every anticipatory realization of it has the character of partial fulfillment of this most basic of human needs. This does not imply that every categorical instance of human communion is the fulfillment of some specific and basic human need, but only that each specific fulfillment of basic human needs ought to be conceived and measured from the horizon of transcendent communion. For example, let us suppose that a particular person's nutritional and health needs are being met with the help of some public program of assistance or development. But if this is taking place in such a context of bureaucratic or ideological insensitivity to deeper needs that the person's simultaneous need to experience communion with others in the sharing of food and drink is not being furthered, or is even being hindered, what is one to say about the fulfillment of basic human needs in such a situation? From the standpoint of the present essay one would have to speak of wasted energies, and even of inner contradictions, in any effort to satisfy specific needs which did not, in appropriate measure, further the most basic need of all. While such a line of reasoning remains somewhat theoretical, its import for affecting attitudes and motivations, and eventually for helping to shape policy, seems clear. The horizon of communion is capable of functioning as a paradigm affecting judgment and decision at many levels, both theoretical and practical, regarding the sharing of food and drink. It makes explicit important aspects of our life together, the neglect of which will leave policy decisions inadequate or unfruitful.

Third, the horizon of communion may provide one way, at least, of linking basic human needs and basic human rights. There are various ways of relating the two terms. One is to see basic needs as a moral category, or almost so, and then to list such needs among the classes of basic human rights. Another is to speak of certain needs as the *basis* of socioeconomic rights. A third tendency is to keep socioeconomic needs at a distance from all conceptions of rights. From the present perspective it is appropriate: 1) to speak of needs as a *basis* for rights, and not formally as a right, since "right" connotes a specifically moral demand where "need" designates a premoral or ontic reality out of which the moral demand arises; 2) to distinguish, with respect to *both* needs and rights, what is transcendent (namely, communion) and what is specific or categorical. Thus the basic need for shared transcendence realized in anticipatory fashion in the fulfillment of specific and basic needs is the ultimate ground of specific and basic rights. Such a ground does not exclude, of course, a more proximate grounding of specific rights in specific needs. What it does is to provide the needs/rights linkage with a foundation which transcends the merely pragmatic and so points to its moral seriousness.

Fourth—and partly as a consequence of this way of relating basic human needs and basic human rights—the claim of this essay may help to deal with the rather common dichotomizing of the two sets of rights described in the United Nations Declaration and Covenants. There may well be a fatal flaw in the usual discussion of these, namely, a dualistic tendency to identify such needs as food and drink, health and housing, as if they had to do only with physical survival and minimal human functioning, and, on the other side, a tendency to omit entirely the category of need where there is question of political and civil rights. Such a division has a certain pragmatic plausibility, in that the first group of needs and rights provides the necessary material, physiological, and psychic substratum which conditions the exercise of all rights. Unfortunately, however, in the process of indicating that certain human needs and rights are crucial to survival (and so, from this viewpoint, basic), we lose that which is most distinctively human about such needs and rights. Thus needs touching food and drink are reduced to the purely material, nutritional, hygienic, and physiological, neglecting the fact that human dignity requires that food be taken in freedom and in communion with others. Once needs and rights touching food and drink, domicile, and the like are identified more broadly from the horizon of human communion, it becomes clear that they are no less deeply human than, say, the need and right to political participation. If, for example, human freedom is taken as a pivotal value, it is verified no less in the sharing of food and drink within the family than in civic participation. Parents are no less affronted in their basic human dignity, as expressed in the right to participate in decisions which deeply affect their humanity, by undue restrictions in what they have to say about the provision of meals for their children than in what they have to say about who exercises legislative office in their country. A related advantage of identifying needs and rights from the horizon of communion is that, without negating such distinctions as private and public, we can prevent such distinctions from becoming separations, and we can affirm the mutual interdependence of diverse needs and rights. Thus, in the present example, the right to political participation and the right to share family meals with integral human dignity are not totally different rights, even though analytical distinction of them is necessary. When the sharing of food and drink is viewed in its integrally human reality, it cannot be reduced to a purely material need; and, as a right, it is not of its nature inferior to those rights commonly classified as civil and political. Thus the notion of human communion, functioning as horizon for reflection, offers a new and interesting standpoint from which to ponder the relationships of the two conventional sets of rights.

Fifth, the notion and role of communion as here described can throw light on the basic conditions required if situations of conflict are to be dealt with realistically and effectively. Here we are brought back to the brief observations on love and justice made in the second part of this essay. The same realism which tests every theory of human rights in the furnace of human conflict must attend to the fact that every struggle over rights presupposes at least a minimal state of communion operative among the parties to the conflict. Otherwise, why would rational arguments and appeals to values be offered as cogent or suasive? What characterizes moral and legal conflict over rights and distinguishes it from recourse to force is its distinctively human character, which includes an implicit recognition that the partners to the conflict are somehow called to be and to some degree are in communion. Far from being a disavowal of radical communion, willingness to struggle through political and juridical processes for the vindication of rights is a sign of basic solidarity with the opponent. One should not underestimate, even in relationships of the most intense hostility and aggressiveness, how deep and tenacious is the belief, in individuals, groups, and nations, that communion is the locus naturalis of humans. I would venture to claim that, short of total psychosis, this powerful dynamism toward communion, while its fulfillment may be seriously thwarted, can never be radically eliminated. If this is true, should it not be given a major place in the resolution of the potentially suicidal conflicts which afflict humanity today?

One consequence of such reasoning: when the sense of human communion is diminished or eroded—and there are numerous signs of this in both domestic and international spheres—intolerable burdens are placed upon the legal and juridical structures and processes which make it possible for human life to go on, particularly in the public sector. Love and communion are no substitute for justice, yet justice and the struggle to resolve conflicts over rights are doomed to frustration unless a basic solidarity is acknowledged and operative between parties in conflict. This is one crucial way in which a basic health in society conditions the viability of a just and workable state and the stability of relationships among the nations.

Sixth, the horizon of communion can suggest a salutary bordering and deepening of the third member of the needs, rights, power triad. [15] A narrow approach to power in the context of basic human needs and basic human rights tends, first, to conceive of power predominantly and even exclusively in military, political, and economic terms (these last two with an accent on the power exercised by structures), to the neglect of many other diverse forms of human power; and, second, it tends to separate sharply the concept of power from the concepts of needs and rights. Such a narrowing of the sense of the concept of power is legitimate and useful particularly for pragmatic and analytical purposes. But it is not, as in the case of needs, the only concept of power possible, and it can coexist with a concept whose source is the horizon of communion and whose relationship with the concepts of needs and rights is more intimate. There is no space here to develop this in detail, but here are a few indications of a possibly fruitful line of reflection.

The goal of transcendent communion impels persons and groups by the power of attraction to seek it through its concrete historical realizations. Hence the truth behind the adage, "Love makes the world go round." The sharing of food and drink is, then, a center where human power is exercised in a notable way. Less measurable by empirical methods, perhaps, than other forms of power, it does not cease to merit and need attention and respect. Furthermore, this compelling power of communion endows human needs, at least when they are recognized, with a power of their own. Needy persons themselves would not be inclined to make their needs known to others unless they were relying, implicitly at least, on the power of communion to evoke compassion and understanding in others. Nor would these others experience as they do the emotional and moral constraints and incentives toward relieving human needs unless the same power of communion were operative. One need only recall what happens when imminent famine and starvation (recently, for example, in Cambodia) activate the forces present in human organizations and in millions of human hearts.

Similarly, human rights may legitimately be viewed as a form of power. In fact, a traditional definition conceives right precisely as *potentia moralis* (moral power). [16] In the presence of my right, others are both morally constrained and morally energized to work for its effective acknowledgment. In this way, too, the radical human thirst for communion is the source of human power of a kind which, even while it cannot substitute for more tangible and extrinsic forms of power, cannot be substituted for by them. Once again, advertence to current history—here the immense energies expended by individuals, organizations, and nations to effectuate respect for the right to food—confirms the claim that human communion, in its interaction with human needs and rights, represents an immense source of human power.

Seventh, while the present essay makes no effort to draw policy conclusions, the basic viewpoint here expressed can eventually find application in setting hard policy directions. A first general area of application is that of *setting goals and objectives* for the broader aspects of food policy. Such formulations, if the present essay is to be heeded, should not stop with the goal of providing physiological sustenance for individuals, but should go on to providing or fostering those basic climates which make it possible for people to make mealtime an experience of human communion. Obviously, the distance from such a broad goal to concrete policies and programs is well nigh infinite, but this is no reason to hold back from courageously setting out on the road.

To this end it might be worthwhile, for example, to engage some human energies and financial resources in a few *pilot projects,* which, though limited in size, would be relatively comprehensive in scope, in that there would be attention to all the major factors which go into the integral human experience of communion in the sharing of food and drink. There would of necessity be question of *community-building,* with its essential components of education for the participants, and careful analysis of the concrete situation from all the points of view which have been described in the first part of this essay. One specific enterprise might be to identify a few existing and vital grass-roots communities, and study the place which sharing food and drink actually has within such communities, and possibly within the family units which may compose them.

In all this I am assuming some of the basic lessons of recent efforts to help deprived people: that the central task is to enable or empower people to do for themselves what no one else can do for them, but which they themselves may not be able to do for themselves unless others remove hindrances or provide auxiliary resources; that efforts to help others must begin by helping people identify and cherish resources which they already have, whether or not they recognize them and utilize them wisely; that the helping person or group must exercise a severe austerity by withholding pressures and suggestions for change which are linked with stereotypes or assumptions not shared by those being helped.

But it would be a mistake to limit our gaze to what needs to be done for others. It might well be that the best contribution that public and private agencies in the developed world could make in the immediate future is an educational effort directed first of all to heightening *our own* sensitivity to the importance of communion in sharing food and drink. Unless the imagination and passion of those who exercise power in the area of food and hunger are caught with the importance of human communion in sharing meals, little significant change will take place in the policies they shape and the programs they administer for the benefit of others. There is question here of changing outlooks not merely in those directly engaged in the fulfillment of food and hunger needs but in all of us. What happens at deep human levels at mealtime in Peoria or Brooklyn eventually has a lot to say about what will happen at the same levels at mealtime in Kenya or Bolivia. We are dealing here, admittedly, with profound and relatively immobile attitudes within different cultures, not with the technicalities and specifics of government food programs. For this reason we need to acknowledge the limitations of what governments can do, and to realize the potential of religious bodies as well as of movements and organizations such as Bread for the World, which aim directly at affecting the consciousness of masses of people.

This is not to say that governmental bodies have no role at all in furthering the values associated with human communion. Especially when such values can be identified humanistically and in continuity with a national heritage, it belongs to government to exercise its considerable and unique power for the furthering of such values.

Eighth, I would expect that a fresh recogntion of the centrality of human communion in the sharing of food and drink would generate new and interesting questions, both theoretical and practical, for ethicians. For example, in the complex of decisions by which scarce resources are made more available for some than for others, should the capacity for a meaningful life, sometimes used as an ethical norm in such decisions, be so defined as to include capacity for human communion? There is also the whole set of ethical questions directly touching on human rights, of which two might be mentioned by way of example: 1) Does each person have a *basic* human right to be in communion with his family, ethnic community, national community, and, if so, how is this right to be ranked and linked among the whole panoply of individual human rights? 2) Is each family and ethnic group the subject of rights, including rights which ought to be termed *basic?*

Ninth, because the present essay has been developed on the basis of only one tradition, that of Roman Catholic Christianity, it raises the question whether a similar horizon of communion is not possible, or better, already implicitly operative, within other religious and secular traditions. Certainly, within Christianity, Roman Catholic theology has no monopoly on the bond of love and communion which is at the heart of Christian faith. [17] Within the various secular traditions, too, there are strong grounds for suspecting the presence and influence of ideas closely akin to that of communion. One thinks, in the philosophy of the Enlightenment, of the notion of *fraternity,* and in the Marxist tradition, of the notion of *solidarity*. [18] However different the rhetoric and accent, these adjacent notions reflect something transcendent within the human spirit, opening up possibilities for a convergence of understanding and aspirations within the human community. A comparison of the notions of communion, fraternity, and solidarity in the three traditions, especially as these are interwoven with the diverse cultures where these traditions have been influential, might open up new vistas at a time when the pragmatic interdependence of peoples and cultures calls for ideological recognition of the common human heritage.

*   *   *

In bringing this long reflection to a close, I would ask the reader to recall what was said earlier regarding complexity, disorder, burden, and frustration in the struggle to satisfy basic human needs and respect basic human rights. In such a situation we need something beyond more reliable statistics, more clever analyses, a shifting of economic and political priorities, significant financial modifications, or realignments of power. Each of these has its importance, but each and all depend for their effectiveness and quality on deeper energies, which touch especially human passion and human imagination. There are moments of crisis, puzzlement, and frustration when pragmatic approaches are incapable of replenishing the wellsprings of commitment, on which everything else depends. New and attractive vistas need to be disclosed, and simultaneously dormant memories must be allowed to emerge and lend energy. Whatever may be said about "ordinary times," it is quite clear that this time of crisis calls for all the resources that reminiscence (return to roots) and dreaming imagination can provide.

More particularly, with respect to the food and hunger question, there are many reasons why recourse to the symbol of human communion might serve as focus for such a replenishment of energies. Communion—being with other humans in loving interchange in the central experience of replenishing human life itself—defines the very experience of being human for all of us. It is central to our personal and communal myths; it contains a wealth of symbolic significance; it calls forth a variety of creative initiatives; it concerns each one of us deeply, as even the mildest hunger pangs will testify; it is a twice- or thrice-daily crossroads where just about every facet of human interest, experience, and skill intersect; it is at once sensate and dreaming, rational and affective, in what it calls for and what it nourishes; especially in the context of family, it stands for both heritage and future; in a word, it is both worthy of the investment of all the resources at our disposal, and capable of disclosing and releasing energies whose existence we have forgotten or whose employment we have despaired of unleashing.

On the attitudinal and motivational level, then, *the release of imagination and the engagement of passion* are what I would see as the principal fruits of admitting deeply into our consciousness the horizon of communion as it finds realization in the sharing of food and drink. Such a suggestion is naturally open to suspicions of utopianism. Who could deny that we are capable of distorting it into a radical disengagement from empirical and rational sanity? But in itself it is by no means incompatible with the legitimate role of science, technology, organizational skill, and the like—which of course themselves came about only through the free play of passion and imagination in the creative minds of their great founders.

I do not expect the specialists of various cadres to abandon what they are doing in order to be passionate and visionary. But, if they are really to contribute to making human life more human, they need occasionally to ask questions not only about the technical intersection of their specialization with other specializations, but also about common horizons of meaning and value. We have had enough experience of the destructive potential of science and technology to be able to assert that whoever is not for the human is against it. And will those engrossed in specialized contributions to the human be able to keep a sense of and appreciation for the human without periodically asking questions about the human in its totality and range?

Then, too, where specialists come into conflict within their own field, and still more with specialists from other fields, some agreed-upon horizon of common interest and concern can serve them not precisely as a rational norm but as a focus of communality, helping them to relativize more limited points of view and to be more open to positive cooperation with those whose specialized avenues toward the human diverge from their own.

Finally, in response to a natural objection, namely, that a shift of attention to the horizon of communion would represent a siphoning off of limited energies from realistic objectives to visionary and problematic goals, I can only respond, on the basis of what has been said, that nothing is so wasteful of resources as despair and frustration, unless it be the locked-in posture of those who are unable to conceive an alternative to the present. It is what one biblical scholar has termed the numbness inherent in the "royal imagination," not the excitement (ultimately both rational and pragmatic) generated by "prophetic imagination," which hinders significant movement. [19] "We are doing the best we can" is a plaint which ought to signal to us that the best is not very good, compared with what is both needed and possible.

Perhaps, when all this has been said, the title of this essay, "On the Need to Break Bread Together," will appear not only as a partial statement of its thesis, but as pointing to what must be, in last analysis, the final argument for commending that thesis. Ultimately, it may well be the actual experience of breaking bread together, with full consciousness of its import and its power in one's personal life and the life of one's community, which offers the decisive argument in favor of the thesis. For North Americans, this may very well come down to a rediscovery of the real meaning of our great American feast, Thanksgiving Day.

NOTES TO CHAPTER 10

1. For the notion of "horizon" in its technical philosophical and theological usages, see David Tracy, *The Achievement of Bernard Lonergan* (New York: Herder & Herder, 1970), pp. 1–21 and *passim.* The present essay makes use of the term less technically, in the general sense of a transcendent goal shaping the categorical perceptions, attitudes, and choices of human beings.

2. The term is, of course, from Paul Tillich, whose view on love and justice will be treated later in the essay.

3. The following material has been found especially helpful for understanding the present food and hunger situation: P. Abelson, ed. *Food: Politics, Economics, Nutrition, and Research* (Washington, D.C.: American Association for the Advancement of Science, 1975), especially the essay of J. Dwyer and J. Mayer, "Beyond Economics and Nutrition: The Complex Basis of Food Policy," pp. 74–78, which highlights the need to enlarge perspectives and relate various disciplines; W. Aiken and H. LaFollette, eds., *World Hunger and Moral Obligation* (Englewood Cliffs, N.J.: Prentice-Hall, 1977); E. Barbotin, *The Humanity of Man* (Maryknoll, N.Y.: Orbis Books, 1975), Chap. 7: "The Meal," pp. 327–338; idem, *The Humanity of God* (Maryknoll, N.Y.: Orbis Books, 1976), Chap. 7: "The Meal of God," pp. 273–305; B. Birch and L. Rasmussen, *The Predicament of the Prosperous* (Philadelphia: Westminster Press, 1978); B. Birch, "Hunger, Poverty and Biblical Religion," *Christian Century* (1975) 593–599; L. Brown and E. Eckholm, *By Bread Alone* (New York: Praeger, 1974); P. Brown and H. Shue, eds. *Food Policy: The Responsibility of the United States in the Life and Death Choices* (New York: Free Press, 1977); *The Catholic World* (September–October, 1977) on "Property and Stewardship"; J. Gremillion, ed., *Food / Energy and the Major Faiths* (Maryknoll: Orbis Books, 1978); M. Hellwig, *The Eucharist and the Hungers of the World* (New York: Paulist Press, 1976); D. Hessel, ed., *Beyond Survival: Bread and Justice in Christian Perspective* (New York: Friendship, 1977); Interreligious Task Force on U.S. Food Policy, *Identifying a Food Policy Agenda for the 1980's: A Working Paper* (Washington, D.C., 1980); G. Lucas and T. Ogletree, eds., *Lifeboat Ethics: The Moral Dilemmas of World Hunger* (New York: Harper & Row, 1976); F. Moore Lappe and J. Collins, *Food First: Beyond the Myth of Scarcity* (Boston: Houghton Mifflin, 1977); R. Sider,

Rich Christians in an Age of Hunger: A Biblical Study (New York: Paulist Press, 1977); A. Simon, *Bread for the World* (New York: Paulist Press, 1975).

4. On the notion of "middle axiom," see C. H. Grenholm, *Christian Social Ethics in a Revolutionary Age* (Uppsala: Verbum, 1973), pp. 86–105. The notion was developed by J. H. Oldham and John Bennett for dealing with the relationship of Christian love to politics and society. A not entirely dissimilar notion of Roman Catholic vintage is that of "prescriptions" (as distinct from principles), as elaborated by Karl Rahner, *The Dynamic Element in the Church* (New York: Herder & Herder, 1964), pp. 13–41.

5. This part of the essay has drawn for the most part on the rather common insights and convictions of the Christian tradition. The accents of such thinkers as Emile Mersch, Pierre Teilhard de Chardin, and Karl Rahner are especially prominent.

6. See D. Hollenbach, *Claims in Conflict. Retrieving and Renewing the Catholic Rights Tradition* (New York: Paulist Press, 1979), pp. 142, 161–166.

7. Council of Trent, Decree on Original Sin in *Enchiridion Symbolorum* ed. Heinrich Denzinger and Adolf Schönmetzer (Herder: Freiburg-im-Breisgau, 1965), n. 1515. For an English translation, see *The Church Teaches,* ed. John F. Clarkson, S.J., et al. (St. Louis: B. Herder, 1955), n. 376.

8. See J. Metz, art. "Konkupiszenz," *Handbuch Theologischer Grundbegriffe,* ed. H. Fries (Munich: Kösel, 1962), pp. 843–851; K. Rahner, *Theological Investigations* 10, trans. David Bourke (New York: Herder & Herder, 1973), pp. 341–348.

9. See, for example, J. Metz, *Faith in History and Society. Toward a Practical Fundamental Theology* (New York: Seabury Press, 1980); I. Ellacuría, *Freedom Made Flesh: The Mission of Christ and His Church* (Maryknoll, N.Y.: Orbis Books, 1976); J. Moltmann, *The Crucified God: The Cross of Christ as the Foundation and Criticism of Christian Theology* (New York: Harper & Row, 1974).

10. J. Segundo, *The Liberation of Theology* (Maryknoll, N.Y.: Orbis Books, 1976), pp. 156–165. For commentary, see A. Hennelly, *Theologies in Conflict: The Challenge of Juan Luis Segundo* (Maryknoll, N.Y.: Orbis Books, 1979), pp. 131–134.

11. See J. Metz, pp. 109–115.

12. See, for example, the juxtaposition in Vatican II's *Constitution on the Church in the Modern World* of the first two chapters, which deal, respectively, with the human person and with community. For commentary on the relationship, see Hollenbach (n. 6), and J. Calvez and J. Perrin, *The Church and Social Justice. The Social Teachings of the Church from Leo XIII to Pius XII* (1878–1958) (Chicago: Regnery, 1961), pp. 101–132.

13. From the many philosophical and theological treatments of love and justice, the brief discussion here draws especially on R. Johann, "Love and Justice," in R. De George, ed., *Ethics and Society: Original Essays on Contemporary Moral Problems* (New York: Doubleday, 1966), pp. 25–47; P. Tillich, *Love, Power and Justice* (New York: Oxford Univer-

sity Press, 1954); D. Williams, *The Spirit and the Forms of Love* (New York: Harper, 1968), chap. 12: "Love and Social Justice," pp. 243–275. See also V. Furbish, *The Love Command in the New Testament* (New York: Abingdon, 1972), especially pp. 194–218; E. Gardner, *Biblical Faith and Social Ethics* (New York: Harper, 1960) pp. 248–270; G. Gilleman, *The Primacy of Charity in Moral Theology* (Westminster, Md.: Newman, 1959), pp. 330–341; D. Hollenbach, *Claims,* pp. 167–178, and in J. Haughey, ed., *The Faith that Does Justice: Examining the Christian Sources for Social Change* (New York: Paulist Press, 1977), pp. 211–215; J. Langan, "What Jerusalem Says to Athens," in *The Faith that Does Justice,* pp. 162–169; G. Outka, *Agape: An Ethical Analysis* (New Haven: Yale University Press, 1972), Chap. 3, "Agape and Justice," pp. 75–92.

14. See D. Christiansen's essay in the present volume; also D. Goulet, "Strategies for Meeting Human Needs," *New Catholic World* (September / October 1978), pp. 196–202; D. Lee, *Freedom and Culture: Essays* (Englewood Cliffs, N.J.: Prentice-Hall, 1959), pp. 70–77; P. Alston, "Human Rights and Basic Needs: A Critical Assessment," in *Human Rights Journal* 12 (1979), pp. 19–67; T. Ogletree, "The Relation of Values to Human Need: An Analysis Based upon Paul Ricoeur's Philosophy of the Will," in *Journal of the American Academy of Religion* XLV /1 Supplement (March 1977), pp. 303–330; P. Streeten and S. J. Burki, "Basic Needs: Some Issues," *World Development* 6 (1978), pp. 411–421. Unfortunately, it has not been possible within the limits of the present essay to develop the organic linkages that exist within the whole spectrum of categorical needs. Such linkages are implicit in the description given in the first part of this essay of the connections between the various systems that contribute to the food and hunger problem and efforts at solution. It is clear that even from less transcendent viewpoints human needs are seen as both varied and interconnected. A case can be made for arguing both psychologically and sociologically that love as communion is a basic human need.

15. On the theology of power, see P. Tillich; and K. Rahner, "The Theology of Power," *Theological Investigations* 4 (Baltimore: Helicon, 1966), pp. 391–409; R. Guardini, *Power and Responsibility: A Course of Action for the New Age* (Chicago: Regenery, 1961).

16. For manual discussion, see M. Zalba, *Theologiae Moralis Summa* 2 (Madrid: Biblioteca de Autores Cristianos, 1957), pp. 205–218.

17. The present essay, limiting itself to a Roman Catholic perspective, has not dealt with recent Protestant works on human rights, nor with the Protestant contribution to a theology of communion. On the former aspect, see A. Miller, ed. *A Christian Declaration of Human Rights* (Grand Rapids, Mich.: Eerdmans, 1977); G. Forell and W. Lazareth, *Human Rights: Rhetoric or Reality?* (Philadelphia: Fortress, 1978): H. Todt, "Theological Reflections on the Foundations of Human Rights," *Lutheran World* 24 (1977) pp. 45–58; G. Krusche, "Human Rights in a Theological Perspective: A Contribution from the GDR," *ibid,* pp. 59–65; Commission of the Churches on International Affairs of the World Council of Churches, *Human Rights and Christian Responsibility; LWF Report* (formerly *Lutheran*

244 *Thomas Clarke, S.J.*

World), (September 1978, 1 / 2); "A Lutheran Reader on Human Rights" (Geneva and New York, n.d.); *WCC Exchange* n. 6, December 1977. A worthwhile ecumenical venture might be the exploration of the relationship between communion and covenant in the Scriptures and in these two Christian traditions.

18. On these and related themes, see: C. Erasmus, *In Search of the Common Good: Utopian Experiments Past and Future* (New York: Free Press, 1977); R. Garaudy, *Marxism in the Twentieth Century* (New York: Scribner's, 1970), idem, *The Alternative Future. A Vision of Christian Marxism* (New York: Simon & Schuster, 1974); G. Girardi, *Marxism and Christianity* (New York: Macmillan, 1968), pp. 51 ff.; W. McWilliams, *The Idea of Fraternity in America* (Berkeley: University of California, 1973); J. Nelson, ed., *No Man Is Alien: Essays on the Unity of Mankind* (Leiden: Brill, 1971); J. Sellers, *Warming Fires: The Quest for Community in America* (New York: Seabury Press, 1975).

19. W. Bruggemann, *The Prophetic Imagination* (Philadelphia: Fortress, 1978).

Drew Christiansen, S.J.

11. Basic Needs: Criterion for the Legitimacy of Development

I. GROWTH AND JUSTICE

For the men and women who study development, a dominant concern the last few years has been the Basic Human Needs strategy. This approach to the promotion of economic and social progress aims at eliminating the worst aspects of poverty by providing the necessities of life to families at the bottom of the economic ladder. Ostensibly, development programs have always been concerned with eliminating poverty, but traditional strategies have attempted to lift the poor out of their misery only indirectly by building up the total economy of the developing countries. Economists had hoped that with the growth of modern industry and agriculture the new wealth of developing countries would "trickle down" to the poor, gradually bringing them employment, education, and health care. Unfortunately, the trickle-down theory proved a vain dream. More often than not, economic development only aggravated inequalities, with some countries, like India, Mexico, and Brazil, severed into two cultures: one urban, modern, and rich, the other rural, traditional, and poor. Moreover, the poor have often been net losers in the efforts of their countries to develop, less able to sustain themselves today than a decade ago. [1]

The Basic Needs approach breaks with previous views of economic development by focusing directly on the conditions in which poor people live. It revives the dormant hope of eliminating poverty by directing government efforts at supplying goods like food, water, and education directly to people in need. Accordingly, the strategy reasserts human welfare as a normative criterion justifying all development, for needs are only the most urgent aspects of personal welfare. Furthermore, the renewed concern for the poor, and particularly the appearance of need as the criterion for development, mark the delegitimation of economic growth as the value that justifies the economic policies of states. The purpose of this essay will be first to examine the moral reasons why growth for its own sake has become morally suspect, and then to outline the limits a principle of need sets for development cooperation in the future.

Growth: The Unkept Promise.   Legitimation is the process of justifying institutional arrangements by appealing to normative values. Police powers, for example, are justified by the need for security. The control of industrial pollution, to cite another case, is justified in the interest of public health. The immediate goals of particular policies make sense only in relation to these larger purposes. In the case of development and development assistance, programs have been put forth in the name of justice, the promise of a better life, and the fight against Communism. A recurrent theme in the legitimation of economic development, of course, has been the elimination of poverty. It was, and still is, a goal with deep-rooted appeal. The appeal of economic growth was that it raised hopes that poverty would be eliminated in the course of doing other more glamorous things, like industrializing the economy. Economists projected that manufacturing and farming for export would bring wealth, wealth would yield additional jobs, and jobs would give people opportunity to improve their lives. But industrialization and agrarian modernization, according to economic theory, would have to precede growth in employment and provision of basic needs. Consequently, over the years growth itself became a normative value, displacing welfare, equity, and the elimination of poverty as legitimations of development. Instead of being a means to certain moral goals, growth became an end in itself. [2]

From the beginning, however, growth was recommended on the ground that it would help alleviate misery. Efficiency and equity were linked together as the warrants for development. It should have been no surprise, then, that political support for growth would wane when it failed to provide the remedies it had promised for the poor. When evidence of the failure of growth began to appear, a reexamination of the purposes of development occurred, in which the unarticulated principle of equity, measured by the service of basic needs, began to emerge out of the shadow of economic efficiency, measured by growth in productivity, as a goal for policy. [3]

The failure of growth to meet the demands of equity was symptomatic of the contrary institutional commitments of the people charged with executing development policies. More often than not, they believed that efficiency and equity were incompatible ideals. For many planners and technicians, the wider purposes of their programs, and equity especially, had little relevance. Their professional commitment was to increased production. Furthermore, economics had for the most part abandoned questions of distribution as insoluble. [4] Consequently, they thought it sufficient for justice that the output of developing country economies should grow. It made pragmatic sense to concentrate on production, because the material value of growth was evident for all to see.

On the philosophic side, growth policy received its justification from a utilitarian idea of justice by which social and economic arrangements are considered just when on balance they lead to an overall improvement in the life of the population. The trouble with this formula was that the improvement was abstract. It was measured by the growth in an average share of society's goods. But averages may rise, as they did under the growth model, without bringing much improvement to those worst off. The poor benefited little, if at all, and this discredited both the economic theory which neglected distribution and the theory of justice which had propped it up. Besides, growth theory left undefined which material improvements counted as increases in welfare. Only the material output of production counted as a measure of social welfare, so that even the majority of the population might grow more hungry, sickly, and illiterate without pulling down the aggregate standard of welfare.

The Case against Growth.   Three sets of empirical findings brought growth-directed development into question: 1) lack of improved living conditions for the poor, 2) the cost of growth to deprived populations, and 3) the success of pioneer needs programs in bringing about improvements for the poor. The first set of evidence indicated that economic growth had done very little to improve the situation of the poor. This was especially true in countries with dramatic rises in productivity. When we look, for example, at income distribution in the four South Asian countries, Bangladesh, India, Pakistan, and Sri Lanka, in the 1960s, we see enormous disparities in three out of four countries, with only slight improvement in the holdings of the poor at the end of the period (Table 1.). Even in Sri Lanka, with an extraordinary drop in the income of the richest five percent, there is only a slight rise in the income of the poorest fifth of the population. Redistributed income was spread, it seems, among the middle and upper classes to the disadvantage of the poor. [5]

Despite a relatively low rate of economic growth, the countries of the subcontinent did realize minimal improvement in the economic standing of their poor. The same cannot be said of nations in other regions of the world. The second charge against growth was that it gave profits to the rich at the expense of the poor (Table 2.). In several countries of Latin America, for example, the share of income received by the poorest fifth of the population either remained unchanged or fell during the sixties. At the same time, in Brazil, Mexico, and Venezuela, countries which turned in strong economic performances, the income of the richest five percent of the population grew substantially. In Mexico, the share of the

TABLE 1:   Income Disparities in South Asian Populations

| | Percentage of National Income by Group | | | |
| | Lowest 20 Percent | | Highest 5 Percent | |
	1960	1970	1960	1970
Bangladesh	7.0%	9.0%	19.0%	17.0%
India	4.0	5.0	27.0	25.0
Pakistan	7.0	8.0	20.0	18.0
Sri Lanka	5.0	7.0	27.0	19.0

Source: The World Bank, *World Tables 1976* (Baltimore and London: The Johns Hopkins University Press, 1976).

top group rose by seven percent; and in Venezuela, its share of income leaped ahead by 13 points, as the share of the poorest fifth fell to a meagre two percent. Development had helped poor people in these countries not a bit. In some cases, they were simply relatively worse off, but in others their situation had deteriorated absolutely. [6]

TABLE 2:   Income Disparities in Central and South American Populations

| | Percentage of National Income by Group | | | |
| | Lowest 20 Percent | | Highest 5 Percent | |
	1960	1970	1960	1970
El Salvador	6.0%	4.0%	33.0%	20.0%
Brazil	5.0	5.0	23.0	27.0
Costa Rica	6.0	5.0	35.0	23.0
Mexico	4.0	4.0	29.0	36.0
Peru	3.0	2.0	50.0	34.0
Venezuela	3.0	2.0	27.0	40.0

Source: The World Bank, *World Tables 1976* (Baltimore and London: The Johns Hopkins University Press, 1976).

The last empirical trend to cast doubt on growth as an end in itself was evidence that a few countries, despite low per capita income and even low rates of economic growth, had measurably enhanced the lives of their poor populations (Table 3.). During a 15-year period, Pakistan showed stronger economic performance than either India or Sri Lanka.

TABLE 3:   Historical GNP Growth and Social Indicators in South Asia, 1960–1976

[DRR means disparity reduction rate; LEB, life expectancy at birth; IM, infant mortality; Lit., literacy.]

	Average Growth Rate	Total DRR Gain	Disparity Reduction Rates		
			LEB	IM	Lit.
Bangladesh	0.4%	---	0.6%	---	---
India	1.3	1.4%	1.7	0.9%	1.1%
Pakistan	3.1	1.3	2.0	1.7	0.4
Sri Lanka	2.0	3.5	3.8	1.8	3.8

Note: The disparity reduction rate indicates the rate at which a country is closing the gap between its social performance and that of the best industrialized countries. [7]

Source: James P. Grant, *Disparity Reduction Rates in Social Indicators: A Proposal for Measuring and Targeting Progress in Meeting Basic Needs.* Overseas Development Council Monograph No. 11 (Washington, D.C.: Overseas Development Council, 1978).

But its rate of improvement in living conditions lagged behind that in the other two countries. In India, progress in the social area kept pace with economic growth, and in Sri Lanka, socioeconomic improvements outstripped economic growth by an average of 1.5 percent a year. Figures like these tended to place in doubt the alleged link between economic growth and solutions for poverty. While the case of Pakistan showed that more must be done than simply promote business, the case of Sri Lanka gave observers good reason to believe that much could be done for the poor, independently of economic performance.

A look at Latin American figures suggest the same pattern (Table 4.). Brazil, with a GNP valued at $1,100 per person and a dramatic growth rate of 4.8 percent, only registered a 1.6 percent improvement in the social area, while poor El Salvador, with a per capita GNP valued

TABLE 4:   Economic Growth and Social Indicators in Latin
America, 1960–1976

	Average Growth Rate	*Total DRR Gain*	*Disparity Reduction Rates*		
			LEB	*IM*	*Lit.*
El Salvador	1.8%	2.5%	3.0%	2.0%	1.9%
Brazil	4.8	1.6	1.8	---	0.5
Costa Rica	3.4	3.7	3.8	4.7	2.5
Mexico	3.0	2.9	2.7	2.9	3.0
Peru	2.6	2.1	1.9	2.5	2.2
Venezuela	2.6	3.4	3.4	1.2	4.3

Source: James P. Grant, *Disparity Reduction Rates in Social Indicators: A Proposal for Measuring and Targeting Progress in Meeting Basic Needs.* Overseas Development Council Monograph No. 11 (Washington, D.C.: Overseas Development Council, 1978).

at $490 and an economic growth rate of only 1.8 percent, showed a 2.5 percent annual improvement in living conditions. The gap between economic growth and social welfare again indicates that other factors than productivity contribute to alleviating poverty.

Growth-oriented development was discredited, then, by three trends: 1) the slight improvement brought to the very poor, 2) the further impoverishment of those worse off in countries where the rich prospered, and 3) the progress of some model nations in reducing poverty despite only modest economic growth. None of these facts by themselves, of course, explain the distinctive appeal of the Basic Human Needs strategy as an alternative to growth, because the needs approach carries with it a significant moral component. For an explanation of the appeal of the needs model, we must look beyond the rhetoric of the failed programs to popular conceptions of justice.

Elementary Justice. The moral appeal of a Basic Needs strategy can be traced to the popular belief that serious deprivation is qualitatively a graver offense than simple inequality, and therefore practically never justifiable. Men and women may accept some degree of inequality or at least tolerate it; but they judge the lack of resources to meet one's own and one's family's needs an intolerable burden, borne in necessity but otherwise never justly suffered. Furthermore, since defending the populace against degrading poverty is one of the tacit ends of governments, a regime which impoverishes its own people or upholds institutions which oppress them is taken to be both unjust and illegitimate. For this reason, in developing countries where traditional notions of justice still persist, policies which jeopardize the basic needs of peasant families have often sparked protests and rebellions. Sooner or later, people have been unwilling to grant authority over their lives and fortunes to predatory leaders and organizations. Accordingly, aggregate measures of welfare, like economic growth, come to be regarded as unjust too, because in their abstractness they fail to reflect the fundamental interest of all people in basic welfare, a matter quite distinct from national prosperity. [8]

As it turned out, the first conclusion that developmentalists drew from surveying the meagre results of more than ten years of development was not that there should be a direct attack on poverty to secure the basic needs of the poor, but that there was need for greater equity in the distribution of national income. Calls for outright redistribution, however, were short lived, mostly because experts saw them to be both politically provocative and economically expensive. Despite the short life of redistributive thinking, the sentiment persisted that unless economic growth served the needs of the poor, commitment to development programs would be unjustified. Growth, this opinion held, is a good thing, but only on the condition that the basic needs of the poor are met first.

Thus, the Basic Needs strategy emerged from a logic latent in the political legitimation of development. From the earliest days, the alleviation of poverty had been a primary goal of the development process. For a long time, however, the welfare of the poor was overshadowed by technical objectives associated with growth and trickle-down theory. But as evidence mounted about the failure of growth to alleviate poverty, attention turned once more to making a direct attack on poverty. This is not merely another shift in technical objectives; it is a clear reordering of priorities, bringing development activities into line with purposes that bring it political support. To use a metaphor from the financial world, the recent concern for basic needs should be understood as a renegotiation of (political) credit, consequent to nonfulfillment of an essential condition of the social contract. Since growth did not make due on its promise to alleviate poverty, the terms of support had to be tightened up. The normative power of the Basic Needs strategy is found in the connection it makes between economic development and the primary goal which gives it political legitimacy, namely, the elimination of poverty as the first step to providing for general welfare.

Need and Justice in American Experience.   In the case of the United States, the late recognition of need as a principle of justice has still other causes besides the general enchantment with growth. Some of these are social and historical; others are ideological. Among the historical pressures inhibiting concern for basic needs are several special circumstances of America's own economic development. For one thing, because of the abundance of a virgin continent and successive waves of cheap immigrant labor, Americans have been able to enjoy a general economic prosperity unparalleled in older and poorer societies. One negative consequence of this affluence has been that Americans have been handicapped in understanding the grinding poverty of other nations and the thirst for economic equality which poverty produces. Second, a distinctive work ethic has made the taboo against malingering common to most societies especially strong in the United States. Moreover, as geographic and social mobility opened up to Americans the routes for escape from failure and the avenues to success, they have tended to overlook the impediments to advancement in poor countries and to attribute economic backwardness to a lack of ambition.

Third, the existence of a broad middle class has meant that Americans have ignored the inherent conflicts between liberty and equality which emerge in more stratified societies, where unrestrained freedom for a few inevitably results in their domination of the many. In such circumstances, equality functions not as a leveler, but as a needed corrective to the excesses practiced in the name of liberty. In the United States, by contrast, liberty and equality have commonly been combined in the facile notion of "equality of opportunity," a formula which transmutes equality into a form of liberty and so deprives it of its critical function with respect to offenses committed in liberty's name. In short, Americans have tended to see others as they would see themselves. They have ignored the special conditions which led to American affluence, attributing success to their own virtue; and they looked condescendingly on the obstacles to development with justice in poor nations, imputing them to moral backwardness. American perceptions of Third World needs, therefore, have been colored by America's own exceptional historical circumstances and have often been unsympathetic to Third World interests. [9]

A Special Bias—Justice by Desert.   Among the ideas which have made Americans unsympathetic, or at least guarded, toward need-based justice, the notion of desert is worth special comment. For probably no other moral idea has stimulated as much bias against need as a principle of just distribution as has the competing idea that goods ought to be allocated solely on the basis of merit. I shall examine this claim in more detail later. Here I want only to note that there is a cultural bias in America against distribution according to need which runs very deep and that this prejudice derives its strength from what is alleged to be the opposite principle of distribution according to desert. This system of belief is associated chiefly with the individualism of market (capitalist) societies of the sort that appeared in the nineteenth century, but it continues to exercise considerable ideological force in the United States today —across society generally and not just in conservative circles. History, of course, has not stood still, and today's capitalist societies have been altered in many important respects, not the least of which has been the place given to need-based concerns in social policy. [10]

While ideology continues to contain strains of reward "by desert alone," our public and private institutions have increasingly recognized the legitimacy of human need as a title for distribution. In practice, acceptance of the need principle has resulted in hybrid policies, which attempt to offer individuals the benefits of a society open to merit at the same time it protects them against severe deprivation through guarantees of basic needs. According to Roger Hansen, the American formula for addressing poverty, though "vague and for the most part inarticulated," has joined "a generalized broadening of equality of opportunity" with the elimination of absolute poverty in a single strategy. In the half century since the Great Depression, Americans have sought to change conditions for the poor not only by opening access to education and employment for minorities, but also by satisfying certain fundamental needs, like that for nutrition through the Food Stamp program, and for medical treatment through Medicare and Medicaid. Americans, says Roger Lampman, "don't really seek any particular degree of income equality, rather [they] seek a system of sharing that recognizes human needs, restrains certain arbitrary or capricious inequalities and serves social purposes." This set of attitudes carries over into the area of foreign assistance, where American public opinion favors types of aid which are "immediate, direct and tangible," such as medical care, education, and farming technology. This preference for substantive forms of assistance conflicts with demands for systematic change which look to the eradication of the causes of poverty rather than the alleviation of its evil effects. [11]

The American formula—needs plus opportunity—has often proved an obstacle to Third World efforts to reverse the cycle of impoverishment in which poor countries are entrapped. In the first place, American literal-mindedness about needs makes it far easier to mount relief efforts in emergencies than to assist systematic reforms which would help people provide for themselves on a self-sustaining basis. There is a one-to-one correlation in humanitarian services, a more or less direct cause-effect relation, which is hard to replicate in the complicated process of development. There are middlemen in relief programs just as there are in development projects, but the main actors remain in view in relief activities and it is possible to see results in a short space of time. Food is donated and a family is fed. A basic needs policy does not provide the American public the same kind of dramatic movement found in emergency assistance programs, and so a higher level of public commitment and understanding is required to make such programs effective.

Again, we can take opportunity for granted, believing it is there for the taking and forgetting that equal opportunity is an illusion without structures of equal access. In the United States, equal opportunity has been built through decades of legal experiment with the social and economic systems. If the American formula for fairness is to be applied on a global scale, there will have to be similar adjustments in the relations between nations. Unfortunately, values like "opportunity," rather than serving as guides to new social and economic arrangements, are often utilized in defense of structures of privilege which prolong the process of impoverishment rather than reverse it. They have been invoked in opposition to increased aid flows, to U.S. government support of internal change in developing countries, to the transfer of technology for development, and to the indexing of commodities under the New International Economic Order. Thus, while the objectives of the Basic Needs strategy correspond to discernible American beliefs about economic justice, there are serious drawbacks to relying on these principles alone to achieve justice either within developing nations or in the relations between rich and poor nations. Systematic changes will be needed both in Third World economies and in the international economic order if basic needs are to be satisfied on a global scale.

The limitations of the principles of justice professed in the United States should not lead us to disregard the significant advance represented by the Basic Needs concept. There has been a steady growth in understanding the priority of needs over other principles of distribution, and greater clarity about the conditions under which that priority holds and those under which it will not. In some ways, need provides merely "a principle of rectification" providing limited remedies for the grossest inequalities. At the same time, the situations it seeks to remedy are so vital that it is a fundamental condition of justice, setting limits on the personal and social injury which can be tolerated in the interest of other values and, in the case of the United States, particularly of the dominant value of equal liberty. This is an important departure from an earlier situation in which need [was] a subordinate consideration of little weight and the philosophers of American public life could lightly dismiss it, in the foreign relations area at least, as a "humanitarian concern." Today the satisfaction of basic needs is a public standard of government performance, whether at home or abroad; this is certainly a major normative shift in the area of public policy.

The emergence of the need principle in the American system of justice opens avenues of communication with other traditions, some of which have seemed incompatible with the dominant American paradigm of equal opportunity, a concept which is closer to the ideal of liberty than to that of equality. The American system, like the Anglo-American tradition which stands behind it, has been idiosyncratic in the balance it has struck between liberty and equality. Other traditions—Social Democracy, Marxism, Roman Catholicism, for example—have laid more emphasis on socioeconomic equality than America's liberal democracy did. The articulation of the principle of needs provides an area of accommodation between American views of justice and these other traditions. Even more, it reunites the liberal tradition with the common moral intuitions of humankind. For there is something like a universal moral sentiment that society ought not to deprive people of the means to satisfy their basic needs. Recognition in the United States of the justice of claims based on need, then, could mark the beginning of a transition away from American exceptionalism toward a more universal understanding of justice. This common principle, moreover, can provide an impartial standard by which to test the legitimacy of development strategies and socioeconomic structures more generally. [12]

Looking Ahead.   Up to this point, I have been trying to show how the principle of need has legitimated development programs, how it has served to criticize growth-oriented development strategies, and how it functions even in the United States as a primary principle of justice. In the remainder of this chapter, I shall take up two further tasks. First, I shall try to analyze the content of the need principle in a way consistent with transcultural norms of justice and the requirements of a realistic development policy. Second, I shall consider the priority of need in relation to some Anglo-American theories of justice. On the one hand, I shall try to show the support for a need principle which can already be found in British and American philosophy, and on the other, I shall criticize those misunderstandings which threaten to vitiate any effective needs policy. In relation to both topics, I shall attempt to formulate some practical maxims for implementing development programs in ways consistent with the real but limited duties imposed by the need principle.

II. "WHAT'S BASIC?" DEFINING HUMAN NEEDS

Basic Needs are claims of an exceptionally persuasive sort cross-culturally, because they point to an evident and compelling concern: survival. "Need" refers to anything required for survival. The range of things to be included in the category of need, therefore, is very wide, so wide, in fact, that one philosopher has proposed treating it as a "convoy concept," by which he means that the term entails a variety of discrete goods (for example, nutrition, health care, sanitation, education, and employment) such that the deprivation of any of them may threaten people with severe hardships. [13]

While the force of appeals to need springs from its connection with survival, as a moral category need goes very far toward taming the often demonic drive associated with survivalism—the assertion that anything is justified for survival. Daniel Callahan has written about the "tyranny of survival." "There seems to be no imaginable evil," he writes, "which some group is not willing to inflict on another for the sake of survival, no rights, liberties or dignities it is not ready to suppress." [14] The appeal to basic needs limits the potential abuses of survival talk in a number of ways. First, it focuses on those men, women, and children who are really in jeopardy, rather than mystifying the danger into a universal threat to humanity or a cause for rivalry between nations. Second, it individualizes the claims of the needy, making personal welfare the realistic standard of moral accomplishment, refusing thereby to validate abstract indicators of social progress. Finally, by giving priority to the poor, it establishes a fairer distribution of life's burdens among the members of a society.

The humanization of survival claims through the notion of basic needs has political relevance, especially in relations between the developed and developing nations. For, on the one hand, it can be used to test the sometimes disingenuous survival claims made by the developed nations of the North in defense of the status quo in international economic affairs; and on the other, it may be used to assess the legitimacy of national security or economic stability arguments made by developing country elites at the expense of their own poor. Furthermore, since these basic needs place minimal, though stringent, claims on political and economic institutions, they should be feasible except in extraordinary circumstances. In short, both nationally and internationally, the fulfillment of basic needs can provide a test of the legitimacy of political regimes and economic institutions alike. [15]

Need and Harm. Survival provides the tremendous motive power of need claims, but in practice need refers to whatever is required to avoid grave harm coming to a person. "A 'basic need'," writes Joel Feinberg, is anything "in whose absence a person would be harmed in some crucial and fundamental way." David Braybrooke, writing of what he terms "course of life needs," says that "they are such that a deficiency with respect to them endangers the normal functioning of the human being." In this sense, needs are things required to survive with dignity. David Miller sums up the protective dimension of needs talk this way: "[When] we ascribe needs to a person, . . . we are thinking not of what a person wants . . . but of the consequences for the person of *not* having what is needed. We are thinking of the harm the person will suffer through not being given what we say he needs." [16]

As moral claims, then, needs are warrants for protection against potential harm. When someone has a need, that person is not merely entitled to compensation in the event that he or she happens to be deprived of the needed good; one has a right to the satisfaction of that need even before harm befalls him or her. Needs, as Braybrooke says, are "the staple considerations of a precautionary social policy." A further point that the precautionary nature of needs claims makes clear is that people are entitled to a predictable future. If something is a need, it is a persistent requirement of a normal human life. It is proper to expect, then, that as far as possible we shall be able to have this need met even when our personal circumstances change so that we are unable to provide it for ourselves. It is for this reason that needs present claims on the community which hold whenever moderate abundance makes it feasible for others to assist in fulfilling the needs of deprived people without comparable harm coming to themselves. [17]

A. I. Melden notes that even for John Locke support of one's fellows in the business of self-preservation was a fundamental assumption, as certain as an individual's own right to self-preservation. With the passing of history, some versions of the liberal philosophy, and particularly those which have been in vogue since the Second World War, have deprecated the responsibilities that accompany personal liberty. The priority of basic needs restates for our own day the conviction of Locke that every man and woman is under obligation to see that others are secure in their lives, liberties, and goods. [18]

The Priority of Need.   Though the mainstream of Anglo-American philosophy has either ignored or rejected need as a principle of justice, a considerable body of philosophical writing, on both sides of the Atlantic, has begun to articulate the priority of need over other principles of justice. This normative priority means that, all things being equal, claims on behalf of need have greater weight in both private and public deliberations than claims based on competing principles of distributive justice, such as merit and incentive. Thus, in the design of development programs provision of basic needs, up to a point at least, ought to count more than stimuli for capital development. Ironically, while Western economists generally assume that welfare provisions and capital development are incompatible goals, improvements in conditions of life in poor countries have, in fact, proved a spur to domestic capital accumulation. In any case, need is a principle of justice which in ordinary circumstances will take precedence over the other principles. This implies that a policy will be just only on condition that it takes suitable action to see that basic needs are satisfied, or conversely, that a policy based on other criteria will be unjust, for example, if it results in hunger, malnutrition, or in many cases, even unemployment. For where unemployment compensation is lacking, the unemployed worker is very likely to be without the means to support his family. [19]

The priority of need rests on a ranking of harms, which Joel Feinberg puts this way: "An actually injurious condition should outweigh a mere change in a harmful direction." [20] An entrepreneur may suffer loss of some financial advantage because of his government's price supports for food, but the unemployed slum dweller suffers more directly when inflation in food prices leads to hunger and disease for himself and his family. The first is merely a decline in potential wealth, the second is a direct and real harm.

Philosophers who have considered the place of need in a theory of justice rely heavily on our normal abhorrence of serious injury and death to make their case. W. G. Runciman, a sociologist and social philosopher, in his book *Relative Deprivation and Social Justice,* contends that if people were ignorant about what their actual position in a future society would be, "it is hard not to visualize them making substantial provision for redistribution according to need." [21] He goes on: "If I know I might, as far as I can tell, find myself unable to support myself and my dependents through no fault of my own, I shall want to reserve the right (which I must also be prepared to concede) to claim some communal provision set aside from the wealth of those more fortunate." In another place, Runciman states his position even more strongly: "If, in a state of nature, I know that I may in due course find myself starving, even though willing to work, while others have the wherewithal to keep me alive, I shall want to assure, not only that I have a claim recognized as just on the basis of need, but that I have a claim which overrides claims made on the basis of either merit or contribution to the common advantage." [22]

A related argument is made by Nicholas Rescher in the course of criticizing the utilitarian conception of justice according to which the basic needs of a minority might be sacrificed for an increase in benefits for the majority. "Is it reasonable," he asks, "that we should in all cases be prepared to sacrifice an 'individual interest' in 'the general benefit' . . . ?" Rescher answers with an emphatic "no!" He explains: "We would surely not want to subject one individual to unspeakable suffering to give some insignificant small benefit to many others. . . . Actual privation offends our sense of justice in a more serious way than do mere inequities." [23] S. I. Benn makes a similar case, arguing that fundamental interests, like basic needs, cannot be traded or compromised the way other interests are, on the simple condition that the procedures under which the trading is done are fair. Basic interests are so vital, he thinks, that they are not merely exceptions to procedural modes of justice (equality of opportunity, for example), but also a limiting condition qualifying the justness of the procedure itself. Thus, a system of justice based on equal opportunity will be unjust if the exercise of the principle leads to a situation in which some groups are left so far behind that they cannot provide for their own needs. [24]

Unfortunately, liberal economic philosophy has quite consciously confused the loss of advantage with losses of a more substantive kind, a step which leads people who are economically favored to take an adversary position toward the poor, because any downward distribution of wealth is perceived as a threat. The future of United States policy in favor of basic human needs will be threatened as long as the exaggerated estimate of loss associated with capitalism goes unchallenged. For while, in a formal sense, basic needs are consistent with equality of opportunity, the competitive psychology which builds on equal opportunity will be stubbornly opposed to accepting need as a rational standard of human action. Both at home and abroad, efforts will have to be made to translate the common moral intuition about the priority of need into an effective public disposition which limits both private and collective greed. Without such a limit, basic needs programs will be doomed to doing no more than offering relief to the symptoms of poverty. [25]

A Moral Minimum: Dignity and Decency. Need sets primary standards for moral evaluation of the institutions of government and society. As David Braybrooke has written, the concept of welfare (basic needs) is indispensable to moral discourse about government. It "is the basic reason for having any government in the first place." [26] Furthermore, need is not only a primary criteria of the legitimacy of governments, it is also a fundamental measure of the equity of the system of justice the government represents. A government may execute its responsibilities in accordance with a certain conception of justice, and yet fail to do justice when the basic needs of the populace go unfulfilled. In such circumstances, citizens are not only likely to rebel against their government oppressors, but also to revolt against the system with the hope of establishing a new moral order in which their fundamental interests will be honored. [27]

What is this minimal welfare which is the fundamental condition of justice? There is wide agreement that it includes at least the means of subsistence for the individual and the individual's family. There is also agreement that subsistence alone is not enough. For to eke out a living is hardly a human life at all. The moral objective of minimal welfare is survival plus sufficient means to be spared the degradation of being made a slave to the struggle for existence. Mere survival leaves people in constant risk of death and debilitating illness. Even more, it drives out the opportunity for those enjoyments which give life its worth. For the ancient Greeks, the difference between freedom and slavery was a matter of whether a person was bound exclusively to providing for the necessities of life. The free person had the leisure to pursue the good life; the slave was bound to the drudgery of daily labor in maintaining a household. For that reason, even poor freemen "preferred the insecurity of a daily changing labor market to regular assured work" because it gave them opportunity to pursue the good life. That ancient notion expresses a perennial truth, namely, that human beings want not just to live, but rather to live fully. The struggle for survival is made worthwhile by other values: love, friendship, skill, art, knowledge, pleasure. Accordingly, basic needs are concerned with providing the minimum requisites for happiness. Security in the conditions of life, in other words, lays the basis for the realization and enjoyment of other values. [28]

Many different things are needed to lay the groundwork for enjoying human life. Various lists have been and continue to be proposed. I do not intend to add to them with my own bill of particulars. Instead, I simply want to propose two corollary principles which seem to be entailed in the notion of a moral minimum. They are the principles of decency and dignity. 1) The *decency principle* requires that no one be forced to endure degrading living conditions because of a correctable maldistribution of resources. 2) The *dignity principle* requires that people not be denied the means to satisfy their basic needs. [29]

Decency refers to the physical conditions which permit an individual to live with the respect of one's fellow citizens. It is, if you will, the minimally acceptable quality of life in a society. Definitions of decency will differ from country to country according to custom and the state of technology, but all societies will have a line demarcating those conditions of squalor which it is disgraceful for human beings to endure. People who fall below that standard will be despised, because they have become unduly subjected to the necessities of life. They are thought to live at a level beneath human beings. In traditional stratified societies, specific classes of workers, such as the night-earth collectors and gravediggers, have been treated with disdain for this reason. In American cities today, derelicts, ragpickers, and shopping bag ladies tend to be regarded in a similar way. The stipulation that no one be forced to endure indecent living conditions because of a correctable maldistribution of resources serves to protect the self-esteem of poor people not only by insulating them from the derision of the better off, but also by assuring them of the kind of security which permits them some limited enjoyment in life. Self-esteem grows first from rising above necessity and second from being able to lead one's own life and pursue one's own satisfaction.

Dignity is concerned, for its part, with the political control of vital resources. The kind of dignity envisioned in the moral minimum pertains to an individual's control over goods vital to him and entails respect on the part of authorities for that prerogative. "Social superiors," notes John Plamenatz, "can behave arrogantly to social inferiors . . . and we are often quick to resent their arrogance as an outrage to human dignity, as a failure to treat man with the respect owing to him merely as a man." [30] One sort of arrogance which is particularly resented is the use of power, influence, or prestige to deprive small people of their livelihoods, as when agribusiness manipulates markets to buy our family farms at a loss to the owners, or when coal mining companies control home building and improvements on land in which they hold subterranean mineral rights. Another reprehensible use of power is found in situations in which superiors employ their control of resources to coerce people into compliance with their wishes, as when the threat of a lay-off or plant closing is used to stifle dissent and protest. Still worse are situations in which control of one vital resource, such as employment, is used to manipulate access to other resources. Take for example, the company store, where factory or mine workers are compelled to buy food and clothing at high prices from their employer under threat of losing their jobs. These practices are an affront to human dignity, first because they manipulate the physical vulnerabilities of human beings. Second, they offend against the personhood of the victims by first limiting their freedom and then exploiting their limitations. Third, the deprivations inflicted on the inferiors rob them of opportunities to pursue the good life by their own lights. "There is," writes Plamenatz, commenting on the indignation felt at the abuse of the weak by the strong, "a feeling that men should deal considerately with one another merely because they are men." [31] In other words, there should be sympathetic understanding of the core interests of the inferior party, and so a refraining from any action which exploits an individual's basic vulnerabilities. The dignity principle states in imperative form the specific kind of consideration that superiors are obligated to show inferiors. It enjoins that men and women not be denied the means to satisfy their basic needs. Conversely, it requires that people be left secure in control of those things necessary to support themselves and their dependents. In traditional natural law theory and even today in Roman Catholic social thought, the rights of private property have been seen in just this way, not as a basis for unlimited accumulation, but as a defense through economic security against exploitation and coercion. The rights of property, of course, are but one instrument for securing the provision of basic needs; and alternative means are necessary, either to supplement or substitute for property, to attain the same end in changing circumstances. Today, for example, ownership of property is not nearly as important as it was in other times, because employment policies, social security, and other entitlements provide the basic security people need to lead a dignified life. In any case, the dignity principle enjoins that people enjoy the control, by entitlement or other means, of those basic economic resources which protect them from serious harm.

No Trade-Offs. While there is probably no more compelling argument for securing basic needs than that to do so shows respect for the common vulnerability of all men and women, a still very important consideration is that dependence on others for basic needs restricts the freedom of people to pursue other values of importance. The less certain we are of our essential welfare, the less liberty we feel to act on our own. The threat of denial of vital resources by the provider will be a strong disincentive to taking any action of which the provider disapproves. Opportunity for education, for religious observance, for companionship, and for political participation, any or all of these can be effectively denied by manipulation of vital services. For when we are forced to a choice between these genuine goods and basic needs, we will usually choose the needs as more urgent. In this way, outside control of necessities culminates in the subversion of other values.

Having security in basic needs means, therefore, that people will *not* be compelled to make trade-offs between those things they need in order to live and those other things which give life its meaning and worth. They should not have to choose between employment and political participation, for example, or between a ration card and union membership. They should not be deprived of housing on account of their religious convictions, nor of medical care because of their intellectual leanings. After all, the purpose of minimal welfare policy is to enable people to live at a human level and to pursue more ennobling activities.

If basic needs cannot be made hostage to more complex human activities, no more may the component needs that constitute essential welfare (food, housing, employment, education) be sacrificed for one another. The need principle demands security across the board. It is, as we have pointed out before, a convoy concept. Short of situations of extreme scarcity, men and women should not have to sacrifice the satisfaction of one need for another, e.g., housing for nourishment. For welfare consists in a number of discrete goods, and satisfying one need does little to satisfy another. Providing fresh water, for example, does nothing to alleviate malnutrition.

While people do choose in extreme circumstances to sacrifice one vital need for another, e.g., medical care for housing, when one is more urgent, forcing people to make such choices is an attack on their basic interests. Such conditional allocation of basic needs reduces people once more to servitude to the biological necessities of life, and as such constitutes a degradation. Such forced choices are inconsistent with the premise on which basic needs count as a criterion of justice, namely, that it is unworthy of human beings to live at the margin of existence. We have to conclude, therefore, that a needs policy conditioned on the denial of other fundamental rights is morally unacceptable. Conversely, while scarcity and underdevelopment may make it necessary for a government to implement a needs policy selectively, say by concentrating at first on food policy and infant health, the moral goal of such policies requires that where it is feasible the population be given security in all matters which affect basic welfare. [32]

Of course, the dignity principle will bring different entitlements in different regions. A peasant might need only a plot of land to till, some credit to carry him through bad seasons, and access to simple storage and transportation facilities for his crop, and with these he will have basic security, whereas an urban worker may require rudimentary school and technical skills in order to be able to find and hold a decent job, and some form of unemployment insurance to help him through bad times. To use an example from another area, the health of the population in some countries may be improved enormously by elementary measures like nutritional programs, immunization, and a safe water supply, while in other countries, clinical services, midwives, and family planning services may be required. Whatever the means, the function of a basic needs policy should be to secure for people, to whatever degree experience shows necessary, immediate control over the means of livelihood and unhampered access to the other components of basic welfare.

A comment is in order concerning the types of programs entailed by the basic needs concept. Three distinct kinds of activity seem to be necessary. There is, first of all, the whole range of programs intended to stimulate employment. The basic needs strategy, you will recall, was conceived as an alternative to the growth (trickle down) model and particularly as a response to its failure to provide a better living for the poor. Employment is rightly conceived as a primary goal of needs policy, not only because it is the surest way to make men and women self-supporting, but also because it is an important element in upholding self-esteem and a sense of purpose in people's lives. The second type of program entailed in the basic needs concept are interim welfare programs of one or another kind: subsidization of basic commodities, public works employment, and so on. These programs are required to fill the gap

between low rates of employment and a satisfactory level of need fulfillment. Sometimes these supplemental programs are seen as opposed to
job-oriented programs. This is a misconception. Assistance is required
simply because employment has grown too slowly in the past to meet the
basic needs. Welfare activities are, in that sense, compensatory for in-
adequacies of the economic system. But as long as jobs are insecure or
nonexistent, then welfare supports will continue to be necessary. [33]

Finally, some needs will have to be met by collective action and
government initiatives, if only by reason of the scale or the character of
the service. I am thinking here of such desiderata as water supply, sanitation systems, public works construction, and schooling. Thus, while employment is a goal of utmost importance, the meeting of basic needs will
also require other programs, involving government and community
initiative.

If growth-oriented development has truly failed to improve the lot
of the poor, and if jobs for the poor still depend significantly on growth,
then it makes sense to rely on nonmarket mechanisms to satisfy basic
needs, because a program built solely on job creation would reduce us
once more to waiting for an unnamed future date when economies flourish, in order to fulfill minimal obligations in justice. Such delays dis-
credit growth-directed development; they would likewise delegitimate any
alternative strategy.

Let me summarize the argument of this section on the definition of
needs. Subsistence in itself is insufficient as a goal of basic needs policy.
As a principle of justice, need aims at giving men and women the economic security to carry on the pursuit of happiness. While fulfillment
of basic needs offers a foundation for the good life, it does not itself
embrace those humanizing goods which make up that good life, things
like religion, art, and politics. Needs are rather only the means which
allow men and women to begin to lead that life. Thus, basic needs represents a minimal, though stringent, criterion of justice. When the definition
extends beyond the essential physical requirements of life to prescribe the
social aspects of the concept, it specifies two distinctively moral expectations. In the first place, it requires that people enjoy sufficient distance
from routine physical insecurity to retain their self-esteem and to receive
the respect of their fellow citizens. Second, it enjoins that the poor
be entitled to a livelihood and to those other basic needs satisfactions
they cannot provide for themselves, so that they will not be deprived of
the humanizing activities of the good life and the freedom to choose the
shape they will give to their own lives.

Finally, on the negative side, the satisfaction of basic needs requires
that people not be compelled to trade away either important values or
the means to satisfy some basic needs to meet more urgent ones. For this

reason, a basic need program will involve entitlements and other individual and popular political controls over the means of livelihood.

Implications for American Policy: The Priority of Need.
What bearing do the ethical elements of the basic needs concept have
for the direction of United States aid programs? In the preceding section
I have endeavored above all else to show the priority of need over other
principles of justice. It follows from this priority that as long as masses
of people continue to live from hand to mouth, American development
plans ought to give priority to basic needs. While in principle U.S.
foreign aid gives priority to basic needs, many political considerations
at home and abroad prevent fulfillment of that goal. Concentration on
basic needs would entail, in the first place, a committed effort to aid in
setting up basic services for the poor, such as water supply, food distribution, and health clinics. Other goals, like attracting investment or
increasing exports, would take a back seat while needs were secured. In
countries and regions where needs have been served, there have been
improvements in the economy as well as in the well-being of the people.

Second, following the dignity principle, emphasis should be placed
on developing programs which will enable the poor to support themselves. While there is some dispute about how employment generation
should take place, there should be no doubt that job creation is an
integral part of the basic needs strategy. What is at issue really is the
kind of policy selected to bring jobs to the poor. From the history of
growth strategies, it should be clear that a trickle-down effect from
capital intensive industry will not produce enough work for all those in
need of steady employment. Under the growth doctrine, productivity by
itself rarely led to a better life for the poor. For that reason, policies
which favor light, labor intensive industries and small farms would be
both morally acceptable and socially effective. Mixed policies would
be morally acceptable on the condition that the capital intensive sector
provides additional new jobs without dislocating workers in older operations. In the basic needs strategy, economic efficiency comes second to
popular self-sufficiency in needs. So, a needs policy, while it tries to
develop the self-reliance of the population, must search for alternate
means with which to do it. [34]

Third, development of basic services and job creation should continue for some time before shifting over to standard economic development
goals. Furthermore, when the time comes to assist in more advanced programs, preference should be given to working with those regimes which
have proved themselves effective in meeting the basic needs of the people.
For those countries will have established a firm base for later development in the health, education, and confidence of their people. They will

also have reduced the likelihood that capital intensive development will be seen as unjust and illegitimate, and American involvement as predatory and self-serving. Conversely, in countries where the advantages of economic growth fall mostly to the upper class and the disadvantages to the poor, it would be prudent for the United States to hold back from assisting with capital intensive development, lest such assistance be seen as abetting injustice. After all, since basic needs are a conditio sine qua non of justice, it is as unjust to defer fulfilling needs for the sake of growth as it is to neglect them altogether. [35]

Norms for Recipient Countries. Following the standards I have sketched, three further stipulations should be applied in assessing development programs in which the United States plans to participate. 1) Before all else, no one should be required, short of extreme scarcity, to sacrifice a basic need or any other basic right for the sake of satisfying another need. Justice demands security across the board in our basic interests. When sacrifices appear to be in order, they should be exacted in areas of surplus, not from needs. 2) Though some transition to other development goals is likely before all the needs of everyone have been met, development plans should be staged so that substantial progress has been made in satisfying the complete range of needs before attention turns to other projects. Scheduling development goals in this way is meant to insure that people are assured some protection from routine insecurity and so enjoy respectable conditions of life. 3) Development programs should lead to provision of basic needs through employment and a system of public services. While some deficiencies may require immediate relief, in the long run the aim of basic needs programs ought to be to make a population self-sufficient in supplying its own needs. Such self-reliance is an important component of self-respect and the best defense against the degradations that often follow dependence.

III. PRINCIPLES OF JUSTICE: NEED, EQUALITY, LIBERTY, DESERT

Up to this point I have been trying to show the illegitimacy of economic growth as a political warrant for development by examining the cogency of need as a primary principle of justice. I have indicated a certain convergence between American ideas about justice and those of peasants and worker elsewhere, and have reported the reasoned defense of need claims made by English-speaking philosophers on both sides of the Atlantic. But I have also acknowledged some inherent tensions in American views which make support for basic needs less than whole-hearted. Several of these themes I have grouped under the rubric of

American exceptionalism: suspicions about poverty, resentment for malingerers, a unique faith in equal opportunity, exaggerated fear of economic loss. At this point, I want to explore a set of resistances against complying with the need principle which result from beliefs that most Americans hold about justice or views that influence elite groups of policymakers.

My approach will be critical. I will be a partisan of the need principle, attempting to preserve its edge against the blunting force of critical objections, and especially of other principles of justice which lend plausibility to these objections. At the same time, I shall admit there are points where need recedes in importance and other principles become more relevant. For when men and women are secure in their lives, then other goods naturally grow in importance. Economic security gives place to liberty or community, for example. This last step is consistent with the position I have already articulated, namely, that basic needs are intended to provide a foundation for the good life. Accordingly, while need in many circumstances sets limits to the realization of other principles, under still other conditions, it may itself be limited by those principles. This transition in guiding ideals will significantly alter the conditions of political legitimacy. Thus, while basic needs are a rock bottom measure of legitimacy both for government and development programs, as conditions improve, expectations about the ends of government will also evolve, leaving basic needs behind as the primary goal or focus of government action.

Equality and Relative Deprivation.   Social theorists have often remarked that the underlying ethical question in the modern world is what balance to strike between equality and liberty in our social institutions. The American tradition, as I noted earlier, has been uniquely supportive of individual liberty as the dominant value and has treated equality, under the formality of "equal opportunity," as a variety of liberty. Accordingly, Americans, though unusually egalitarian in their manners, have tended to be suspicious of egalitarian economic policies as infringements on personal liberty. Basic needs programs have often been taken to be a variety of egalitarian social policy with unfortunate results for the poor. For when the two principles of need and equality are confused, need programs are undermined. Ordinarily, Americans will accept the justice of need-based programs as protections against deprivation, but they are disturbed at the prospect of legislating uniform social conditions, which would exclude individual advancement on the basis of effort and achievement.[36] As a result, need programs are discredited because they appear to demand too much. It is worthwhile, then, to consider briefly whether "need" is only a code word for equality or whether, despite the connection between the two concepts, need is a distinctive principle of justice with characteristic features all its own.

Egalitarian political theorists make one of two mistakes. Either they confuse the principle of need with the principle of equality or they subsume need under equality. Joel Feinberg illustrates the latter error. He writes:

> The principle of need . . . in most of its forms is not an independent principle at all, but only a way of mediating the application of the principle of equality. It can, therefore, be grouped with the principle of perfect equality as a member of the equalitarian family and contrasted with the principles of merit, achievement, contribution, and effort, which are all members of the nonequalitarian family. [37]

W. G. Runciman also makes need a subordinate norm to cover exceptional cases, with equality as the key principle of justice. He holds that "[In] a socially just society there will be a continuous transfer of wealth from richest to poorest," not only provision of basic needs. [38] David Miller goes perhaps the farthest in the direction of equating need with equality. He proposes that "the logical extension of the principle of need is the principle of equality, interpreted as the claim that every man should enjoy an equal level of well-being." [39]

The difference between the positions of these authors and the one articulated in this paper has to do with whether need is intrinsically related to the principle of absolute or perfect equality. In other words, is a basic needs program simply one step in a grand egalitarian strategy? For Runciman, to take a single example, equality is the basic principle of justice; and need, though the first of several subordinate norms, is a principle only for a class of exceptional cases, such as helping the handicapped. From the perspective of a needs-based theory of justice, however, the most important form of equality and the one which makes the most serious demands has to do with fulfillment of basic needs. It is qualitatively different from other forms of equality, from equality of income, say, precisely because it deals with fundamental human vulnerabilities. Thus, while an equal incomes program, like that proposed by Runciman, may be desirable, the provision of needs would be obligatory. Again, consider Miller's utopian proposal that need results in claims to equal levels of well-being. It is easy to see how powerful an influence egalitarian beliefs have exercised on Miller's understanding of need. By contrast, a need-based theory of justice upholds the difference between welfare and well-being, admitting strong claims only in matters of welfare, so that expanded notions of equality, such as equality of result, would be optional, debatable ideas.

On the need theory, society may structure itself according to a variety of conceptions of equality in matters that do not affect the fundamental requisites of life. Any number of social goals might lead to justifications for forms of acceptable inequality above the level of minimal welfare. But they may never lead to the conclusion that it is just for people to be deprived of their basic needs when means are available to meet them. Inequalities in basic needs will matter very much; inequalities of other sorts will matter less; some will matter not at all; and still others will be valued positively.

In the end, it turns out, even David Miller views the relation between need and equality a good deal more modestly than his ambitious proposition about equal well-being would lead one to believe. He concedes: "The safest conclusion is that the 'needs' conception of justice and the principle of equality stand in a peculiarly intimate relationship to one another which is still less than identity. . . . One could say that the principle of need represents the most urgent part of the principle of equality." Miller reasons that the urgency attached to the fulfillment of needs leads to the conviction that basic needs are a primary component of justice, while disagreement over the moral status of wants results in their receiving considerably less warrant. This seems to me to be the heart of the matter. While there is an egalitarian element to the need principle, it is a weak equality based on security from deprivation and the requirements of dignity in society. It is not a strong sort of equality which would force redistribution of wealth toward a mean, and it is certainly not a utopian equality which guarantees a like standard of well-being for all. The provision of basic needs results only in equality in the basic conditions of a human life, with lots of room beyond that point for individual and group variations, and thus inequalities of less harmful and even beneficial kinds, including those resulting from the competition compatible with equal opportunity. [40]

A common motive for expanding ("inflating") the definition of basic needs beyond the level called for by the need principle is the notion that the level of need rises with the general level of affluence in society. Joel Feinberg, for example, writes: "The more abundant a society's material goods, the higher the level at which we are required (by force of psychological needs) to fix the distinction between 'necessities' and 'luxuries'; what *everyone* in a given society regards as 'necessary' tends to become an actual, basic need." Feinberg argues that if society stimulates "artificial needs," then "it is only fair that society provide all with the opportunity to satisfy them." [41]

Thus, the distinction between needs and wants is forced into perpetual retreat. "The view that standards of need must change in some approximate ratio to rising prosperity is at least as old as Adam Smith," says Runciman. It is immaterial to Runciman's way of thinking what "the level of so-called absolute need" happens to be: "It may be that progressively more extravagant wants often come to be felt as needs because progressively higher comparisons become plausible; but there is no necessary reason why a sense of need deriving from an external reference group should be less 'absolute' or less valid." He goes on to explain why he sees the search for a valid nonrelative standard of need as inappropriate. "The way to vindicate a feeling of relative deprivation," he writes, " . . . [is] by showing that the inequality which is perceived is one which offends the canons of social justice." Relative definition of needs, dependent on intragroup comparisons, will be legitimate, therefore, when they meet the requirements of justice. They will be illegitimate only if the inequalities in question do not result from just causes, namely, equality, need, merit, and contribution to common good. [42]

Runciman's argument is misleading, it seems to me, insofar as it suggests that judgments about deprivation are wholly formal in nature. What counts as a need is only derivatively a matter of rules. It is first off a material judgment about harm suffered. At issue is loss, danger, injury, and disability. These are all things which are usually plain to see or easy to measure. Difficulties of definition arise only as needs become expanded to cover the enhancement of life and we depart from the underlying paradigm. [43]

Liberty, Preferences, and Basic Needs.   The clearest opposition to need-type principles comes not from political philosophers with idealistic visions of an egalitarian society, but from economists, whose defense of existing economic arrangements makes them fearful of distribution according to need. Their views about taste and consumer sovereignty, as we shall see, have encouraged many people to be more assertive about realizing their own preferences even when it deprives others of their needs. [44]

A cardinal belief shared by neoclassical economics and the liberal tradition in politics is a conviction that no one knows what is good for another person. This notion exhibits a certain healthy agnosticism about social management. Certainly a great deal of evil has been done down the ages by people who believed they knew what was indisputably good for everyone and then imposed their ideas on others. In that sense, it is a gain to let men and women judge for themselves what is good for them. The economic version of this belief, however, assumes that all decisions, like those of the consumers in the marketplace, are matters of preference. It does not acknowledge differences between informed, uninformed, and misinformed opinions. Neither does it admit any distinction between needs and wants. In the end, it says all differences in preference reduce to matters of choice and all the arguments about some choices being more worthwhile than others are useless quibbles. [45]

The market model assumes that all decisions between alternatives are like a shopping spree, that is, that they are simply matters of taste, like the woman who buys a calico dress rather than a paisley blouse. The extended application of the market model to explain all economic transfers is erroneous in two respects. The first error we might call the fallacy of arbitrary choice. Because in theory, at least, economics is unconcerned with how people choose to allocate their money, it wrongly assumes that there are no significant reasons why people choose to purchase some goods rather than others. It regards all purchases as equally unmotivated or perhaps as equally well motivated. Whatever the usefulness of this model for purposes of economic analysis, it is misleading for ethical evaluation of public policy, where the alleviation of fundamental deprivations ought to weigh more heavily than the satisfaction of idle desires.

The second fallacy associated with economic views of the consumer is the mistaken assumption that the individual is free to choose whatever he likes. This is the fallacy of uncoerced choice. The economists' ideal shopper may happen on a store and on impulse buy a chess set rather than a book. This kind of choice, however, is trivial. Most economic decisions, whether by individuals or public bodies, are weightier matters demanding careful deliberation about competing goals. But even more to the point, there are situations where people have no choice at all but to buy the things they need. One does not have a choice about whether to buy food, or to heat one's home, or to seek remedies for illness. These things are forced upon us all, and if we neglect them we suffer. The poor woman cannot neglect her needs and those of her family, and so her limited means must be spent to satisfy them. It is a distortion to imagine this as a situation of choice, as the economists would. The poor cannot choose what to buy like an affluent consumer. Their choices are so constrained as to be nonchoices. Like the ancient Greeks, they understand economics as a matter of necessity and constraint, for their economic dealings are tied to the struggle for survival, not to the expression of personal freedom and individuality.

A special distortion of the market model is that it places demand for superfluous commodities on the same level as the need for essential goods, thereby increasing the cost of supplying basic needs. This is not to say that both kinds of goods cannot be produced in one economy, but rather that where basic needs are measured only by the univocal standard of market demand they will be subject to strong pressures to reduce their share of the economy. For that reason, basic need programs, if they are to be effective, will require protection against this kind of market imbalance in order to maintain the supply of basic commodities at a relatively constant level despite other shifts in market structure. Such economic restraints are rational because of the qualitative difference between gross poverty and mere inequality. Were there not such significant differences in the harm done, then other principles might apply; but given the material harm inflicted by deprivation of basic needs, other principles, like liberty, at least in the form of preference or market demand, are rightly subordinated to need.

Economics is also at odds with basic needs policy because it measures social welfare in terms of aggregate preferences and so is willing to sacrifice individual and minority group welfare (basic needs) to satisfy the preference gratification of the majority, which is in some cases merely the preference of those with the greatest purchasing power. As we have seen many times in this paper, on the normative side at least, deprivation of basic needs is so serious a matter that it counts as a fundamental violation of justice. In a situation of abundance, an increase in satisfaction for the majority, leaving other considerations aside, is likely to represent a morally acceptable improvement in living conditions, but only because minimal conditions of welfare have already been satisfied. Otherwise the improvement enjoyed by the majority will be unjust. Obviously, any advance in preference satisfaction for a minority where there is not marked improvement in satisfying basic needs of the majority would always be unjust. In this sense, the core conditions of justice do not count it an infringement of liberty for market freedom to be curtailed for the sake of basic needs, for the provision of basic needs lays a foundation of equal liberty. Security in basic needs guards against coercion by deprivation at the same time that it makes possible the pursuit of individual preferences.

This set of problems about social welfare suggests, I think, how important it is to develop and utilize new kinds of social indicators (like the Physical Quality of Life Index and Disparity Reduction Rates) suited to register improvements in basic welfare as distinct from measures of overall economic performance. Without them, it will be hard to know what real progress is being made toward upholding elementary justice in the midst of development or affluence.

The primary tension, then, between the need principle and the principle of liberty as understood by economics concerns the conception of liberty within the market system. On the one hand, economists allege an ideal freedom for the consumer akin to the fancy of the window shopper; morality, on the other hand, looks at the idle shopper choosing on impulse as untypical of the way most people, and poor people especially, make their choices. The difference is a sharp one. For behind advocacy of distribution according to need will be found a picture of men and women who because of their poverty not only lack effective freedom but also are the victims of exploitation and domination; and behind the simplification of market activity into consumer preference lies the powerful psychological reality of unrelenting desire, forever dissatisfied and seldom if ever ready to sacrifice its freedom of self-gratification for others' sake. These two are opposed images of the human condition. Between need and other conceptions of liberty or between need and other principles, like equality and desert, some common ground can be found. But between need and the capitalist idea of freedom, there seems to be no point of accommodation. For ultimately, a system of justice which includes a need principle justifies curbs on the accumulation of wealth for the sake of liberty, thus enhancing economic security for all, while in the main capitalist economics opposes intervention in the market as a violation of certain individuals' right to do what they want. The case I have tried to make about basic needs is that liberty is a vain ideal unless all people have sufficient means to begin to enjoy living and to sustain their independence against outside manipulation. In other words, basic economic security, like public safety, is essential to assuring equal liberty for all.

Liberty and Need in Recent Political Philosophy. Among American political philosophers the chief question in recent years has also been what balance should be set between liberty and equality. The most famous contemporary American theorist, John Rawls, proposes a conception of justice in which liberty takes priority over equality—at least in economically advanced societies. Rawls offers two principles of Justice. First, there is to be the most extensive liberty for each person compatible with a similar liberty for all. Secondly, there should be equal access to economic and political institutions. In addition, while equality is the rule in social and economic affairs, inequality will be acceptable on the condition that it brings improvement for the population as a whole. This condition is further defined by what Rawls calls "the difference principle," namely, that departures from equality must yield benefits for those who are least advantaged. The difference principle is a mechanism for linking innovation and risk-taking with the alleviation of poverty. [46] Despite this accommodation to the claims of the poor, Rawls is criticized for making no provision for basic needs. The difference principle, it is charged, requires only that some benefit accrues to the poor whenever there is a movement away from equality. It sets no minimal standards below which people should not fall. Distribution according to need, however, would demand guarantees for the necessities of life.

Rawls describes the priority of liberty as the long-term trend of his theory. In the short term, liberty possesses only a conditional priority, subject to a society's attainment of a modest level of wealth. In citing the condition of moderate affluence, Rawls appears to take the part of the advocates of need. "Until the basic wants of individuals can be fulfilled," he writes, "the realistic urgency of their interest in liberty cannot be decided in advance." [47] In another place, he puts it this way: "The denial of equal liberty can be accepted only if it is necessary to enhance the quality of civilization so that in due course the equal freedoms can be enjoyed by all." [48] Furthermore the level of wealth which will satisfy the condition for liberty to take priority is to be settled by appeal to the demands of the least advantaged. Thus, while he sees a situation of equal liberty as the norm for moderately affluent societies, Rawls acknowledges not only that liberty may be curtailed in the interest of a minimal, need-based equality, but also that the question of how long liberty must be subordinated to need depends on improvement in the welfare of the poor. Unfortunately, he nowhere elaborates a system of justice for less than affluent societies, leaving development ethics more or less unaided with respect to assessing the balance between liberty and need in poor countries.

For neglect of a need standard and the inapplicability of his theory to situations of underdevelopment, Rawls has been justly criticized. J. Roland Pennock argues against him that if a person is asked to lay down ground rules for a society, it will be plausible for him to look for guarantees in the area of basic needs. [49] W. G. Runciman has also, as we have seen, urged the primacy of a need principle in the original position. "If, in a state of nature," he writes, "I know that I may in due course find myself starving, . . . I shall want to ensure not only that I have a claim recognized as just on the basis of need, but that I have a claim which overrides claims made on the basis of either merit or contribution." [50] In other words, anyone who is ignorant of what her actual social condition will turn out to be will find it reasonable to protect herself against grave deprivation before trusting her fortunes to a welfare linkage mechanism like the difference principle or economic growth. For Pennock and Runciman, and for many others, need is a primary principle of justice corresponding to common intuitions, and no theory of justice, no matter how intricate, may avoid meeting its demands. Rawls' theory is deficient, it would seem, in that it proceeds as if gross poverty were an insignificant moral fact without a special hold on us.

In defense of Rawls, Frank Michelman has proposed a reading of his intentions which would give primacy to the satisfaction of basic needs. (We should be careful to note, however, that the argument, though constructed out of Rawlsian ideas, is Michelman's own.) "The theory as a whole," writes Michelman, "reflects a degree of risk aversion . . . (such that) the question of generally amplifying one's income simply is not reached until adequate assurance has been made for what one specifically needs in order that his basic rights, liberties, and opportunities may be effectively enjoyed, and his basic self-respect maintained." [51] The argument falls into two parts. The first deals with risk aversion; the second with self-respect.

First, Michelman's case about risk aversion is that any group conservative enough to choose a social minimum will want to see that its basic needs are secured, not merely, as Rawls proposes, to have a guaranteed income. After all, what use is a guaranteed income which is insufficient to meet basic needs? Michelman is arguing, it seems, that the intention behind the social minimum is in fact to provide security in basic needs and that any guarantee which falls short of that goal ought to be reformulated with explicit reference to need.

Second, Michelman says, self-respect is the preeminent social good found in *A Theory of Justice.* All the principles (liberty, opportunity, difference) "are elaborated and justified in terms of their tendency to instill and safeguard self-respect. . . . " Correspondingly, all three entail a need criterion as a means of preserving self-respect. "The opportunity and liberty principles imply welfare rights," says Michelman, "as more objective, less relativistic biological entailments. . . . " [52] In other words, for people to enjoy advantage of equal opportunity and liberty, it is first necessary for them to be freed of the burden of subsistence living and the deficiencies and disabilities which accompany it, and to possess sufficient means to exercise their rights. Lacking those prerequisites, as I have argued, they will find themselves degraded and exposed to exploitation. Self-respect is defended, however, when men and women are not forced to toil only to survive and where they may not be forced back to such toil except out of genuine necessity.

Another interpretation of *A Theory of Justice* which moves Rawls toward a need-based understanding of justice is proposed by Ronald Dworkin, who suggests that Rawls' "deep theory" of justice is that the legitimacy of social institutions, including the major items of the social contract, rests on a fundamental right to equal consideration and respect. The concept of equality, as Dworkin formulates it, requires that "government must treat those whom it governs with concern, that is, as human beings who are capable of suffering and frustration, and with respect, that is, as human beings who are capable of forming and acting upon intelligent conceptions of how their lives should be lived." [53] I would assume that these injunctions, since they are basic ones, would apply not only to governments but also to other organizations, like business corporations, and private individuals too. This "deep theory" buried beneath Rawl's superstructure, if we are to believe Dworkin, is nothing more than the common "intuitive notion" of justice made explicit. [54]

In the work of Dworkin, the liberal tradition joins hands with many other traditions round the world that make use of the same intuition. For the majority of noncapitalist societies, as I have been at pains to point out, judgments about justice have to do above all with having the means to lead a decent and dignified life, rather than with equality of opportunity which is the American ideal. Equal opportunity and liberty in some of its other forms are subject to the test of basic equality. Their acceptability is conditioned, as I proposed in connection with the priority of basic needs, on their compatibility with equal consideration and respect. If they do not meet that test, they fail to contribute to justice.

The novelty in Dworkin's theory is to deny that justice involves anything like a general right to liberty, a view which would seem to set him at odds with those who advocate an unqualified priority for liberty. There is no right to liberty as such, Dworkin claims; there are only those particular liberties which are consonant with the right to equal concern and respect. [55] While Dworkin makes no mention of basic needs, his fundamental principle certainly covers the same vital interests, with equal concern touching the avoidance of deprivation and degradation, and equal respect dealing with the pursuit of the good life. Like Rawls, however, Dworkin fails to offer priority rules for balancing competing demands of concern and respect as they would apply in situations of dire need and serious poverty. What he does contribute is a proposition about how the liberal tradition ought not to make liberty an obstacle to greater equity; and this, of course, opens up possibilities for greater agreement between Americans and people of other nationalities who find that Americans' excessive preoccupation with personal and corporate liberty very often contributes to injustice.

Need and Desert.   Besides the tension between liberty and need, there is in the American ethos another tension of great importance, that between need and desert or merit. While equality of opportunity receives its political justification by appeal to maximal liberty, its genuine motivating power derives less from aspirations for personal freedom than from the prospects for material reward. Liberty, if you will, provides an acceptable rationale for commercial purposes. Working within a market economy, Americans' first practical consideration in matters of justice is not what anyone needs, but what a person deserves by virtue of his productive labor and social usefulness. Now the British philosopher, David Miller, in his book *Social Justice,* contends that need-based justice is fundamentally at odds with systems of justice, like the American one, based on desert. The notion of social justice, Miller says, includes both concepts (need and desert), but in an unstable combination. " 'Deserts' and 'needs'," he writes, "are *necessarily* in conflict since (accidents apart) no society can distribute its goods both according to desert and according to need. . . . The conflict between the two different specifications of ideal justice seems to be ineradicable." [56] Because the principle of desert is a major factor in American thinking on justice, I want, if only for a short space, to look now at the alleged tension between desert and need.

After positing "ineradicable" opposition between the two principles, Miller admits that a country may "distribute part of its good according to desert and part according to need"; but he thinks such arrangements are inherently unsatisfactory. In particular, he notes that welfare-state capitalism tries to see "that everyone's basic needs are . . . satisfied . . . before any surplus (is) distributed in proportion to desert." But he believes it is psychologically difficult to preserve this understanding of social justice, "since it is made up of two dissonant elements. It is easy to return to regarding the needy as objects of charity. . . . This is particularly true of the unemployed, whose deserts in the form of contribution are nil. . . ." [57] In other words, as long as we routinely reward people for their contribution and their labor, then people who are unable to support themselves and their dependents and who fail to contribute to the common good run the risk of being regarded as shirkers.

Even if we grant that poor people are wrongly perceived as lazy, we can expect there will be a major problem in gaining social support for their interests in a desert-based system. People don't look first for excusing conditions, but make snap judgments on the basis of their everyday routine. Baseless suspicions, when they become routine, however, are only prejudices. While we must deal realistically with misperception, suspicion, and prejudice as strong social forces, they do not settle by any stretch of the moral imagination what justice requires be done for men and women in need. That demand can only be identified by considering what it is reasonable to do for people who would in other circumstances work to sustain themselves and their families, but who are for the foreseeable future, whether because of physical incapacity or social constraints, unable to do so.

American society is by no means unique in the prohibitions it places on malingering. Most societies, including primitive ones, employ such taboos. Even today's socialist countries impose penalties for "parasitism." Societies with need-based systems of justice, therefore, also require that people do their fair share. So it is not true that need-based justice relieves people of the responsibility to labor on their own behalf. Furthermore, insofar as self-reliance is a necessary condition for maintaining one's dignity in society, the concept of basic needs itself entails a presumption that, when people have the means, they will work to support themselves. When we assist people who are unwilling to support themselves, even thought they have the capacity to do so, then we are no longer carrying out our obligations in justice, which after all involve the sharing of the burdens and benefits of a life lived in common, but are rather exercising charity. Basic needs, by contrast, prescribe stringent duties in justice only as long as the conditions of incapacity and lack of opportunity are met.

A final word about a special kind of desert, namely, economic incentives. Desert covers a variety of considerations: labor, skill, contribution, risk-taking. The paradigmatic item here is certainly labor. But a society may also arrange to give special rewards for exceptionally productive workers or for those who take on hazardous labor. By extension, those who make a greater contribution by their inventiveness and skill may also receive more in return. In no case do any of these special rewards have priority over basic needs, except perhaps where they make a direct and marked contribution to supplying those needs. The supremacy of need in these cases still rests on a judgment of substantial harm, while potential losses of surplus income may count only as changes in a harmful direction.

The claim of investors to a return on their capital is an appeal for reward, advanced on grounds of contribution and risk-taking. Now investment is one step removed from the kind of meritorious labor for which special payment is given. And it is a fairly long step. For the worker contributes of his time, talents, and strength, the very substance of his life, while the investor contributes only of his surplus wealth. Thus, if the contribution, effort, and skill of laborers is subordinate to the need principle, all the more should the abstract interests of investors be deferred or suppressed until basic needs are fulfilled. This is not to say that there is never any place for capital, rather that no major place out to be made for it until basic needs are fairly well met.

Need and Other Values Reassessed. I began this paper noting how Americans have viewed the rest of the world from the perspective of their unique material advantages. The result of that perception, I said, has been misunderstanding of social forces and historical and physical conditions in other nations. The purpose of this last section has been to try to reassess some perduring sources of suspicion about basic needs resulting from America's unique constellation of values. In the field of equality. Americans sometimes suppose that needs-based justice would result in a social uniformity inimical to competitive achievement and individual initiative. To that objection, I answered that basic needs have to do, as the term itself suggests, with establishing security in the basic conditions of life, not with establishing a leveling sort of equality. In other words, they aim only to see that people have the means to lead a decent life. This minimal form of equality is compatible with various degrees of acceptable inequality, including among others the pattern of unequal status resulting from America's own equality of opportunity. Thus, need-based justice is consistent with equal opportunity in the American style, but it also will fit with more strongly egalitarian kinds of justice. Support for need in principle, therefore, really tells us little about the overall direction of a society.

Second, it is frequently alleged that basic-needs programs lead to interference with individual freedom and particularly the process of market demand. In response to these charges, I answered first that market preference is an inadequate model for the exercise of personal freedom. Further I noted that relying on demand as a measure of allocation imposes grave deprivations for the sake of trivial gains, and sacrifices the essential welfare of minorities (and sometimes of majorities) to those who possess greater purchasing power.

Turning to the priority of liberty in political philosophy, we find that qualifications of the liberty principle dovetail with the criticism of the market economy I just offered. I pointed out that the priority of liberty, when it is legitimate, assumes from the start that basic needs are being satisfied. Further, philosophers in the liberal tradition propose that self-respect is a core value lying behind all the principles in the liberal understanding of justice. Consequently, the material readjustments required to sustain self-respect would warrant such curbs on nonessential forms of liberty as redistribution of wealth and limits on speculation. Similarly, this "deep theory of justice" would also deny there is any general right to liberty, save for those particular liberties compatible with equal consideration and respect for all persons. All in all, these contemporary philosophical readings of the principle of liberty tend to admit that in situations of poverty and destitution, liberty is subordinate to elementary considerations of distributive justice and especially to the fulfillment of basic needs as a condition of self-respect. [58]

Third, the opposition posited between need and desert was shown to be based on the false assumption that a need-based conception of justice excluded the duty of self-help. That belief was shown to be incorrect, because even socialist countries, where justice is proportioned to need, have prohibitions against laziness. Even more to the point, it is mistaken to view a basic needs policy as abetting indolence, because self-reliance is an intrinsic part of the dignity which needs policies try to promote. Indeed, several developing countries have made popular self-reliance the cornerstone of their development programs. [59]

Further Implications for U.S. Policy. What guidelines can we derive from this review of competing ethical principles for United States foreign policy? First, it should be clear that there is no direct connection between the adoption of basic needs policies and inclusion or exclusion at later points of equal opportunity and the open market. While not every society will choose equality of opportunity as suited to its situation once the basic needs goals have been met, there is a reasonable expectation that having security in basic needs will lead to desires for greater self-expression and individual freedom. But whatever balance emerging societies later choose to strike between equality and liberty, Americans should not take offense when other people prefer giving priority to basic needs in the shaping of their own economic policies, because to provide basic needs is to do the basic work of justice. This caution is especially important in the case of revolutionary societies, like contemporary Nicaragua, and polarized ones, like Chile before the coup of 1973, where American anxiety and hostility often affect the future possibilities of millions of poor people. Still more, the United States should refrain from penalizing countries which emphasize basic needs at the expense of business and other special economic interests. It would be desirable to go even further and encourage business and financial institutions to collaborate with governments in trying to meet basic needs of poor people. But short of affirmative policies, it is elementary justice to refrain from opposing or taking action which would interfere with basic needs policies. [60]

Second, both the public and public officials should bear in mind that limitations on market freedom should in no case be confused with curbs on more fundamental liberties. The market is a mechanism of limited use, and its deficiencies are nowhere more apparent than in the failure of economic growth to supply basic needs. When market preferences are allowed routinely to supersede basic human welfare, a grave injustice is done. For that reason, restrictions on business and financial practices do not count as violations of essential liberties and human rights. From a moral standpoint, economic freedom is contingent on the provision of basic needs, as I have tried to show, and so restrictions on economic activity will be legitimate when they are undertaken for reasons of human welfare. It would follow from the subordination of economic liberty to basic welfare that the United States should be wary about supporting the interests of narrow-based middle class political and economic groups against the poor majority, when such groups feel threatened by basic needs initiatives.

Finally, common agreement on the notion of self-help in both need- and desert-based theories of justice suggests that U.S. supported basic needs programs, while not ignoring the needs of children, the aged, and the disabled, should aim at building systems of self-support for the poor. Of course, work requirements should not as a rule function as penalties for recipients of aid, but should rather be a way for them to win control over the resources from which they gain support in keeping with their dignity. Lastly, the theme of self-reliance could well be used to persuade the American public of the worth of needs strategies, dispelling the suspicion that they are giveaways.

IV. HOPES FOR UNITED STATES POLICY

Time and again, pollsters have shown that the American people are willing to pay a greater price for development if only the aid goes directly to the poor. The Basic Human Needs strategy aims at doing just that. The adoption of basic needs goals in U.S. foreign assistance and international economic policy offers, therefore, the prospect of gathering substantial popular support for the American role in development. The single most important task for these new policies is to make it absolutely clear to the American people that the men, women, and children who benefit are poor. It will be vital, too, that aid programs put the poor back on their feet, so that they can support themselves in the future without dependence on outside assistance. A development policy which takes poor people seriously, and by that I mean a policy that promotes their self-reliance, will go a long way toward winning popular approval for U.S. involvement abroad. On the other side, when a development program makes visible progress in establishing decent conditions of life, the program and its government sponsors are more likely to be perceived as just, with the result that there is less civil strife, more room for political maneuver, and more time for gradual, nonviolent change, outcomes Americans strongly favor. [61]

At the same time that basic needs strategy wins approval for U.S. foreign policy at home, we can expect it will also earn respect for American intentions abroad. It does not take great learning to understand the indignity of dire poverty, nor special insight to see injustice when powerful institutions keep people chained in their misery. Men and women everywhere know, even when their leaders and alleged experts do not, that it is wrong to deprive people of their basic needs. The basic needs policy embodies a simple truth: hard-working people should be able to make a decent life for themselves and their families. Programs directed at enabling people to support themselves, as basic needs programs do, are sure to be welcomed by poor people everywhere, because they do simple justice simply.

Not every Third World leader, of course, is likely to accept basic needs programs as willingly as the common people might. Elites with vested interests are shrewd enough to see that security for the poor could be the undoing of exploitative regimes. For when men and women are sure of having the necessities of life they are less willing to suffer abuse, and they are readier to defend their liberties in defiance of their rulers. While needs policy may, by building up the confidence of the people, result in some unrest and topple a few regimes, it should for the most part lay solid foundations for peace, because the restlessness that springs from injustice will be quelled naturally. People will be able to turn their hands to making a better life, and to leave behind them the struggle for survival.

Since World War II, the United States has too often supported petty despots because they promised to bring order and stability to their region. This policy imitates one followed in ancient Rome. Of that strategy the historian Tacitus wrote "they made a devastation and called it peace." [62] It is time American officials realized that the legitimacy and stability of governments depends on their justice, and that order must be matched by equity. "What are kingdoms without justice," wrote Saint Augustine, "but bands of robbers?" [63]

The Basic Human Needs strategy will not end all American worries about the Third World, not even all the exaggerated ones, but it does have a good chance of changing situations of political instability for the better. It builds the conditions of long-term stability on the economic security of the poorest people in society. The satisfaction of the needs of the poorest derives advocates of violence of a legitimate cause and strengthens those interested in gradual change. What unrest remains once basic needs are being met is likely to be for the sake of greater liberty, a cause which will meet with sympathy among Americans. In sum, a basic needs policy, pursued with conviction over an extended period of time, offers the promise that by promoting justice we will also serve the cause of peace.

NOTES TO CHAPTER 11

1. For some influential reports using the basic needs concept, see *The Planetary Bargain: Proposals for a New International Economic Order to Meet Basic Human Needs,* Report of an International Workshop convened in Aspen, Colorado, July 7–August 1, 1975 (Aspen Institute for Humanistic Studies, 1975); *Reshaping the International Order* (New York: E. P. Dutton, 1976); *Employment Growth and Basic Needs: A One-World Problem,* prepared by the International Labour Office (ILO), with an Introduction by James P. Grant (New York: Praeger, 1977). Also, Roger D. Hansen, "Major U.S. Options on North-South Relations: A Letter to President Carter," in John Sewell et al., *The United States and World Development, Agenda 1977* (New York: Praeger, for the Overseas Development Council, 1977), pp. 33–36, 60–86, 117–121.

For a perceptive history of American ideas about development, see Robert A. Packenham, *Liberal America and the Third World* (Princeton, N.J.: Princeton University Press, 1973). The persistence and aggravation of poverty under growth strategies are discussed in Roger D. Hansen, "The Emerging Challenge: Global Distribution of Income and Economic Opportunity," in James W. Howe et al., *The U.S. and World Development: Agenda for Action, 1975* (New York: Praeger, for the Overseas Development Council, 1975), pp. 157–188.

On the failure of "trickle down" approaches to development, see Hansen, "Challenge," pp. 167–168, and Philip Alston, "Human Rights and Basic Needs: A Critical Assessment," *Human Rights Journal* 12:19 (1979), pp. 10–67.

2. Legitimation is analyzed with some care by Peter L. Berger and Thomas Luckmann, *The Social Construction of Reality: A Treatise in the Sociology of Knowledge* (New York: Doubleday/Anchor, 1967), pp. 92–128. The role of legitimacy in development is treated by David E. Apter, *The Politics of Modernization* (Chicago: University of Chicago Press, 1965), especially pp. 12–16, 225–228, 236–237.

3. According to David Apter, efficiency and equity are the twin norms by which the legitimacy of governments is established (*Politics of Modernization*, pp. 236–237). Sociologist Daniel Bell sees these two values in conflict in post-industrial America, with rationalist technocrats competing with egalitarian populists over which value will be dominant. See his *Cultural Contradictions of Capitalism* (New York: Basic Books, 1976), especially pp. 3–30, 269–274; also, on equity as an international issue, see Zbigniew Brzezinski, *Between Two Ages: America's Role in the Technetronic Era* (New York: Viking, 1970).

4. The supposed insolubility of distribution questions was formulated in 1939 by economists Nicholas Kaldor and J. R. Hicks. See Nicholas Rescher's account of "The Kaldor-Hicks Criterion" in *Distributive Justice: A Constructive Critique of the Utilitarian Theory of Distribution* (Indianapolis: Bobbs-Merrill, 1968), pp. 14–18.

5. See Hansen, "Challenge," pp. 168–170.

6. On some welfare economic grounds (Pareto efficiency), performances of this type would be judged inadequate. See Rescher, *Distributive Justice*, pp. 12–14. Also David Braybrooke, *Three Tests for Democracy: Personal Rights, Human Welfare, Collective Preference* (New York: Random House, 1968), pp. 129–133.

7. The Disparity Reduction Rate is a measure devised for calculating the progress of less developed countries in eliminating poverty. It measures the rate at which poor countries are closing the gap with rich countries in key social indicators. The target levels are the highest figures advanced nations are expected to reach by the year 2000. James P. Grant, *Disparity Reduction Rates in Social Indicators: A Proposal for Measuring and Targeting Progress in Meeting Basic Needs,* Monograph No. 11 (Washington, D.C.: Overseas Development Council, 1978).

8. The connection between political legitimacy and basic welfare is discussed by Barrington Moore, Jr. in his book, *Injustice: The Social Bases of Obedience and Revolt* (White Plains, N.Y.: M. E. Sharpe, 1978), p. 38. Notions of justice among peasants in relation to political activity are treated by James Scott, *The Moral Economy of the Peasant* (New Haven: Yale University Press, 1976), pp. 13–43, 157–192. Moore's *Injustice* also reviews the multiple factors affecting the legitimacy of governments, the toleration of illegitimate ones, and the unleashing of rebellion and revolt. The logic of political revolution is analyzed in scrupulous detail by Ted Gurr, *Why Men Rebel* (Princeton, N.J.: Princeton University Press, 1970).

9. See David Porter, *People of Plenty: Economic Abundance and the American Character* (Chicago: University of Chicago Press, 1954), for the classic exposition of the exceptionalist thesis about American history. For more recent applications of exceptionalism to U.S.-Third World relations, see John W. Sewell and John A. Mathieson, "What Are American Interests in Third World Development?", a paper in preparation for a University of Sussex volume on developed nations' interests in the Third World (forthcoming); and Bruce C. Birch and Larry L. Rasmussen, *The Predicament of the Prosperous* (Philadelphia: Westminster Press, 1978).

. 10. David Miller, *Social Justice* (London: Oxford University Press, 1976), pp. 286–317.

11. Hansen, pp. 158–159. Lampman, cited by Hansen, p. 159. See also Robert J. Lampman, "Measured Inequality of Income: What Does It Mean and What Can It Tell Us," *Annals of the American Academy of Political and Social Science* (Sept. 1973), pp. 90–91; also, Benjamin Ward, *The Ideal Worlds of Economics: The Liberal Economic World View* (New York: Basic Books, 1979).

12. On the relation of liberty to equality, see J. R. Pennock, *Democratic Political Theory* (Princeton, N.J.: Princeton University Press, 1979), pp. 16–58; R. H. Tawney, *Equality* (London: Allen and Unwin, 1952), pp. 254–268; and Donald Dworkin, "What Rights Do We Have?" in *Taking Rights Seriously* (Cambridge, Mass.: Harvard University Press, 1977), pp. 266–278.

Harlan Cleveland and the authors of the Aspen *Planetary Bargain* quite deliberately used basic needs as a common standard for international cooperation (pp. 3, 16–19). The other reports cited in n. 1 seem to proceed from the same premise.

13. On the special force which survival gives to 'need' claims, see A. R. Louch, *Explanation and Human Action* (Berkeley and Los Angeles: University of California Press, 1966), pp. 70–73. The notion of welfare (basic needs) as a "convoy" concept is presented in David Braybrooke, *Three Tests for Democracy,* p. 92. See also, See also, Nicholas Rescher, *Welfare: The Social Issues in Philosophical Perspective* (Pittsburgh: University of Pittsburgh Press, 1972), p. 5, where the author speaks of welfare as a "profile" produced by the satisfaction of component needs.

14. See Daniel Callahan, *The Tyranny of Survival* (New York: Mac-

millan, 1973), p. 92. I have set out some further tests of survivalism in an article co-authored with C. P. Wolf, "Environmental Ethics: The Problem of Growth" *The Encyclopedia of Bioethics,* Warren Reich, ed. (New York: Macmillan/Free Press, 1978), 5 vols., Vol. 1, pp. 395–397.

15. *Planetary Bargain,* p. 3. Also, see Hansen, "Challenge," pp. 184–187. See Chap. 4 in this volume on the importance of institution building to the fulfillment of human rights.

16. Citations on harm: Joel Feinberg, *Social Philosophy* (Englewood Cliffs, N.J.: Prentice-Hall, 1963), p. 111; David Braybrooke "Let Needs Diminish That Preferences May Prosper" in Nicholas Rescher, ed., *Studies in Moral Philosophy* (Oxford: Basil Blackwell and University of Pittsburgh, 1968), p. 90; David Miller, *Social Justice* (Oxford: Clarendon Press, 1976), p. 130.

17. Braybrooke, "Let Needs Diminish," p. 92.

18. A. I. Melden, *Rights and Persons* (Berkeley and Los Angeles: University of California Press, 1977), pp. 237–242.

19. On the economic benefits of basic need policies, see William Rich, "Smaller Families through Social and Economic Progress." Monograph No. 7 (Washington, D.C.: Overseas Development Council, 1973). John W. Ratcliffe gives a detailed report on the impact of basic needs policies in one region of India; see his "Poverty, Politics and Fertility: The Anomaly of Kerala," *Hastings Center Report* 7 (February 1977), pp. 34–42.

20. Feinberg, *Social Philosophy,* p. 31.

21. W. G. Runciman, *Relative Deprivation and Social Justice: A Study of Attitudes to Social Inequality in Twentieth Century England* (Berkeley and Los Angeles: University of California Press, 1966), p. 261.

22. *Ibid.,* p. 264.

23. Rescher, *Distributive Justice,* p. 29.

24. S. I. Benn, "Egalitarianism and Equal Consideration of Interests," in J. Roland Pennock and John W. Chapman, eds. *Nomos IX: Equality* (New York: Atherton Press, 1967), pp. 71–78.

25. On fear of loss as a motive in liberal capitalism, see Sheldon S. Wolin, *Politics and Vision* (Berkeley and Los Angeles: University of California Press, 1960), pp. 325–331.

26. Braybrooke, *Three Tests,* p. 86.

27. Moore, *Injustice,* p. 38.

28. On the insufficiency of minimal subsistence as a goal of needs policy, see Alston, "Human Rights and Basic Needs." Also, Braybrooke, "Let Needs Diminish," p. 92.

The Hellenic conceptions of freedom and slavery are discussed in Hannah Arendt, *The Human Condition* (Garden City, N.Y.: Doubleday, 1959), pp. 27–34.

29. I adopt a position here on the scope of need which some may find too narrow. The two principles I specify in this section, decency and dignity, are an attempt to define need claims within the range of obligations reasonable men and women would admit they owe one another. Such a

definition is both practicable and in keeping with a traditional western moral convention of distinguishing obligations of justice from those of charity.

While I attempt to hold the conception of need to some minimal content, I also avoid defining the term in solely material terms. Thus, decency is linked not just to material standards of living, but to social standing and self-esteem as well. Similarly, dignity is not linked simply to independent control of resources, but to the choice of activities and the potential to enjoy other values. For a more ambitious conception of need, making spiritual good the object of obligation, see Chap. 10 in this volume.

30. John Plamenatz offers the distinction between dignity and decency I have tried to amplify here. See his "Diversity of Rights and Kinds of Equality," *Nomos IX: Equality,* pp. 90–93. Citation, p. 92.

31. Economists sometimes argue as if choice among necessities were, like the other decisions we make in the market, genuine preferences. This assumption is attacked by Braybrooke, who writes: "Needs sometimes conflict and one must choose between them. But forced choices of this kind would not be described in ordinary language as 'matters of preference.' One would say, 'I had to give up y, though I needed it . . . I had no choice but to give up one or the other, x or y.' One's preferring x would then be irrelevant; the moral or prudential question would be, which of the conflicting needs was then most urgent." ("Let Needs Diminish," pp. 94–95.)

In connection with the question of pseudo-choice, it is well to recall that basic needs (welfare) is a "convoy" (Braybrooke) or "profile" (Rescher) concept, embracing several different types of goods. Accordingly, one's welfare can be negatively affected by falling beneath a minimum standard even with respect to one of these goals. A well-paying job is of little help, for example, if health care is out of reach; and support payments cannot compensate for lack of education. Also, see Braybrooke, *Three Tests,* pp. 123–133, especially p. 133.

32. For an application of this principle to an ethical analysis of the emergency state sterilization campaigns in India, see Drew Christiansen, "Ethics and Compulsory Population Control," *Hastings Center Report* 7:1 (February, 1977), pp. 30–33.

33. See Chap. 4 in the companion volume, *Human Rights and Basic Needs in the Americas.*

34. The most important statement on the place of employment in basic need strategies is undoubtedly *Employment, Growth and Basic Needs: A One-World Problem,* prepared by the ILO with an Introduction by James M. Grant. (New York / London: Overseas Development Council / Praeger, 1977).

35. Henry Shue distinguishes three classes of duties associated with the right to subsistence which may well serve as guidelines for policy. He lists them this way:

I. Duties not to eliminate a person's only available means of subsistence—duties to avoid depriving.

II. Duties to protect people against deprivation of the only available means of subsistence by other peoples—duties to protect from deprivation.

III. Duties to provide for the subsistence of those unable to provide for their own—duties to aid the deprived.

Henry Shue, *Basic Rights* (Princeton, N.J.: Princeton University Press, 1980), p. 53.

36. See n. 13 above. My colleague John Langan has arged for guarantees of socioeconomic rights on the grounds that they make possible the enjoyment of more essential liberties. Similarly, Henry Shue has argued that "basic rights" need to be served and protected as the condition of enjoyment of any other rights. See Langan, Chap. 4 of this volume and Shue, *Basic Rights*.

37. Feinberg, *Social Philosophy*, p. 111.

38. Runciman, *Relative Deprivation and Social Justice*, p. 268.

39. Miller, *Social Justice*, pp. 143–144.

40. *Ibid.*, p. 149.

41. Feinberg, p. 110.

42. Runciman, p. 252.

43. John Weeks and Elizabeth Dore discuss the notion of "absolute poverty" in their essay "Basic Needs: The Journey of a Concept," *Human Rights and Basic Needs in the Americas,* Chap. 4. They share with me the view that poverty differs in kind from relative deprivation.

44. See Duncan MacRae, Jr., *The Social Function of Social Science* (New Haven: Yale University Press, 1976) for a more detailed analysis of the ethical assumptions of utilitarianism and welfare economics and the influence of these beliefs on contemporary democratic theory. Other helpful studies are Brian Barry, *Sociologists, Economists and Democracy* (Chicago: University of Chicago Press, 1978) and John Plamenatz, *Democracy and Illusion* (London: Longman, 1973) for explication and criticism, respectively, of the links between liberal democracy and the market model.

45. MacRae, pp. 138–145.

46. Rawls lays out his principles at several places in *A Theory of Justice* (Cambridge: Harvard University / Belknap Press, 1971), pp. 60–65, 150–161, 175–183. For application of his theories to basic needs, see Frank I. Michelman, "Constitutional Welfare Rights and *A Theory of Justice*" in Norman Daniels, ed. *Reading Rawls* (New York: Basic Books, 1974), pp. 319–347.

47. Rawls, p. 543.

48. *Ibid.*, p. 542.

49. Pennock, *Democratic Political Theory*, pp. 51–53.

50. Runciman, p. 264.

51. Michelman, p. 347.

52. *Ibid.*, p. 346.

53. Ronald Dworkin, *Taking Rights Seriously* (Cambridge, Mass.: Harvard University Press, 1977), p. 272.

54. *Ibid.*, pp. 181–182.

55. *Ibid.*, pp. 266–278.

56. Miller, pp. 27–28.

57. *Ibid.,* p. 28.

58. Other political philosophers have also attempted to reconcile liberty with redistribution of wealth and income. See, for example, Ernest Loevinsohn, "Liberty and the Redistribution of Property" *Philosophy and Public Affairs* 6:3, pp. 226–239.

59. Denis Goulet, "Looking at Guinea-Bissau: A New Nation's Development Strategy," Occasional Paper No. 9 (Washington, D.C.: Overseas Development Council, 1978) is a study of one such country.

60. Shue's discussion of subsistence duties in *Basic Rights.*

61. One important survey on attitudes of United States citizens to development is Paul A. Laudicina, *World Poverty and Development: A Survey of American Opinion,* Monograph No. 8 (Washington, D.C.: Overseas Development Council, 1973).

62. Tacitus, *Agricola,* 30.

63. Saint Augustine, *City of God,* IV.4.

CONTRIBUTORS

Drew Christiansen, S.J., is currently visiting professor of social ethics at the Jesuit School of Theology at Berkeley in the Graduate Theological Union, Berkeley, California. From 1977 to 1980 he was Research Fellow of the Woodstock Theological Center, where his investigations concerned the place of basic needs in human rights policy. He is currently completing a doctoral dissertation on autonomy and dependence in old age for the department of religious studies at Yale University. He has been associated with the Hastings Institute of Society, Ethics, and the Life Sciences, and with the Kennedy Institute for Ethics at Georgetown as well as with the Aspen Institute for Humanistic Studies. He served as book editor and as special editor for *Theological Studies* from 1970 to 1973. He is a contributor to the *Encyclopedia of Bioethics* and has published articles in the *Journal of Humanistic Psychology, Soundings, The Humanist,* and the *Hastings Center Report.* He has taught at Yale and at Georgetown.

Thomas Clarke, S.J., was a research fellow at the Woodstock Theological Center from 1977 to 1981. He received his doctorate in theology from the Gregorian University (Rome). For 20 years, he taught as professor of systematic theology at Woodstock College, while also serving as associate editor of several periodicals and presenting numerous lectures and workshops both in the United States and abroad. He is the author or editor of four books, and has published many articles in professional and popular journals. His special area of interest has been spirituality and its relationship to society, a field in which he is an internationally recognized authority. He is currently spending a sabbatical year in Alabama and California.

Ignacio Ellacuría, S.J., was born in the Basque region of Spain and has lived and worked in Central America for over 25 years. He studied philosophy in Quito and Madrid and theology at Innsbruck, Austria. He holds a licentiate in theology and philosophy and a doctorate in theology. At present he teaches at the Universidad Centroamericana in Managua, Nicaragua. He is on the editorial board of *Estudios Centroamericanos* and has published articles in periodicals and lectured in universities throughout Latin America and Europe. His best-known book in English is *Freedom Made Flesh: The Mission of Christ and His Church* (Orbis, 1976).

John C. Haughey, S.J., has been a research fellow at the Woodstock Theological Center since it opened in Washington in 1974. Before that he was Associate Editor of *America* and taught theology at Fordham and Georgetown Universities. He has been actively involved both in the charismatic renewal and in social action ministries. He has written two theological books: *The Conspiracy of God* (1973) and *Should Anyone Say Forever?:*

On Making, Keeping, and Breaking Commitments (1975). Father Haughey has also edited and contributed to two volumes in the Woodstock Studies series: *The Faith that Does Justice* (1977) and *Personal Values in Public Policy* (1979). He has organized and directed a number of Woodstock programs promoting reflection and dialogue on the ways in which ethical and religious values influence public policy and the work of government officials. He holds a doctorate in theology from the Catholic University of America.

Monika Hellwig is professor of systematic theology at Georgetown University and has long been interested in liberation theology and other contemporary socio-critical theologies. She has engaged in a number of workshops with Latin American clergy involved in action for social justice. She holds a doctorate in Theology from the Catholic University of America, and her published writings include *The Eucharist and the Hunger of the World* (Paulist Press), *Tradition: The Catholic Story Today* (Pflaum), and *The Christian Creeds: A Faith to Live By* (Pflaum).

Alfred Hennelly, S.J., is currently a research fellow at the Woodstock Theological Center. He holds a doctorate in religious studies from Marquette University, a licentiate in theology from Woodstock College, and a Master of Arts from the Ateneo de Manila. He taught and studied for six years in the Philippines, and has also taught at Marquette University, Fordham University, and Le Moyne College, Syracuse, where he attained the rank of associate professor. His specialty has been religion and social change in Latin America, which led to field research in Jamaica and Peru. This research has resulted in a book entitled *Theologies in Conflict* (Orbis, 1979) and articles in *Theological Studies, Cross Currents, America,* and other periodicals.

David Hollenbach, S.J., is currently assistant professor of moral theology at the Weston School of Theology in Cambridge, Massachusetts. He holds a doctorate in religious studies from Yale University. In 1975–76 he was a Research Fellow at the Woodstock Theological Center, and he has continued to be associated with the Center since then. In 1979, his book on the Catholic tradition of human rights *Claims in Conflict* appeared. He is currently engaged on a comparative study of Christian, Jewish, and Islamic approaches to human rights, for which he has done research in the Middle East. He has lectured extensively on social ethics in this country and in India. He serves on the Peace and Justice Commission of the Archdiocese of Boston, and he has been a consultant for the Inter-religious Peace Colloquium.

John Langan, S.J., has been a research fellow at the Woodstock Center since 1975. He has a doctorate in philosophy from the University of Michigan, where he specialized in the history of ethical theory. He has contributed essays to two volumes in the Woodstock Studies series, *The Faith that Does Justice* (1977) and *Personal Values and Public Policy* (1979). His articles on ethical theory and on applied ethics have appeared in *Theological Studies, Harvard Theological Review, Journal of Religious Ethics, Religious Studies Review, Commonweal,* and *Christian Century*. He has organized a series of seminars on ethical issues in foreign policy and has served as a consultant to the U.S. Catholic Conference and the United Methodist Law of the Sea Project. He serves as a lecturer in the philosophy and theology departments at Georgetown University.

Dr. Hernán Montealegre is a Chilean lawyer who specializes in human rights and international law. In 1967, he received an award from the Chilean Institute of Criminal Law as the best student in that discipline. In 1968 he was awarded the Montenegro Prize instituted by the University of Chile for the best student in the graduating class of the law school. He entered the diplomatic corps and served as Consul to Great Britain until 1973. Returning to Chile, he joined the Peace Committee and defended hundreds of political prisoners from 1974 until 1976, when he himself was imprisoned for six months. Upon release, he joined the Academy of Christian Humanism and in 1979 under its auspices published a 775-page treatise entitled "La Seguridad del Estado y los Derechos Humanos." This book has elevated him to the rank of an authority on the relationship of international law to the doctrine of national security. At present he is executive director of the Interamerican Institute for Human Rights in San Jose, Costa Rica.

Philip Rossi, S.J., has been assistant professor of theology at Marquette University since 1975. During the 1979–1980 academic year, he was a visiting fellow at the Woodstock Theological Center and participated in its research project on Human Rights and Basic Needs in the Americas. He holds a doctorate in philosophy from the University of Texas, where he wrote a dissertation on the moral philosophy of Kant. He has been an active member of the American Philosophical Association, the American Society of Christian Ethics, and the College Theology Society. Father Rossi has published several articles on social ethics and medical ethics and is currently working on a book on moral imagination and the foundations of moral theology. He has published articles in *Linacre Quarterly, Renascence, The Journal of Religious Ethics,* and *The Modern Schoolman.*

Max Stackhouse is an ordained minister of the United Church of Christ and is professor and chairman in the department of religion and society at Andover-Newton Theological School in Newton, Massachusetts. He holds a doctorate in religious ethics from Harvard, where he has also served as lecturer. From 1976 to 1980, he was executive secretary of the American Society of Christian Ethics. He has served on the boards of the Division of Church and Society of the National Council of Churches, the Massachusetts Civil Liberties Union, and the Boston Industrial Mission. His books include: *Ethics of Necropolis* (1971) and *Ethics and the Urban Ethos* (1972). He participated in the Woodstock Center's conference on theoretical foundations for human rights in January 1980 and is currently completing a book on religion and human rights.